CHINA EMERGES

A CONCISE HISTORY OF CHINA
FROM ITS ORIGIN TO THE PRESENT

STEVEN WARSHAW

diablo press

©1964, 1974, 1979, 1990, 1992 , AND 1994 DIABLO PRESS, Inc.
Berkeley and San Francisco
P.O. Box 7042, Berkeley, California 94707

ORDER DESK
American International Distribution Corporation
P.O. Box 20, Williston, VT 05495-0020. Telephone (800) 488-2665
EDITORIAL DESK
P.O. Box 4042
Berkeley, CA 94707, Telephone (510) 653-5310

PRINTING HISTORY
First edition as part of ASIA EMERGES
First Printing, 1964. Second Printing, 1966. Third Printing, 1967
Revised and expanded as CHINA EMERGES
1974
Second printing as CHINA EMERGES
1974
Third printing as CHINA EMERGES (Revised)
1979
Fourth printing as CHINA EMERGES
1985
Fifth printing as CHINA EMERGES (Revised)
1987
Sixth printing as CHINA EMERGES
1989
Seventh printing as CHINA EMERGES (Revised)
1990
Eighth printing as CHINA EMERGES (Revised)
1991
Ninth printing as CHINA EMERGES (Revised)
1992
Tenth printing as CHINA EMERGES (Revised)
1994

Library of Congress Cataloging-in-Publication Data

Warshaw, Steven.
China emerges.

(The Asia emerges series, 4)
First published in 1964 as part of the Asia emerges
series; rev. and expanded.
Bibliography: p.
1. China—History. I. Title.
DS735.W36   1986   951   86-16783
ISBN 0-87297-001-9 (pbk.)

Printed in the United States of America

CONTENTS

Contents

4
ANARCHY AND RESTORATION: THE SUI, THE TANG, AND THE SONG DYNASTIES, 44-61

5
THE MONGOL EMPIRE (1269-1368) AND THE MING DYNASTY (1368-1644), 62-71

6
THE AGE OF THE MANCHUS: THE QING DYNASTY (1644-1911), 72-83

Contents

China Emerges

11
THE NEW CHINA, 155-186

The cities. The countryside. Civil rights. Religious freedoms.
Corruption. The revival of classes. Increasing unrest.
The struggle of women. Environmental degradation.
Foreign relations, 171
The United States. Russia. Japan. Taiwan.
Tibet and India. Southeast Asia.
The Future of Communist China, 184-186

APPENDIXES

PREFACE & ACKNOWLEDGMENTS

"Recommended with enthusiasm."
>—National Project on Asia in American Schools (Columbia University) and the Association for Asian Studies.

IN SO JUDGING THIS WORK, the National Review of Asia in American Textbooks crowned years of labor with words that it rarely grants. The credit is to be shared: the present volume, along with its three companions in the *Asia Emerges Series*, could only have won the accolade with the cumulative efforts of many people, a few of whom are cited below. The same must be said of the other three volumes, which also won the agency's recommendations.

That a National Review was organized at all is a sign of a growing recognition of Asia's increasing power to change the world. Japan led the way in the consciousness of the West until recently, but now it is China, a new rising dragon among Asian countries. The last chapter of this book indicates China's immense potential to help shape the life of every human on earth.

Not only China, but also Japan, India, and the nations of Southeast Asia have begun to expand their roles in world affairs. By numbers alone, and often by the amazing economic growth now being recorded in Japan, China, Taiwan, Hong Kong, Singapore, and Korea, Asia is claiming more attention in the West. The next century is likely to be much more of an Asian century than the present or past ones.

Aiming to be a clear, concise introduction rather than original scholarship in depth, the Series began informing Western readers about the Far East when Americans were going to war in Vietnam, new holocausts were developing in Southeast Asia, China was entering the world community, Japan was registering some of the greatest commercial triumphs in history, and India and Pakistan were joining the nuclear powers. Thoroughly tested for accuracy and improved over this long period, it has grown with events.

The Series attempts to show how environment, culture, and external pressures may interact to shape an unfolding history. Thus the four books offer glimpses of Asian art, language, philosophy, law, and education as well as the account of Asian political and economic developments which is found in more standard histories. Conscious of their own limitations, the author and researchers hope that these glimpses will send readers to the many more profound texts available, or at least to gain a new point of view.

The present revision of the Series might never have taken place without the specific encouragement of the members of two faculties: Sister M. Naomi Schreiner O.S.U., of Cleveland's Villa Angela Academy; and John Szablewicz, Social Studies Chair at the Fairfield College Preparatory School in Fairfield, Connecticut. They saw a need for a work which was simple yet broader in scope than most. They called for republication, and their willingness to read the revisions in manuscript form proved immensely helpful. David Driscoll, who is also at Fairfield and has long been a teacher of Asian history, added many insights.

In the same generous spirit, Tom Koberna, a distinguished author and the editor of many texts, analyzed the material. Mr. Koberna's incisive questions concerning data and his penchant for plain English did much to improve all four manuscripts. Other readers, of course, chiefly focused on the one manuscript of the four in whose subject they are noted. They reviewed the material for accuracy. The approval of scholars known throughout the world for their efforts in a field as complex and subtle as this was heartening. However, any faults in the material are the author's, not theirs. Revisions in the present work were read, in addition to those listed above, by Dr. Joyce Kallgren, Chair of the Center for Chinese Studies at the University of California, Berkeley, and, these others carefully screened the materials on ancient times, in which they are especially knowledgeable: Dr. S. J. Chen, a noted poet and historian as well as Professor of Chinese at the University of California, Berkeley; Esther Morrison, Professor of History, Howard University, Washington, D.C.; Edward Schafer, Professor and Chair of the Department of Oriental Languages at the University of California, Berkeley; A. Elgin Heinz, Asian specialist and teacher of history in the San Francisco school system; and Kenneth F. Folsom, reader in the Department of History at the University of California, Berkeley. This group reviewed the material up to and including Chapter 6, "The Age of the Manchus."

The effectiveness of the work was greatly increased through the superb help of Shau Wing Chan, Professor of Chinese, Emeritus, Stanford University. His profound concern with China's long history and his desire to share it with American students prompted him to make a vital contribution to *China Emerges*, which he screened for balance and emphasis as well as for accuracy. Before the first publication careful attention was given to the text, too, by Dr. Edward LeFevour, Professor of History—Asian Studies, Mills

College; Dr. John Bryan Starr, then Chair of the Asian Studies Group at the University of California, Berkeley; and Nancy Dyer, then Research Assistant in the Department of Asian Studies at the University of California, Berkeley.

During the updating of text, accurate transliterations of Chinese words into *Hanyu Pinyin* could not have been accomplished without the conscientious aid of Christa Chow of the University of California's famed East Asiatic Library, Berkeley. Finally, the unique collection of illustrations was assembled with much expert help. Consultants in the selection of photographs included Dr. Raymond N. Tang, also of the East Asiatic Library, and Chang-Soo Swanson, who was on its staff at the time the earlier editions were first published. The Associated Press, United Press International, The Asian Student, The Asia Society, and the late Felix Greene, who traveled widely in China, all made contributions, direct or indirect, to this effort. The maps on pages 6-7, 15, and 104, as well as the chart on the structure of China's government on page 136, are Copyright 1981 by the U.S. Government and are contained in the following source: *China: A Country Study*, prepared by Frederica M. Bunge and Rinn Sup Shinn, editors, for Foreign Area Studies, the American University, published by the U.S. Government Printing Office for the Department of the Army.

A Note on the Spelling of Chinese Words in this Book

All of the type in the present edition of *China Emerges* has been reset to reflect the English renderings preferred by the People's Republic of China, that is, in *Hanyu Pinyin* ("Chinese language spelling"). Among older generations which have become accustomed to such traditional spellings as Canton and Chiang Kai-shek, the new forms, Guangzhou and Jiang Jieshi, must of course be relearned. Against this disadvantage the editors weighed the needs of the younger readers. The new generations, which are most likely to be using the book, seem best served by learning what is now an authorized method of transliteration and is strongly supported by over a billion Chinese speakers. Readers who continue to prefer the previous renderings, chiefly developed in the nineteenth century by Sir Thomas Wade and Herbert Giles, may find Appendix A, which compares methods, useful. Moreover, the text parenthetically cites the traditional spellings of many words after their first appearance in Hanyu Pinyin.

—SW
Berkeley

Across the mountains of North China, thousands of laborers are building roads. Their efforts show modern China's determination to become a 20th-century power.

"The Middle Kingdom"

CHAPTER 1

CHINA IN PERSPECTIVE

CHINA TODAY IS A DIVIDED NATION. One part is on the continent of Asia; the other is off the continental shore, on the island of Taiwan. The China of the mainland—known as the People's Republic of China—is by far the larger of the two parts. It occupies that region which, until recently, was the only China known for centuries; it came under the control of the Communists in 1949. The other China—known as the Republic of China—is ruled by a refugee government that formerly held the mainland.

While the people of Western nations have until recently thought of China as remote, the Chinese have long regarded their country as the center of the civilized world. Since before the birth of Christ, the Chinese have called their land *Zhongguo*—"Middle Kingdom"—as if to say that other cultures were satellites of theirs. China's comparative isolation from the nations of Europe led to the development of a unique civilization, encouraging the Chinese to think of themselves as culturally superior. With one exception, the frontiers of China have long been secure. To the west lay Tibet and Central Asia; to the north, Mongolia; to the northeast, Manchuria; and to the east and south, the Pacific and Southeast Asia.

The weakest of China's borders was on the northwest. There, wild Central Asian nomads often overran the frontier. The Gobi Desert was a main invasion route into North China. It was blocked, however, by a great Chinese emperor, Qin Shihuangdi (259—210 B.C.), who during his reign (221—210 B.C.) extended the Great Wall from the Pacific in a westerly direction. The wall was, for a time, an effective barrier against the nomads, who fought on horseback with bows and arrows and had no artillery or siege weapons.

On other frontiers of the nation, natural boundaries hindered contact with foreign peoples. High mountains and dense upland jungles cut the land off from India and Southeast Asia. For centuries the vastness of the Pacific, to the east, discouraged most European nations from sending ships to China. In fact, until the sixteenth century the Chinese considered the sea a "back door," closed to the outside world. This distinct landward orientation, in the face of the threat from Central Asian nomadic tribes, helps to explain why the Chinese did not develop a strong seafaring tradition. China has produced some famous sailors, however, and the country's long, rugged coast has been well used by Chinese fishermen.

Despite its isolation, the Chinese nation has become a blend of many Asian peoples. Beginning in a small river valley, the Wei, the earliest Chinese civilization expanded to include the Yue on the south, the Tai on the north, and the Mongols and Dongu on the northeast. The powerful and sophisticated Chinese culture eventually absorbed many others, drawing even invaders and conquerors into its way of life. Today, as a result, China unites eighteen ethnic groups. Some of these groups do not use the most widely spoken Chinese dialect, Mandarin, but all consider themselves people of China.

China is the most populous nation on earth. According to estimates of the United Nations, by 1990 there were more than 1,100,000,000 Chinese on the mainland alone. They increase at the rate of about 16,000,000 a year, which is almost as many people as live in New York State. The People's Republic announced in 1989 that about 22 percent of the population of the entire world was Chinese. Though enormous, this is far less than had been expected just ten or twenty years ago. Using the powerful forces of law and social pressure, China has succeeded in limiting its annual growth to less than 2 percent in recent years. Even at that rate the population will double in 36 years.

Before World War II, China's enormous population was dominated by a few wealthy landowners and foreign investors. Less than 3 per cent of all Chinese owned one-third of the total land. This unjust situation enabled a few Communists to gain widespread support. The Communists, who considered land distribution to be the country's greatest problem, threw out the landlords when they came to power in 1949. Seizing control of all lands, they killed many landlords in the process.

Nevertheless, the Communists then had the enormous task of increasing agricultural output fast enough to feed the growing population. To solve this problem, they reorganized the whole society. Regulating all aspects of social and economic life, they expected people to dedicate themselves to the state and so raise standards for all. The masses of Chinese were more strictly controlled than ever before in their history. Millions of peasants were brought to work ceaselessly on new dams, levees, and hydroelectric and reforestation projects.

Conditions did improve, but not fast enough. While the people of China were wondering when their sacrifices would end, the country's revolutionary leaders demanded even more rigid controls. At last a change of leadership took place, enabling the government to modify its policies. Some, though not all social and economic regulations were relaxed.

China's economy now mixes Communist and capitalist methods. Under recent changes people must still meet government quotas, but may keep whatever they produce above them. Such incentives to work harder have greatly improved the standard of living. For the first time since their revolution the Chinese have the right to own substantial property, and they are pouring new energies into production. Politically, too, the Chinese Communists seem to be relaxing their controls. Political freedoms are still far from those considered essential in Western democracies, but are greater than they were from 1949-79.

THE LAND

The 3,690,546 square miles that make up modern China are 33 per cent larger than the continental United States. Still, China's arable, habitable land is no greater in area than the ten largest American states. Almost half of the country is covered by mountains, canyons, and hills. All but one-third of the rest is too dry or windswept to support large populations. Considering the number of people it must house and feed, China is dangerously limited in farmland and living space.

Many of the mountains of North China are steep and barren. Over them and adjacent desert plains, ancient Chinese built the Great Wall.

The mountains extend from the mighty ranges of Central Asia, in Tibet and Xinjiang, across western China. From Mount Everest (29,028 feet), the highest point in the world, whose summit China shares with Nepal, the ranges descend toward the Pacific. At their base to the north, on the high plateau of Mongolia, the Gobi and several lesser deserts stretch for one thousand miles in a broad arc around the north of China. Craggy mountains separate them from the broad, grassy plains of Manchuria, to the northeast.

In ancient times, it was necessary to guard China's northerly frontiers through the construction of the Great Wall. Today, lands far beyond the Great Wall are part of China. Eighteen provinces south of the wall are even now called "China Proper," or "Central China." China Proper includes four major centers of population: North China, South China, the Red Basin, and the Guangzhou Region. Life in each of these four areas is closely tied to one or another of the three principal rivers of China. From north to south, these rivers are the Yellow (Huang), Yangzi (Yangtze), and Xi (West). The main regions of China include these sub-regions:

Western China and Mongolia. The world's highest mountains stand to the west of China, in Tibet. There, most of the land is above 16,000 feet and the average altitude is 15,000 feet. The mountains consist of the mighty Pamir and Himalayan ranges on the west and south and the Kunlun Range on the north. Tibet is so steep, arid, and cold that it has only one agricultural region, the valley of the Zangbo—the Tibetan name for India's Brahamaputra River, which rises there.

The Zangbo Valley is in the south of Tibet. To the east of it are other valleys which receive summer rainfall, and where the Mekong, Salween, and Yangzi rivers originate. The Mekong and Salween rivers flow down from Tibet into Burma. The Yangzi surges across the Daxueshan, or Great Snowy Alps at the Chinese border. Then it cuts into the lower but still formidable mountains of China's Sichuan Province.

To the north of Tibet lies Xinjiang. This outer Chinese province, with a land area of 633,000 square miles, is crossed by the Tianshan, or Heavenly Mountains, which range eastward into China for 1,000 miles. On either side of its 20,000-foot high peaks, in Xinjiang, are basins that extend from the Gobi Desert. Their sandy floors are still dotted with oases which, in ancient times, were waystations on the main land routes between China and Europe.

East of Xinjiang and north of China is Inner Mongolia, a newly acquired Chinese province. The Gobi Desert occupies most of this land, stretching into Outer Mongolia and dipping southward into China Proper. Below the Yellow River, it is called the Ordos Plain.

Loess, the powdery soil that is blown into North China from Mongolia, is made fertile by Chinese peasants.

Those parts of the two Mongolias that are not desert are arid mountains.

Northeast China. Manchuria, which includes three Chinese provinces with a total land area of 404,000 square miles, lies between one of the world's longest rivers, the Amur, and China Proper. Although mountains encircle most of it, Manchuria has at its center a rolling plain that is moist and fertile, which is bounded on the south by the Yellow Sea. Not all of this plain is arable, however. Much of it is swampy or permanently frozen.

North China. Descending from the Inner Mongolian border, the Yellow River (or Huanghe) flows through the Yellow Plain. The land is almost entirely flat. It spreads for 150,000 square miles, forming China's oldest and largest agricultural area.

Thick brush once grew along most of the Yellow River's 2,700-mile length. Before recorded time, the first farmers cut and burned this brush to extend their lands for planting. For centuries the river has been carrying away rich soil from banks thus stripped of vegetation, depositing some at the bottom of the bed and some in the delta. Fragments of soil give the water a yellowish hue—thus the river's name. Lacking the vegetation to contain it, the riverbed has risen steadily, and despite dikes laboriously constructed for centuries, the stream has often overflowed its banks.

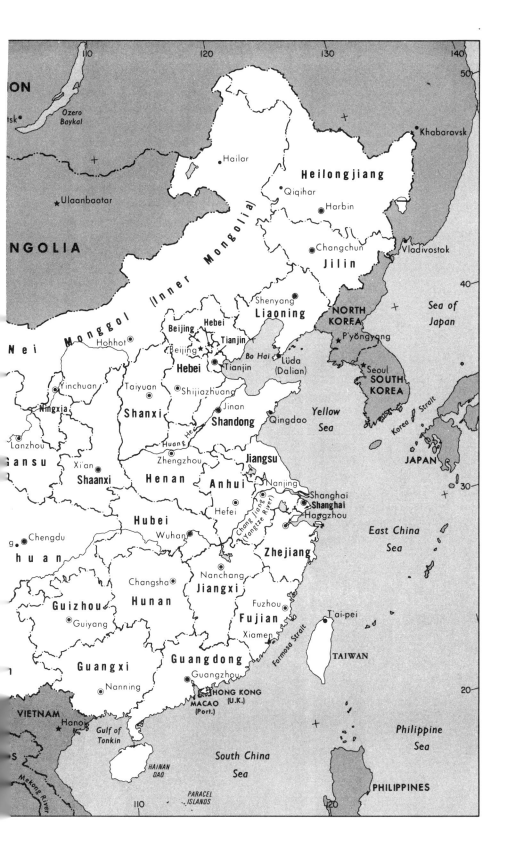

Along the northerly course of the Yellow River, in Shaanxi and Shanxi provinces, lies a region of about 100,000 square miles known as the loess plateau. "Loessland" also includes large areas of western Gansu and northern Henan provinces: it reaches as far to the northwest as Xinjiang. The word "loess" comes from the German verb losen, to dissolve or to loosen. Over the ages, cold, dry winds from the desert have deposited layers of dust over this region, to a depth in some places of 300 feet. The loosened soil, highly porous and fertile, is easily eroded. Some of the land in Shaanxi Province is so soft that it cannot support an oxcart. Carts have worn roads in it thirty feet deep. Farmers have hollowed caves into for centuries, creating makeshift houses despite the many who have died in them during earthquakes. They remain because much of the porous soil can be made highly productive.

The presence of loess has had an immensely important influence on life in North China. Picked up by the Yellow River, the light soil is carried for miles before it is deposited in the river's bed. Thus in the delta, the bed is too shallow for the river after the heaviest rains. There, flood waters have often broken through even the broadest dikes built by humans.

The Shandong Promontory, spreading to the east of the delta, is largely a plain over which mountains rise more than 5,000 feet. This promontory is about 100 miles wide at its junction with the mainland. Yet the mouth of the Yellow River, now north of it, has flowed past its southern end, too. The riverbed has shifted to that extent, the last time in 1856. In addition to the problem of flooding, farmers of this region suffer from the intrusion of briny sea water into their fresh water supplies.

The Yellow Plain is bounded on the south by the Qinling Mountains, which extend from Tibet into the center of China. Although not high by Asian standards, the chain's peaks near the Yellow River soar to 12,000 feet above sea level, towering over the valley of a lesser river, the Wei. Rising in the path of the rain-bearing monsoons, the Qinling Mountains are one important reason why North China is dryer and colder than South China and why the loess of the North has never spread to the South. The mountains separate the Yellow River from the Yangzi and slope down into the Yellow Plain.

South China. On the southern slopes of the Qinling Range, green hills extend southward. There, the elevations are known as the Tapa Mountains. The population of this region is concentrated along the lower course of the Yangzi River, which winds among the hills until it enters its delta. Farmers, terracing and irrigating up the hillsides, have made this one of China's most important rice-

The Yangtzi Delta is often flooded. Farmers make high earthen dikes in order to grow rice in it. Here, women are building a reservoir.

growing areas. For 150 miles between the hills and the seacoast, the Yangzi flows through the rich, alluvial soil of its delta. This intensively farmed and irrigated area is the most populous in all China. It includes Shanghai, which, with its 12 million people, is the largest Chinese city. Down the coast from this metropolis are the other large ports of Hangzhou, Ningbo, Wenzhou, Fuzhou, and Xiamen.

The Red Basin. In western China, the Yangzi River flows through the Red Basin, an almost circular plain that is 2,000 feet above sea level and 1,500 feet below sheltering mountains. The Red Basin is so named because of the color of the sandstone that lies beneath its rich topsoil. The number of people living in this region is not known, but it probably exceeds sixty million.

Below the Red Basin the Yangzi drops into steep mountains, cutting deep gorges through which it bubbles and foams; here the river is navigable only by skillful sailors in small boats. Below the "Gorge Mountains," however, the Yangzi broadens and is joined by the Han, Xiang, and Gan rivers. At the confluence of each of these rivers are three busy inland ports, Wuchang, Hanyang, and Hangzhou, each nearly six hundred miles from the Pacific Ocean.

The Guangzhou Region. The southern coast of China twists and bends more than the northern, and many small islands lie offshore. Land there is generally hilly. Toward the southwest, mountains run parallel to the coast, covering all but 15 per cent of the region. The largest river of this area, the Xi (West), rises 1,650 miles from the coast, in Tibet.

With two other rivers, the Dong (East) and Bei (North), the Xi flows into a delta where the metropolis is Guangzhou (Canton), a huge commercial center of about 5,250,000 people. Guangzhou sprawls across a large stream of the delta, the Zhu (Pearl). The Zhu is not deep enough for ocean-going vessels, but Western seamen have been able to reach Guangzhou by means of other rivers of the delta and have historically favored it as their Chinese port. The Portuguese did so in 1557, when they became the first Westerners to settle in China. They set up trading stations on the peninsula of Macao, in the mouth of the Xi River near Guangzhou. Today the Portuguese colony of Macao covers about six square miles and has 300,000 people.

Opposite Macao in the Xi River delta, ninety miles southeast of Guangzhou, lies the rocky island of Hong Kong. The British acquired Hong Kong in 1841 after a war with China, and in 1898 they forced the Chinese government to lease them 355 square miles of adjacent mainland. Both the island and the mainland area, which is part of the Kowloon Peninsula, must be returned to China when the lease expires in 1997. Until then the British will continue to administer these lands from the city of Victoria, on Hong Kong.

The Chinese province in which the Xi River delta lies, Guangdong, includes a long, narrow peninsula which points toward the large offshore island of Hainan. Covered by steep mountains, Hainan, by contrast to the rest of China, is sparsely populated. Few immigrants have come to settle on it. On the mainland to the northwest of Hainan, beyond the Chinese border with Vietnam, lie the important Chinese provinces of Guangxi and Yunnan. Mountainous but extremely moist and fertile, they produce much of China's rice and silk.

Taiwan. Midway between the southern port of Guangzhou and the northern one of Shanghai, opposite the province of Fujian, lies the island of Taiwan. It is 110 miles offshore, beyond a series of craggy isles called the Penghu, or Pescadores Group. The island of Taiwan slopes toward them from a rocky eastern side that rises to almost 13,000 feet. Located in a humid, semi-tropical climate, Taiwan is richly covered with vegetation. The name Formosa ("beautiful") was given it by Portuguese sailors in the sixteenth century. Asians continue to call it by the older Chinese name of Taiwan, however.

CLIMATE

In China's most populous areas, the climate resembles that of the eastern United States. North China has cold winters and brief summers with little rain. South China has much more rain than the North and is much less windy, but its heat and humidity often are intense and oppressive. On the South China coast, cyclones and hurricanes often form and cause widespread destruction.

Extremes of temperature prevail in the far north and south. Throughout Tibet, Xinjiang, and Mongolia, the land is cold and dry, with some exceptions caused by the terrain. The Guangzhou Region in the south, on the other hand, extends almost into the tropics. Although it experiences some frost, it is hot and humid for at least eleven months of the year.

Winds from the north, and monsoons from the south, are important factors in these climatic changes. During every month but July, cold air blows into China from the Arctic. Moving at speeds between thirty and sixty miles an hour, it sweeps over North China, carrying loess dust from the Ordos Plain. At the Qinling Mountains the air is shunted eastward; at the coast, it becomes warmer.

While North China often appears brown, the ground cover of the South is more likely to be green. Beginning every June, summer winds bring heavy rainfall below the Qinling Mountains. Rainfall there may be sixty to eighty inches, more than twice as much as in the North. But throughout China the autumns are likely to be brisk and the winters cold, with windblown snows.

So much of China is mountainous that, to grow enough food, the farmers terrace the hillsides.

AGRICULTURE

Chinese agriculture began of the banks of the Wei River. There, the Qinling Mountains sheltered early farmers from continual winds and caused the moist air to precipitate rain. As population grew, these farmers spread down the course of the Yellow River, clearing thick shrubbery from the land as they went. The pioneers of North America were fortunate to discover fertile plains, meadows, and hillsides ready for planting. The settlers of China needed centuries to prepare the land.

More than 70 per cent of China's terrain is too dry, cold, or mountainous for agriculture. Half of the remaining acreage, or 15 per cent, was all that remained to be tilled by Chinese farmers for centuries. By contrast, more than 50 per cent of the land in the United States is arable. When computed on a per capita basis, China has only one-tenth the arable land in the United States. Some Chinese lands can sustain neither humans nor animals. Meanwhile a single square mile on the fertile river plains may support more than five thousand people and two thousand animals.

Despite its huge population, China has relatively few cattle or beasts of burden. Good grazing land is scarce because all available farmland must be used for crops. Farmers therefore concentrate on raising animals that are small and cheap to feed. Scavengers such as pigs, chickens, and ducks are numerous throughout China. Oxen and water buffaloes supply energy, not food, though some are used for their dairy products. The Chinese have disliked dairy foods until very recently. This aversion has deprived them of calcium and other minerals in their diets, causing them to be a relatively small people.

Since the beginning of agriculture in China, certain crops have been favored—particularly rice (originally introduced from Southeast Asia), sorghums, and millets. Over the centuries, other important crops have been added. Two of these, maize and sweet potatoes, reached China by way of the Philippine Islands, where they were brought by Spaniards from the Americas.

Cotton and soybeans are now important in Chinese agriculture, too. Wheat has long been the main crop in the north; it grows in areas where water is less plentiful. Ricefields spread over the humid areas of South China, while millets (including *gaoliang*, a grain sorghum) are thick in the northwestern and central valleys. In

Millions of tons of fertilizer are needed to make China's poor soil productive. The Communists have organized ways to distribute it.

addition, silkworm-raising has long been practiced in the Yangzi Valley, where the mulberry trees on which the worms feed are cultivated.

Chinese agriculture depends on plentiful human labor and on skillful irrigation. About four-fifths of the population toils in the fields and paddies, working almost every inch of arable soil. The hills have been terraced, often by bare hands, to make room for wheat and rice. Water is coaxed from the rivers by means of water-wheels and other primitive devices. It is channeled throughout the land by means of intricate networks of canals, which may be counted among China's greatest achievements. At least 300,000 miles of them, some centuries old, have transformed the land and increased the agricultural potential by many times. There were canals in the delta of the Yangzi River as early as the eighth century B.C. By the second century B.C. a Chinese emperor was proclaiming that his government had the historic obligation to "cut canals, drain the rivers, and build dikes and water tanks to prevent drought."

The most important artificial waterway in China, the Grand Canal, was started during the sixth century A.D., and the government has been maintaining and improving it ever since. At times, up to one million Chinese have labored to improve this waterway, until today it extends from Beijing in the North to the port of Hangzhou in the South. In a nation with few roads, the Grand Canal is used primarily for transport, but it also irrigates much of China Proper.

Most Chinese soil is worn out and must be replenished by the use of fertilizers. Since the country is poor in livestock, little animal manure is available for this purpose. Moreover, straw and plant stalks must be used as fuel rather than for fertilization. Farmers therefore commonly use human wastes—so-called "night soil"—to enrich their lands. This has sometimes caused epidemics, but such primitive, often dangerous methods of agriculture are still widely used in China. Despite recent efforts to industrialize, China remains primarily a farming nation, and its economy is borne on the backs of millions of toiling peasants.

MINERALS

Having concentrated on agricultural production for centuries, China has spent little time searching for minerals and has not been a successful producer of them. Coal is one exception. China's deposits of this mineral, among the most extensive in the world, were well used long before Europeans burned coal. When Marco

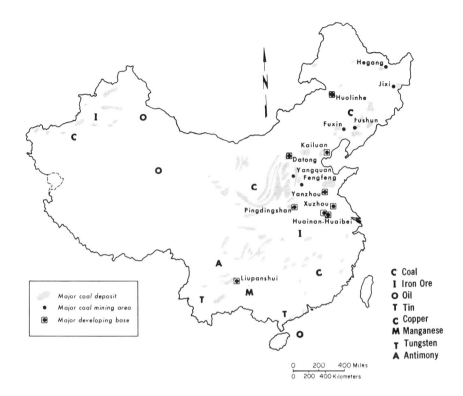

Hegang
Jixi
Huolinhe
C Fushun
Fuxin
Kailuan
Datong
Yangquan
Fengfeng
Yanzhou
Xuzhou
Pingdingshan
Huainan-Huaibei
I
I
O
C
O
O
C
I
A
Liupanshui
M
T
C
T
O

Major coal deposit
Major coal mining area
Major developing base

C Coal
I Iron Ore
O Oil
T Tin
C Copper
M Manganese
T Tungsten
A Antimony

0   200   400 Miles
0   200   400 Kilometers

MINERAL RESOURCES OF CHINA

Polo visited China in the thirteenth century, that famous Italian traveler wrote: "It is a fact that throughout the province of Cathay there is a sort of black stone, which is dug out of veins in the hillsides and burns like logs. These stones keep a fire going better than wood."

During recent efforts to industrialize, China has redoubled its search for minerals. The country has long been known to have good deposits of copper, tungsten, lead, zinc, manganese, tin, and limestone. It also appears to have most of the world's antimony, which is used to harden soft metals. Yet in modern times, these are secondary minerals. In a machine age the world needs iron, steel, oil, gasoline, and plastics, which are often made from petroleum.

Until after World War II, China was thought to have little oil and almost no coking coal or iron ore. Today, Chinese geologists are reported to have turned up immense supplies of all three of these minerals. With advice from Western and Japanese technicians, they have found substantial oil deposits under Chinese seas. One iron ore deposit, in Shanxi Province, is said to have more than three times the amount of ore taken from the rich mines of Minnesota between 1892 and 1950.

The discovery of these minerals does not necessarily mean that China can use them. The problems of mining, refining, and transporting mineral products are enormous. In an effort to use scrap and low-grade iron ores, the government encouraged people to build small backyard furnaces during the 1950's. The experiment was a failure, however, because of the difficulty of gathering and distributing the product.

CHAPTER 2

THE ORIGINS OF CHINESE CIVILIZATION

MYTHOLOGICAL

CHINESE LEGENDS SAY THAT THE FIRST MAN, called Pangu, lived eighteen thousand years, and that he spent his lifetime creating the earth and the sky. He kept growing, according to legend, until his tears were so heavy that they became the Yellow and Yangzi rivers, his breath the wind, and his words the thunder. Upon his death, the parts of his body became the Five Sacred Mountains of China, his flesh the streams and seas, his hair the plants, and his eyes the sun and the moon.

The legends assert that three equally awesome rules followed Pangu: the lords of heaven, earth, and man. The first two also lived eighteen thousand years; each had twelve heads, the bodies of serpents, and the feet of beasts. They served to prop up the sky with the mountains of Tibet and to prepare the earth for the coming of humans.

With their introduction of the Lord of Man, China's legends give more clues to the country's pre-history. They state that during the ten epochs of his 45,600-year rule, the major problems of civilization in China were solved. During the first part of his reign he slew the flying beasts and then the dragons. Next he taught humans to wear clothing and to build houses high in trees, above floods. From these houses they were able to fish. They also learned a form of writing—the Eight Trigrams—as written symbols for heaven, earth, fire, water, wind, thunder, marsh, and mountain.

During the tenth and last epoch of the Lord of Man's reign, an emperor began the division of China into provinces and districts. This ruler, the so-called Yellow Emperor, appointed administrators for these divisions. By doing so he revealed a Chinese passion that has never ceased—the desire for social order. In addition, he and his wife are said to have been the first to make silk in China and to have introduced calendars, coins, canoes, and chariots. Even today the Chinese honor the Yellow Emperor and Empress as founders of their high civilization.

The Yellow Emperor is said to have been succeeded by a ruler named Yao. Needing help in the administration of his growing kingdom, Yao chose a peasant named Shun to be his first minister and heir-apparent. The ancient texts say that he chose Shun after putting him to the most extraordinary tests of courage, including a threat of a forest fire. Having passed these tests, Shun was assigned to help the Chinese people roll back the floodwaters and to drive off the beasts that stalked their land. With the aid of four brave lieutenants, Shun burned down the wilderness. He plowed the soil, sowed in it, and labored to control floods which endangered the people and were later mastered.

The legends, some of which are still current in parts of China, refer to the lieutenants as princes. One of these men, Prince Millet, trained people in agriculture; his name refers to one of the wheat grains still widely planted in North China. Another taught the Five Principles of Chinese Society. These principles have been restated many times in Chinese literature and remain important in Chinese life. They urge integrity of government, love of family, the knowledge of one's place in society, the respect of the young for the old, and loyalty among friends.

One of Shun's princes was named Yu. After Shun's death, Yu founded a dynasty, or line of kings, which ruled on the threshold of recorded history in China. This dynasty, the Xia, appears to have ruled in North China from 2205 to 1766 B.C. During the reign of its kings, the people of China were discovering how to make bronze, to use the wheel, and to domesticate animals. The names of surrounding tribes communicate a feeling of life in those times. To the east were enemies of the Xia, the Yi (archers), to the north the Di (dog users), to the west the Rong (spear users), and to the south the Man (silkworm cultivators).

The Chinese have been telling stories of these cultural forefathers for centuries. In doing so, they show their pride in a civilization deeply rooted in the distant past. Thus basic ideas established long ago have been made to command the loyalty of millions of Chinese. These ideas were developed during the legendary period and were first recorded during the dynasty that succeeded the Xia. Over the generations since then, the Chinese have always looked to the past for the wisdom that would enable them to live in the present. They have seen themselves as a continuation of a society that began before history was written—the oldest continuous civilization surviving in the world.

YELLOW RIVER CULTURES: THE SHANG DYNASTY (1766—1122 B.C.)

Near modern Anyang, in Henan (Honan) Province, a people called Shang became powerful in the eighteenth century B.C.

Advancing down the banks of the Huan River, a tributary of the Yellow River, this mystical people, who claimed to have been descended from a heaven-sent swallow, developed a culture for which the first records still exist. With the advent of the Shang Dynasty, history begins in China.

The Shangs, like many other clans of the Yellow Plain, became discontented with the rule of the Xia kings. By 1766 B.C. the last of these monarchs, King Jie, was so openly corrupt that he lost the support of the people. He spent most of his time, and much public money, on a notorious concubine. Even at this early period of Chinese history there was established the teaching that homage is due to a good ruler but that the right to rule—the "Mandate of Heaven"—may be withdrawn from a bad one. Accordingly, a rebellion began against King Jie. It was led by Prince Tang of the Shang people and was encouraged by the king's own family.

With their victory the Shangs (later renamed the Yins) began China's second dynasty. Sending expeditions far into the plains, they subjugated many tribes, ranging from Mongolia to the Pacific Ocean. They were not always successful in warfare and occasionally were driven back to the river. Nevertheless the Shang kings, who were worshipped as gods, sacrificed animals, and probably

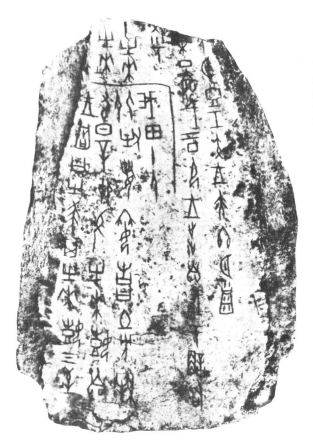

The earliest form of Chinese writing was inscribed on tortoise shells by court oracles.

humans, too, in order to arouse the people for battle. They sent out brigades of infantrymen and charioteers dressed in strong leather armor, furnished with bronze weapons. In those days armies consisted of from three to five thousand professional soldiers; the hunters and farmers stayed home.

The Shangs were as notable for their peaceful skills as they were for their valor in war. With a fine technical sense, they were able to alloy metals and hew stones for building materials. They used vessels mounted on bronze and earthenware legs throughout their houses. Thousands of these artifacts, in addition to many bows, knives, spears, and parts of chariots, have been found recently along the banks of the Huan River. Despite their age, modern artists still admire their vigorous shapes and marvelous symbolic designs.

Late in the Shang Period, about 1300 B.C., members of the court concentrated at Anyang. They organized a new capital for the empire, a complex city with temples, palaces, public buildings, and houses. Its structures were made of stone and wood columns, sidings, and roofs; its foundations were made of earth. Here the Shang kings ruled by means of a calendar, based on phases of the moon, that enabled the people to know the time to plant, harvest, hunt, and make war.

Development of writing. The Eight Trigrams, which Chinese legends say existed from pre-historic times, provided a basis for a more complex form of writing. These figures, as we have seen, were symbols for heaven, earth, fire, water, wind, thunder, marsh, and mountain. Through them the Chinese understood that both objects and ideas could be represented in writing. People of the Shang Period required both for mystical purposes.

They wanted to see into the future. For an unknown reason, they believed that the flat, bottom shells of tortoises could help them in this quest. Shang kings ordered the turtles brought to them, and oracles marked the shells. When certain points of the shells were heated, cracks would appear. The oracles claimed to be able to read the future in these cracks, much as modern seers may claim to read the lines in hands or the patterns in tea leaves.

Using sharp tools, the oracles often inscribed both the question, such as—"Will I be successful in the hunt?"—and the answer that they read in the shells. These would be placed on the turtle shells themselves, or, when the animal shoulder bones were used, as they sometimes were, across the bones. Their desire to make these inscriptions led the Shang people to develop Chinese writing.

Most visible classes of objects, such as birds or trees, were easily drawn. By the time of the Shang Period they were rendered in the form of what are now called pictographs. Acts or ideas, however, are more difficult to show because they are not visible. The Shang people solved this problem by combining different pictographs. The idea for "words" for example, they represented by showing a pictograph for a mouth with another pictograph for vapor emerging from it. Modern comic strips do approximately the same.

Additional combinations were needed to make the more abstract ideas meaningful when written. The result, called an "ideogram," is shown when the Chinese symbols for "words" and "tongue" are used together to make the word "speech." Finally, a class of words called "phonograms" was developed. It enabled the Chinese to use the sound of one word for another having the same sound but an entirely different meaning. In English, the effect would be the same if the word "horse" were represented by a picture of the animal and if the same picture were used to express the word "hoarse." Much confusion would result from this unless the second word were given an additional mark, or determinative, as linguists call it. This the Chinese did.

Over the more than three thousand years of its development, Chinese writing has been greatly elaborated. It now includes at least forty thousand characters. The earliest pictographs have been altered and stylized to such a degree that it no longer always possible to see in them the pictures from which they were evolved. Thus the Shang inscription for sun ⊙ has passed through these stages: ⬭ and ▭. To make it more easily written with a brush, the writing tool used by later Chinese calligraphers, it next was changed to 日. In addition to such changed words, thousands of new characters have been added to the language.

Despite modifications in them, Chinese characters are still built on the same basic principles first introduced by the Shang scribes. Each is a composite of several "keys"—one of which gives the sound, or pronounciation, while another (or several) supplies the meaning. Until recent times Chinese was written in vertical columns, from right to left. This practice can be explained by the fact that early Chinese "paper" was made of strips of bamboo. A few of the old, simple pictographs remain in current use.

Early religion. The Shangs developed an important religious concept which has affected the Chinese people ever since. It is the idea of a Supreme Being, or *Di*, who the Shangs believed created and ruled the universe. They believed that the spirit of the Di dwelled in their kings.

Chinese monarchs later claimed they were the "Sons of Heaven" and deserved power because of the "Mandate of Heaven." Many of them reminded their people of this invincible support by placing

As writing developed in China, letters were drawn on bamboo strips. They were bound vertically; thus, the writing became vertical, too.

the word Di after their names. Still, neither the Shangs nor succeeding Chinese believed that their kings were gods. The Chinese held that like any son, a king could displease his father, the Supreme Being. They developed this principle more fully during later dynasties. An innate harmony existed between heaven, earth, and humans, they reasoned. In their view, floods, plagues, or droughts meant that human misconduct had thrown nature out of balance. They held the king responsible for the disorder because it was his duty to set an example of right conduct. If the country's troubles persisted, they declared the right to remove the king and to replace him with someone whose virtues would restore the natural harmony.

CHINESE CIVILIZATION: THE ZHOU DYNASTY (1122—256 B.C.)

Near the source of the Yellow River, in the valley of its tributary, the Wei, lived a people called the Zhou (Chou). Their recent ancestors had been western nomads who had settled inside of China to become farmers. The Iron Age was just beginning in this part of the world; new tools, both for farming and for warfare, were available to them. So great was their energy and skill in using these tools, in agriculture and in conquest, that their king, Wen, was called "Chief of the West."

Members of the Zhou family became powerful enough to marry women from the royal Shang court. They were not pacified by this, however; their charioteers had often beaten back the invading

Huns of the north and were ready for fresh victories in the south. Chinese historians say that the Zhou people decided to attack the Shangs because of the corruption and cruelty of the Shang king, Zhou Xin. Probably the accounts were influenced by the Zhou's victory, and the real reason lay in their readiness to expand. In any case, King Wen ordered his troops to attack King Zhou Xin.

The Zhou people were at first defeated; their king, whose name was Wen, was briefly imprisoned. Soon, however, Wen's son, Prince Wu, resumed the fight and burned the Shang palace while Zhou Xin was leading his troops nearby. Zhou Xin, hearing of the attack, hurried back to the capital. There, the inscriptions relate, on hearing of the defeat of his palace guard, he fled to the still burning structure, "climbed onto the Terrace of the Stag, arrayed himself in his pearl and jade, and hurled himself into the flames."

For the next three years Prince Wu marched against the nobles of the tottering Shang Empire. While defeating them he also captured or slaughtered the roaming leopards, tigers, rhinoceroses, and elephants that had made life intolerable in many parts of the kingdom. A complex empire was established. After Wen's death Wu became its sovereign, the first emperor of the great Zhou Dynasty. He, his father, Wen, and his brother, Tan, who was called the Duke of Zhou, have a place in Chinese history that resembles sainthood in Western culture.

Social developments. King Wen is credited with changing the ancient custom under which a ruler's heir was his brother rather than his son. This custom often tempted the heir to slay his brother, the king, when he himself was too old to wait for legal succession to the throne. From King Wen, legitimate power passed to Prince (later Emperor) Wu, and then to Wu's eldest son, Zheng. The Emperor Zheng was only a boy, however, when he came to power. His uncle, the Duke of Zhou, respected social custom and served as regent rather than as emperor until the boy came to maturity. Ever since, Chinese families have granted their first-born sons positions of immense esteem.

Another field of government that concerned the Zhou Dynasty, beginning with its first emperor, was the administration of land. The Emperor Wu recognized that some distant noblemen continued to be loyal to the traditions of the Shangs. To win them over, he boldly appointed them the administrators of the outlying districts. Approximately 1,600 members of his own family and court also were given lands to control.

The result was the development of feudalism, which to the Zhou rulers seemed the best way to govern distant places. The Zhous appointed five grades of nobility—dukes, marquis, earls, viscounts,

King Wen and his son, Prince Wu, held regular audiences for noblemen, thus establishing a system of civil service that was to endure.

and barons. They divided the land and put it under the control of nobles in amounts which varied according to grade. The largest grants, 100 square *li* (a li was about one-third of a mile), went to the dukes. The barons received the smallest grants, about 50 li each.

Later tradition claims that the feudal states subdivided their lands into units of nine parts each, using a method called the "well-field system." This system is illustrated by the Chinese character for a well: 井. Under it, eight families lived around the central square. After farming the center, which was owned by the states, they were permitted to till the outer squares for themselves. Whether the ancient system of land division was so ideally uniform is open to question.

The Zhou rulers therefore created a circular chain of loyalty. First, the peasants made their strongest commitment to their families. Peasants gladly accepted this because they shared the responsibilities for labor with members of their families and, in the Chinese way, usually developed profound affections for them. Second, families were committed to the nobles, from whom they received protection from enemies, hunger, and sickness in exchange for labor. The nobles also had to guarantee that every able-bodied Chinese could work on land. The nobles were responsible to inspectors who held them to their duties. As the king's representatives, the inspectors supervised agricultural production, and they also distributed pensions to the sick, aged, or orphaned. In pyramidal fashion, these inspectors were responsible to the king himself. He checked on them and sought to gain the loyalty of the people by visiting the countryside every five years.

In modern times, China's feudal system seems amazingly complete. Relying on a uniform or autocratic society rather than on a diverse one, however, it had basic weaknesses. Such a system would either remain stable or, if disaster struck the farm economy, would collapse entirely. Nobles might take advantage of the peasants and escape detection, especially if the central government were weak. "Nothing is put aside for emergencies such as sickness, funeral expenses, and extra taxes," Li Kui, a minister in the Wei River Valley, wrote sadly. "Consequently, the farmers are always in a state of poverty."

Civil servants. One of the most important of Chinese institutions was evolved from the organization of feudal inspectors. It became known as the examination system and developed in this way:

The Chinese considered it a sacred trust to serve the country through the emperor. Because appointment to the civil service was considered such a distinction, no single person, not even the king, had the right to judge candidates. Those chosen were expected to be loyal to China rather than to a person. Committees of scholars were formed, therefore, to interview the candidates. All Chinese males, including commoners, were permitted to apply. The government offered elaborate courses, complete with complex educational materials, on the workings of the civil service. A Zhou nobleman described a class conducted by the king for aspiring civil servants:

> *Just before the dawn the king would enter his court while the candidates were ushered in. Then, at commands from the king, the court historian would hold up strips of bamboo on which various texts and instructions were written. With great ceremony he would recite rules and regulations: "One horse and one roll of silk are exchanged for five slaves. . . ."*

The Chinese have endeavored to learn the formal rules and ceremonies of their country since ancient times. They think of governing as one of the most worthy occupations. Civil servants of the Zhou court planned and helped to carry out irrigation and road-building projects, financing them through taxes. Chinese emperors often paid foreigners to join their armies, but civil servants were loyal to China for more reasons than payment. They looked to the leaders of Chinese culture—to the founders of one of the world's earliest and most important systems of ethics—for guidance.

The Zhou Dynasty ruled for a total of 772 years. At first its monarchs governed from their ancestral home in the Wei River Valley, in the west. This period, which lasted until about 771 B.C., is known as the "Western Zhou." During this time barbarians raided the northeastern coast, threatening the lower river valleys. The border states of the Zhou Empire formed their own armies to combat the menace. These provinces, especially those of Chen and Qin, toughened by constant warfare, became rebellious and asserted their independence from the central Zhou government. Even after the government moved its capital to Luoyang, where it endured for almost three centuries as the "Eastern Zhou," its deterioration continued, and the barbarians won greater successes.

There followed an age of the dissolution of the empire—the Warring States Period (480—222 B.C.). Ancient skills in government and the arts deteriorated. Soldiers rebelled against their commanders and seized power. Codes of chivalry, which had been respected in feudal times, were swept away. No longer was combat a genteel affair, marked by formal challenges and duels. The era of the "gentleman" was over. Bandit armies ranged the countryside. They were made up of uncouth archers and swordsmen who suddenly appeared on horseback at the gates of cities, intent on bloodshed and plunder. This type of rough-and-ready warfare was perfected by a king of the province of Zhao. He had found it most effective against the barbarian invaders and soon turned it against the Chinese people.

CHINESE PHILOSOPHY: CONFUCIANISM AND DAOISM

Like the classical age of ancient Greece, the late Zhou Period was a time notable for the number and quality of its philosophers. Most of these teachers came from the Qi and Lu region (modern Shandong Province), the mountainous land that juts into the Pacific above the delta of the Yellow River.

Confucianism. The greatest philosopher-teacher of the Zhou Period, and of all other times in China, was Confucius. Born in 551 B.C., Confucius opened a school for the sons of noblemen when he was twenty-one years old. He did this at great personal sacrifice: he was a descendant of a Shang king and is said to have been Minister of Justice in his native state of Lu. Rather than staying in the government, of which he disapproved, he risked his career and possibly his life in order to teach.

Confucius lived in a violent time, and he made it his mission to plead for peace. In his opinion, a stronger civilization could be developed if individuals could be taught to accept the idea of *ren*, or humanitarianism. The settled ideas of the past, rather than the controversies of his lifetime, could be used to advance *ren*, he thought. Accordingly, he claimed no originality, but only to be the transmitter of ancient wisdom to his contemporaries.

For generations since Confucius lived, his followers have asserted that he was able to search back for literature dating from the mythological ruler Yao. They say that he compiled the material and the wisdom of the Shang and early Zhou dynasties in five sacred books. In large measure, the texts were ancient writings that he brought together. Parts of them, however, appear to have been inserted into the work by his followers after his death. In any case, millions of Chinese ever since have believed in the Five Classics, which describe what has come to be called Confucianism. These books are:

1. The *Yijing (I Ching)*, or Book of Changes, is said to contain the thinking of prehistoric oracles, as revealed in mystic hexagrams. The appendixes, or "wings," are said to have been written by Confucius.

2. The *Shujing*, or Book of History, is thought to include the statements of rulers and ministers from the days of Yao to Zhou. Many of the statements, however, seem to have been added long after Confucius died.

3. The *Shijing*, or Book of Odes, is an anthology containing 305 poems, folk songs, and ceremonial lyrics dating from the Shang and the early Zhou Dynasty periods.

4. The Ritual. This is a group of texts, the best known of which is the Book of Rites, which offer a practical guide for living in the ways of Confucius.

5. The *Qunqiu*, or Spring and Autumn Annals, is a brief chronicle of events in the state of Lu during the years 722 to 481 B.C., and was compiled by Confucius from official records.

The essence of Confucianism, as it developed, was allegiance to human values rather than to any religious rites. Confucianism, therefore, was more a system of ethics than a religious movement, although it has probably attracted more followers than any of the religions of the world. Its ideals in relation to government and the family are expressed in the Book of Rites:

> *When the Great Dao prevails, the world becomes a commonwealth; men of talents and virtues are elected, and mutual confidence and harmony prevail. Then people not only love their own parents and care for their own children, but also those of others. The old people are able to enjoy their old age; the young are able to employ their talents; the juniors respect their elders; widows, orphans, and cripples are all well taken care of. The men have their proper occupations, and the women their homes. If the people do not want to see their wealth being discarded under the ground, they do not*

have to keep it for their own use. If they labor with their
strength, they do not have to labor for their own profit. In
this way, selfish schemings are repressed and cannot develop;
bandits and burglars do not show themselves; and as a result,
the outer doors remain open and need not be shut at night.
This is the age of . . . the Great Commonwealth.

Thus Confucianism offered a way to world peace through the extension of family love. In addition to the Five Classics, the Four Sacred Books, recorded by followers of Confucius, related this message as the essential one of his teachings. Having the family as its foundation, these books urged the improvement of the masses rather than the enrichment of a few rulers. Confucius made education almost holy to the Chinese, who ever since have excelled in scholarship. In the *Analects*, a thin volume that is perhaps best known of the Four Sacred Books, the followers of Confucius noted that he said:

Those who are born with the possession of knowledge are
the highest class. Those who learn and readily get possession
of knowledge are next. Those who are dull and stupid and yet
do not learn, they are the lowest of men.

Everyone, said Confucius, has a place in society. To know this place with regard to family, nature, and government, is to be wise and good. The Master, as Confucius was called, is said to have been asked what one word might be applied to the conduct of a good life. Confucius said: "Perhaps the word 'reciprocity.' Do not do to others what you would not want others to do to you."

This idea, so similar to the teaching of Christ, was instilled by Confucius in the heart of Chinese society. It runs as timelessly and as surely through the history of China as the Yellow River runs to the sea. If all humans know their place and respect the authority of their superiors, the world is serene.

Confucianism reminded China of the ancient principle which held that people stand in five basic relationships to the world: to parents, brothers, mates, friends, and government. In each there are no quarrels, provided that all people respect the established authorities. The son does not quarrel with his father; the father is always right. The children do not quarrel among themselves; they abide by the father and the eldest brother. The husband rules the wife and the older friend the younger one, in the hierarchy of Confucian society. The emperor is the ultimate authority, but the people do not follow him blindly. Indeed, they have the obligation to disobey him when he becomes tyrannical or breaks the ancient law. "When a prince's personal conduct is correct," Confucius said, "his government is effective without the issuing of edicts. If his conduct is not correct, he may issue edicts, but they will not be followed."

Thus, while a strong authoritarianism pervades Confucian society, authority is based on ideals and behavior rather than on physical power. When men are not true to the highest ideals, they may be deposed. Confucius hoped to put his ideas into practice, or at least to influence the ruler of his province. But although he gained widespread respect for his wisdom and virtue, rulers thought his teachings impractical and ignored him. Petty rivalries and dynastic struggles continued for 250 years after his death in 479 B.C.

Two men were chiefly responsible for spreading Confucianism after the Master's death. The first of them, Mencius (371—289 B.C.), is sometimes called the Chinese Saint Paul. In China he is known as the "Second Sage"—second, that is, to Confucius. Mencius elaborated the Confucian doctrines of government. It is true, he said, that kings rule through a "Mandate of Heaven." But the king must respect that mandate or be deposed. Like Confucius, he urged the people to rise up and overthrow tyrants: "When a ruler treats his subjects like grass and dirt, then it is right for his subjects to treat him as a bandit and an enemy." And he said: "The humble individual, however humble, has a share in the responsibility for the prosperity or the downfall of the empire." Thus, like Confucius, Mencius envisioned society as resting on a bond between the people and the ruler. He thought of every human being as essentially good—born with "four beginnings," which, if developed, could become the four great virtues stressed by Confucius: human-heartedness, righteousness, propriety, and wisdom.

The second great apostle of Confucianism was Xunzi (298—238 B.C.). He differed from Confucius and Mencius in that he advocated stricter government control of the population. Unlike Confucius and Mencius, Xunzi considered the nature of man to be evil. Hence, he urged that education be used to correct humans. His was a purely rationalist philosophy. The state, he thought, should control the evil power that existed everywhere. As we will see, this idea later took root in Chinese life. Developed by the Legalists, it led to the founding of a powerful and tyrannical government.

Daoism. Another of the great philosopher-teachers who lived during the Zhou Dynasty period was Laozi (Lao-tze). Little is known of his life. Tradition, however, sets the date of his birth at 605 or 604 B.C. Laozi lived at a time of fierce conflicts, of mass pillaging, and of sudden death by fire and sword. In the state of Qin, three chieftains, Han, Zhao, and Wi, had divided among

This tomb painting of the Han Period shows a legendary meeting of two great philosophers, Confucius and Laozi, in Shandong Province.

themselves lands that were far from the capital of the Zhou Dynasty and beyond the reach of the royal authority. This region was at the border of the empire and was under constant threat of barbarian invasion.

Laozi probably was in the service of the Wei court. Evidently he inherited noble blood from his father. The Wei government was at war, and Laozi became sick at heart as he witnessed the continuing strife and bloodshed. He left the court to preach peace. Later, he did negotiate an armistice between the Wei rulers and their adversaries. By the end of the fifth century B.C., his teachings were widely accepted among intellectuals. His thoughts had been collected into a book expressing his ideas on how to achieve an end to political strife—as well as how to find peace of mind and a good life.

The book of Laozi's teachings was given the name *Daodejing*, which means "Classic of the Way and Values." The word *dao* had long been used in Chinese society to mean right conduct that would lead to peace. In their classic book, the Daoists urged people to renounce their brutal ambitions, aggressive designs and desires, and to strive to regain the inner balance, harmony, and wise passivity which exist in nature.

Laozi's teachings were an attempt to achieve inner peace in the midst of the savage conflicts of his times. To reassert the importance of personal values, pleasures, and happiness—in contrast to the emptiness, the pitiful transitoriness of worldly achievements—one of his followers wrote:

What is a man's life for? What pleasure is there in it? Do we live for the sake of being cowed into submission by laws and penalties? . . . We move through the world in narrow grooves, preoccupied with petty things we see and hear, brooding over our prejudices. . . . Never once do we taste the wine of freedom. . . . In life all creatures are different, but in death they are the same. Alive they are wise or foolish, noble or base; dead they all alike stink, putrefy, decompose, disappear. . . . Thus the myriad of things are equal in birth and death. In the end all are rotten bones, and rotten bones are alike. Then let us make the most of these moments of life that are ours. . . .

The final truth cannot be learned, the Daoists claimed. The moment that it is grasped, a new truth appears.

You look at it, but it is not to be seen;
Its name is Formless.
You listen to it, but it is not to be heard;
Its name is Soundless.
You grasp it, but it is not to be held;
Its name is Bodiless.
These three elude all scrutiny,
And hence they all blend and become one.

The "one" is Daoism (pronounced dah-o-ism). The followers of this mystical philosophy, which was designed to reject the less subtle, more practical attitudes of Confucianism, held that the best government is "the one known only to the people"—that is, no government. Since life is changing constantly, they saw no virtue in social order. They viewed the world as made up of two balancing forces, *yin* and *yang*. In human life, yin represented the female and passive elements in nature and was symbolized by the earth, darkness, even numbers, or a broken line. Yang embodied the male and active element and was symbolized by heaven, light, odd numbers, or an unbroken line. All human experience includes elements of the two categories, each modified by the others. No human sensation is exactly like another.

Laozi and his followers urged their pupils to proceed in as *neutral* a way as possible, to balance the differing forces of yin and yang, to be at peace with themselves and the world. Daoism affirmed that a man should act spontaneously, prompted by his intuitions rather than conscious, rational thought. One should not study *how* to do something, but instead think about it and so become one with it. The artist who paints bamboo, for example, should think about it until, in a sense, he "becomes" bamboo—until he gains a feeling for its essence. But no thing is knowable. A famous Daoist epigram declared: "The greatest square has no corners, the greatest pot is the slowest made, the greatest melody makes the smallest sound, the greatest image has no shape."

The Daoist, being yin and yang in equal measure, harbored no force within himself to attack others. He was detached from life, but in the words of one early writer, "despises all things and values life." The great Daoist mystic Zhuangzi (329—286 B.C.), in the supreme expression of this skepticism based on the transitory nature of things, wrote:

> How can we know if the self is what we call the self? Once upon a time I dreamt I was a butterfly, a fluttering butterfly, and I felt happy. I did not know I was Zhuangzi. Suddenly I awoke and was myself, the real Zhuangzi. Then I no longer knew if I were Zhuangzi dreaming he was a butterfly, or a butterfly dreaming it was Zhuangzi.

The Daoists applied ideas such as this to their thinking about society and government. Since life may be nothing more than a dream, it should be observed and not controlled, they said. They urged people to withdraw from activity and to consider nature rather than social organization, which they thought could only lead to slavery. Whoever could not accept the more rigid discipline of Confucianism, with all of the responsibilities that it gave to the Individual in society, tended to accept Daoism.

The "Hundred Schools." The conflicts and unrest of the late Zhou Dynasty period led other philosophers to offer different solutions for the problems of the time. Daoism and Confucianism were only two schools of philosophy in a period in which, it was said, "a hundred schools contend."

These hundred schools were each groups of philosophers and their followers. The leading ones were the Legalists, Mohists, Occultists, and Sophists. The last two named were last important: the Occultists had a magical belief, similar to that of some ancient Greeks, that earth, wood, fire, metal, and water are each associated with a period in human history. The Sophists (so-called by Westerners because their teachings resembled those of the Greek Sophists) were primarily politicians.

The Legalists, led by Hanfeizi, were active in the final centuries of the Zhou Dynasty and after. They believed in law and in severe punishments to insure strict obedience to it. They favored a form of highly centralized government administration that would impose laws on society with an iron hand. Society would be organized to enhance the power of the state. The Legalists heartily detested the Confucians and Confucian theories of reciprocity between ruler and ruled. Under them, the king would be an absolute despot, unrestrained by codes of virtue or human consideration for his subjects. The Qin Empire, which followed the Zhou, was largely modeled on Legalist concepts, and Legalism continued to be influential in later Chinese history.

The school of Mohists, led by Mozi (470—391 B.C.) attracted the poor who could not accept the austere detachment of the Daoists, the altruism of the Confucianists, or the authoritarianism of the Legalists. Mozi was probably one of a class of liberated slaves; he believed in the common masses and in their essential goodness. He was a practical man who taught that people should judge ideas and courses of action by the standard of usefulness. He wrote:

> *For testing an argument there are three standards . . . to trace it, to examine it, and to use it. Where to trace it? Trace it in the authority of the ancient sage-kings. Where to examine it? Examine it in the facts which the common people can see and hear. Where to use it? Put it into practice and see whether it is useful for the benefit of the country and the people. These are the three standards for argument.*

Mozi taught the love of humans in words close to those of Western religions:

> *The main reason for good behavior should be fear of the Lord on High, of Him who sees all that passes through the woods, in the valleys, and in the hidden retreats where no human eye can penetrate. He it is that one should strive to please. He loves good and hates evil, loves justice and hates inequity.*

Mozi was so eager to bring peace to humanity that he would walk for days, until his feet bled, in order to talk with a ruler who was known to be preparing war. If the ruler disregarded him, Mozi was known to bring his followers to the aid of the people who were attacked, often with success. "To kill a man in order to save the world is not acting for the good of the world," Mozi said. "To sacrifice oneself for the good of humanity—that is acting rightly."

CHAPTER 3

THE RISE OF EMPIRES: THE QIN AND HAN DYNASTIES

THE QIN DYNASTY (221—206 B.C.)

T HE HISTORIC TASK of uniting the warring states of China fell to the state of Qin. Because it was threatened by the nomadic tribes of the Asian steppes, to the west, Qin had developed a mighty army. Invading forces found it difficult to climb to its high land in the valley of the Wei River. A Chinese historian, Sima Qian, who died about 80 B.C., wrote: "The country of Qin was a state whose position alone predestined its victory. Rendered difficult of access by the girdle formed around it by the Yellow River and the mountains, it was suspended a thousand li above the rest of the empire."

On this high rugged land, every soldier of Qin was a match for many opponents. The Qin army was brutally disciplined. A fourth-century B.C. regent who tried to institute a milder military regime and to encourage agriculture was punished by being "torn limb from limb between chariots." The rulers of Qin were merciless tyrants: "Those who offered criticism were put to death with all their kin; the executed bodies of those who held meetings in secret were exposed in the marketplace."

The armies of Qin slowly brought the lands of the Wei Valley, between the Han and Wei rivers at the foot of the Qinling Mountains, under their control. Slaughtering hundreds of thousands of their foes between 331 and 260 B.C., Qin became known as the "wild beast" of China. In 259 B.C. the Qin's Prince Zheng became king, though he was only thirteen. Between his twenty-fifth and thirtieth birthdays, having been thoroughly schooled in the arts of slaughter, he conquered all of central and eastern China.

Zheng's conquests laid the foundations of the great Chinese empire. He took the name Qin Shihuangdi, which means "First Emperor of the Qin Dynasty." Although his rule lasted only eleven years, Qin Shihuangdi decisively altered the course of Chinese history by centralizing all authority. Ending feudalism with one stroke, he created a nation of forty-two administrative units made up of prefectures and towns. To control these units he appointed administrators who seized the weapons of the feudal barons; they

34

An early woodcut shows the restless Qin Shihuangdi (259—210 B.C.), who unified China.

even melted the armor of warlords armor to make bells. Next he standardized weights, measures, and wagon-wheel gauges and set a goal for what was to become his greatest achievement—a uniform language for China. Qin Shihuangdi eliminated provincial styles of script and so bound the Chinese people together through a single enduring form of writing. In 220 B.C. the emperor ordered the construction of an efficient transportation system, created by conscripts who linked previously isolated regions with tree-lined roads, fifty paces broad. Later, he put his skilled engineers to work designing the famous Great Wall. Thousands of laborers toiled to build this massive defence against the Huns of the north. The wall extended an incredible 1,500 miles across the country from the sea to the mountains, joining old feudal castles in its path. Guard towers loomed above it at intervals, and a wide roadway, over which troops could be rushed to points threatened by invasions, ran down its center.

Qin Shihuangdi lived in fear of assassination and searched for some means to gain immortality. His huge castle in Shaanxi (Shensi) had secret passages to help him escape any attempt on his life. It was not surprising that this tyrant, who was so despised and feared by his subjects, was a disciple of the Legalist philosophers rather than the Confucianists. His personal philosopher, Li Si, adhered closely to the Legalists' concepts. In 214 B.C. Li Si induced his master to murder 460 scholars who taught Confucian doctrines. In the following year he succeeded in persuading the fearful emperor to seize all Confucianist books that could be found and burn them.

Because of these savage persecutions, China's scholars have despised this early emperor ever since. Yet his achievements in molding an empire stand out above the barbaric havoc and suffering that he inflicted. In search of spiritual peace, this strange, tormented man often retired to the mountains or the sea, whose restlessness resembled his own. Despite his claim to immortality, Qin Shihuangdi died in 210 B.C. He was buried in a huge tomb, along with his wives, workmen, and art treasures. Many centuries later this tomb, near the city of Xian, was excavated. Its vast area was found to contain thousands of lifelike figures. They had been created out of painted ceramics to provide Qin Shihuangdi with an enduring world of relatives, friends, a court, and an army after death.

THE HAN DYNASTY (206 B.C.—A.D. 220): THE EARLY HAN

Though Qin Shihuangdi laid the foundation of a great Chinese empire, anarchy followed his death. Subject peoples revolted, and the old feudal lords reasserted their authority. New governments sprang up in the six states that the emperor's government had created.

During this turbulent period a new dynasty, the Han, slowly gained the upper hand. Its leader was Liu Bang, an uneducated peasant. As chief of ten villages in the state of Zhu, he was in charge of bringing convicts to continue the work on the tomb of Qin Shihuangdi. Liu Bang is described as "a man with a prominent nose, the forehead of a dragon, and a handsome beard." While leading the column of convicts to Shaanxi, this striking figure unchained them, called them his soldiers, and announced himself their general. "He annointed his drum with blood," the story goes, "and took red for the color of his standards."

Liu Bang had been a bandit, but he soon became an ally of his state's ruler, who needed his help to quell rising violence. Having a legal authority and a large army behind him, Liu Bang marched against the old capital in the province of Shaanxi. There, he met and destroyed the armies of Xiongnu, his only rival for the empire.

In 202 B.C., five years after the start of his rebellion, Liu Bang became emperor. To gain the support of the feudal barons, Liu Bang appointed some to high administrative posts in his empire. Others who would not cooperate were put to death.

The next two centuries, until the time of a usurpation in A.D. 9 are usually known as the Early Han. During this period, fierce barbarian Huns (the Xiongnu) were raiding the empire from Mongolia. They penetrated as far as Shaanxi, where Liu Bang had established his capital. Not even Liu Bang's loyal army could resist the Huns who surrounded and laid siege to Shaanxi. The emperor barely escaped. The capital later was besieged again. Wounded by the Huns, Liu Bang, who hated doctors as much as he hated the literati and other intellectuals, refused medical treatment. He died at the age of fifty-two.

After Liu Bang's death, power passed to his widow. Appointed empress in 188 B.C., she controlled China for eight years. In 180 B.C. she was succeeded by Wendi, a Daoist who ruled until 157 B.C. This gentle monarch was followed by Jingdi (156—141 B.C.), who adopted many Legalist ideas and so strengthened the central government. Then began the long reign of his famous successor, the great Wudi (140—87 B.C.)

Reign of Han Wudi. Wudi's first goal was to break down the power of the feudal barons, and he did so by compelling them to divide their lands equally among their children, rather than to the eldest, when they died. This so split up the larger estates that few barons dared to challenge Wudi during his forty-seven-year rule. The emperor, a dedicated Confucianist, strengthened the civil service system by basing appointments on written examinations which tested knowledge of Confucianism. He trusted his officials, who often were educated commoners, rather than nobles.

Qin Shihuangdi had begun the conquest of South China, but his generals had set up their own southern state, with their capital at Guangzhou, after his death. Wudi continued this expansion to the south through military victories which added Annan (in modern Vietnam, where it is called "Annam"), the five states of South China, Xinjiang, and Korea to Chinese territories. In the course of his campaigns, the emperor's emissaries contacted peoples of distant lands. In 138 B.C., for example, Wudi sent an ambassador named Zhang Qian to the Yuezhe, a people of Central Asia, in order to make an alliance against the Huns. This envoy carried with him the Chinese crossbow, as well as the peach and the apricot—items which later reached Western Europe. He brought the grape and alfalfa back to China. Zhang Qian failed to negotiate the alliance, but his journey helped to establish a trade route to the

Middle East. Over it, Chinese silk could be traded for Western products. A later chapter will describe how Marco Polo eventually traveled this overland route—the famous Silk Road.

Wudi's wars steadily drained the resources of the empire. As he grew older, he became vain and senile, wasting funds and energies building grandiose monuments to his power. The empire foundered. After Wudi's death, corrupt and depraved court nobles seized power.

THE HAN MIDDLE PERIOD: WANG MANG AND LIU XIU

In the year A.D. 1 a Confucian scholar, Wang Mang, became regent to a Han child emperor. Eight years later, Wang Mang usurped the throne and proclaimed himself emperor or China. A remarkable and competent Confucianist, Wang Mang redistributed land to the peasants and established state monopolies to control salt production, wine growing, and lending institutions. Through his so-called "Five Equalizations" he tried to stabilize prices, limiting interest rates and taxing only one-tenth part of profits. In addition, he standardized funeral ceremonies and provided state funds to defray the costs.

But Wang Mang failed to realize that he could not undertake such sweeping reforms without arousing resistance. Confucian scholar-officials refused to support his programs. Their sons, including most government officials, were more loyal to them than to the state that they were hired to serve. In this family loyalty, the scholars and their sons were practicing the ways of Confucius. Resentment flared; rebellions against the reforms broke out. A series of droughts and floods caused severe epidemics and further imperiled Wang Mang's financial experiment. Finally, a band of rebels, painting their eyebrows red as a symbol of defiance, attacked his army and seized the lower Yellow River Basin. The success of the "Red Eyebrows," as this rebellious group became known, encouraged uprisings by members of the Han ruling family, Liu Xuan and Liu Xiu, in the provinces of Henan and Hebei. In A.D. 22 they combined forces and attacked the emperor's palace. Wang Mang fled to a tower, but the rebels found him there and killed him. During this episode at the capital, the Red Eyebrows also captured Liu Xuan and strangled him.

Chinese historians have since regarded Wang Mang as a renegade who interrupted the course of the Han Dynasty. They have preferred to think so because the dynasty, fully restored, seemed to them never to have surrendered the "Mandate of Heaven." In Chinese belief the Mandate, once lost, can never be regained.

It was left to Liu Xiu, as surviving leader of the Han family, to bring the dynasty back to power. He did so brilliantly. Regrouping his army, he drove the Red Eyebrows back to the east and became master of China. Liu Xiu was a Confucianist who believed in education and a competent government. While working toward these goals, he did not neglect China's foreign policies. He stationed armies from Mongolia in the north to Annan in the south and skillfully negotiated a treaty under which the Huns became allied with China. Because of this agreement, Huns defended the Great Wall for more than two centuries, leaving the Chinese free to develop their country internally.

THE LATER HAN PERIOD: IMPERIAL POMP AND DECAY

The most effective Han general was a dashing cavalryman named Ban Chao (A.D. 32—102). Using persuasion and force, he subjugated tribes as far as the outposts of the Roman Empire on the Persian Gulf. His troops moved along the gulf, far up through southern Asia, then across modern Iran and southern Russia. Confucian officials in the imperial court disapproved of Ban Chao's military expansion, but he died a popular hero in A.D. 102. His brother and sister gained almost equal fame, as historians.

Ban Chao's son, Ban Yong, took up his banners after his death. This young soldier, continuing his father's thrust into Central Asia, gave added protection to the increasing numbers of Chinese merchants traveling on the Silk Road. These merchants drove camel caravans between a string of oases in the basin of the Tarim River. The main threat to them came from nomadic tribes who plunged down from the north in lightning raids on horseback, terrifying their rich convoys. To the Confucians who criticized his military action in Central Asia, Ban Yong pointed out the importance of the land to China, saying:

> *If you abandon the Tarim Basin, you leave it to the Huns. This would be to give them back their stores and their treasures, to refix their severed arm. The day would soon come when the barbarians once more treated our frontiers with contempt and the gates of our cities were kept closed in broad daylight.*

Because of Ban Yong's determination, the Silk Road remained open as an avenue of commerce with the Roman Empire. Over this long route, traders carried rich silk fabrics for the togas of Roman senators and the gowns of their wives. For the Romans, China and silk were so closely identified with each other that they used their

A tomb of the Han Period includes a drawing of a funeral procession in which legendary animals, as well as humans, are seen marching.

own word for silk, Seres, to refer to the Chinese. The Roman writer Virgil wrote of "the delicate wool that the Seres comb from the leaves of their trees."

Success in international trade proved as dangerous as it was profitable, however. Wallowing in riches and puffed up with military victories, the Han Dynasty gradually sank into decay. Fear and corruption engulfed both the nobles and the people. The court became a center of conspiracies among royal wives, mistresses, and eunuchs. Meanwhile, the population lived in dread of epidemics, Hunnish invasions, and bandit attacks.

Bewildered and seeking solace from the misery of the times, thousands of educated Chinese turned to various forms of mysticism. This period witnessed the emergence of Popular Daoism, with numerous cults devoted to special diets and rituals of physical hygiene. In the upper Han River Valley a family called Zhang promised magical cures for epidemics. Members of this family preached a simple remedy—drink pure water. Thousands of people took this advice and, feeling themselves cured, became ardent followers of a cult. Soon the Zhang family had sufficient power to take over some of the functions of local government, such as roadbuilding.

This local usurpation of royal authority signaled the end of the Han Dynasty. In Shandong, Hebei, and the basin of the Huai River, followers of the Zhang formed an army and rose in revolt. They called themselves the "Yellow Turbans" because they wore yellow bands over their foreheads. The royal army defeated the Yellow Turbans, but only after a bloody struggle. The Han government never fully recovered from the blow.

HAN CULTURE: RISE OF THE GENTRY CLASS

Life in China took on a rigid form during the Han Period. By this time, Confucian doctrine had established fixed rights for most individuals. The father, as the head of a family, sought to earn the respect of his community and was guided more by Confucian doctrine than by state laws. Some of his main tasks were to control his children, educate his sons, and continue the family name through them. These ideas became so important that most fathers would not consider a divorce, even if they were desperately unhappy. Often a man would take a second woman into his house, ignoring the wife who failed to please him. Unable to earn a living, the wife would remain in the house with her rival, suffering without complaint.

The rich, or "gentry" class increasingly shaped the goals of society during these times. Membership in this class depended chiefly on wealth and education rather than on hereditary positions or titles. The gentry placed a much higher value on learning for its own sake than on commercial success, and they instilled Chinese society with contempt for merchants. As mandarins gained power in government, they wrote laws reflecting their prejudice, favoring agriculture rather than commerce or industry. Their hostility towards commerce was evidenced by high taxes and government monopolies that penalized merchants. A few people in business and industry managed to educate their sons by lending money during hard times. Still, not even education gained them the friendship of the gentry.

Han science. Science made astonishing advances during this period. Inventors created precise sundials which showed the phases of the moon, the months of the year, and the solstices and equinoxes. They devised waterclocks to record the passing hours. The philosopher Wang Chong (A.D. ca. 27—97?) predicted lunar and solar eclipses, astutely reasoning that they had natural rather than supernatural causes. Another astronomer, Liu Xiu, calculated the length of the year precisely to 365.25 days. Meanwhile, other Chinese astronomers noted and studied the phenomenon of sunspots, and Han mathematicians perfected a system of place values for writing numerals.

In A.D. 100, the Chinese invented paper and began to use it to replace wood, bamboo strips, and silk as a writing material. Progress in the techniques of printing accompanied this memorable development. About A.D. 175, long before anything similar was invented in Europe, Han printers were using stone plates to create engravings.

Architecture and the arts. Under the Han, the art of building reached new levels of accomplishment. The Chinese imported bricks, which had been developed in the ancient Middle East and used widely in the Roman world. Creating factories to manufacture them, they used bricks as well as precious gems and intricately wrought marble, in the huge palace of the Emperor Wudi. The Han court employed professional painters and sculptors for royal buildings and tombs. In recent times, archaeologists have found the remains of beautiful lacquered tiles and table tops decorated with scenes from everyday life. Other remarkable Han artifacts include delicate clay figurines of human beings, birds, and animals, and examples of glazed pottery.

Chinese of the Han period also improved music. They introduced many new instruments, the most important of which, the pipa, resembles a lute; it has four strings which are made to vibrate with a plectrum. The pipa seems to have been invented in the Greek colony of Bactria and brought to China by way of the Silk Road. Along with it, the Chinese added different kinds of flutes, mandolins, and zithers to their orchestras.

Han literature and historical writing. People of the Han poured new energies into literature. The Chinese, with their Confucian love of the past, preferred history to fiction, and during these times they produced their first great historian, Sima Qian. His *Memoirs of an Historian* covers the period until 100 B.C. Sima Qian, like such early Greek historians as Herodotus and Thucydides, was among the first to interpret history instead of chronicling events. He and his followers developed an important concept in Chinese thought: the "dynastic cycle."

The principle of the dynastic cycle fit in well with the Chinese tendency to honor the past. It suggested that the past constantly repeats itself. In the view of Sima Qian and his school, history does not evolve in a line from "ancient" to "modern." Rather, each dynasty goes through a cycle of internal peace and prosperity, then

The pipa, a favorite instrument of the Han Period, was modeled on the Greek lute, which was imported from the colony of Bactria.

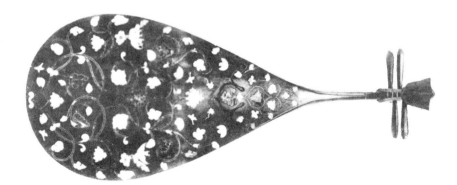

expansion and heavy government expenditure, followed by fiscal bankruptcy, social decay, and bureaucratic corruption. Administrative and economic reforms only seem to postpone the inevitable collapse.

Western historians have long sought to discover cycles in world history, but few have been persuaded as completely as the Chinese that cycles exist. The idea of dynastic cycles has endured in China until modern times and no doubt still has a hold in modern China. According to some of China's most influential thinkers, the country has never ceased striving relive the "Golden Age" formed by the Xia, Shang, and Zhou dynasties. Their perspective has been based, no doubt, upon the many centuries of Chinese civilization, as well as on the country's continuing respect for the past.

On a lesser but immensely important plane, scholars of the Han period compiled national bibliographies on such subjects as poetry, philosophy, science, and medicine. Court scribes polished love songs and ballads, incorporating them into new collections, and painters and calligraphers produced some of the most beautiful work in the nation's history. Their efforts demonstrated the lasting commitment of the Chinese people to their culture.

CHINESE PHILOSOPHY: THE ADVENT OF BUDDHISM

During the Later Han Period, the Chinese acquired one of the most momentous and meaningful concepts in their history—Buddhism. This philosophy first flourished in India, where it gained a large following. Under the liberal Han ruler Mingdi (A.D. 58—75) two Indian Buddhist monks were permitted to enter China. Buddhism won a great number of converts in China after the fall of the Han Dynasty. Twelve Indian monks translated 350 Buddhist texts into Chinese, and these collections were widely circulated.

"Buddhism," an historian has pointed out, "taught the sanctity of animal life, transmigration of the soul, the law of moral retribution *(karma)*, the value of asceticism, and meditation. Among a people accustomed to revere the ethical and political wisdom of Confucius and exalt filial piety, such ideals must initially have appeared incongruous and alien." Buddhism, however, offered greater spiritual consolation than Confucian ethics. It appealed to intellectuals, particularly in times of social and political decay. A growing number of Chinese monks crossed the Himalayan mountains to visit Buddhist shrines and teachers in India and Tibet.

CHAPTER 4

ANARCHY AND RESTORATION: THE SUI, THE TANG, AND
SONG DYNASTIES

SOCIAL DISORDER: THE SIX DYNASTIES PERIOD (A.D. 222—581)

Mᴏʀᴇ ᴛʜᴀɴ ᴛʜʀᴇᴇ ᴄᴇɴᴛᴜʀɪᴇs of chaos and bloody anarchy followed the downfall of the Han Dynasty. They began when a general named Dong Zho seized the Han court, burned the royal castle and its valuable art collection, and appointed himself regent for the young emperor. To oppose him in the north, an army officer named Cao Cao rallied troops in the Yellow River basin. Meanwhile, two other generals, Sun Quan and Liu Bei, held the basin of the Long River in the south and the highlands of Sichuan in the west.

Liu Bei, a member of the Han family who claimed the throne, is considered one of the greatest figures in Chinese history. His efforts to win back the throne for the Han is the subject of a famous epic called *The Romance of the Three Kingdoms*, by Luo Guanzhong. Like the hero of the French epic, *The Song of Roland*, Liu Bei, in the Chinese legend, is said to have fought bravely against desperate odds, aided by two loyal friends. The story goes on to glorify the ideas of legal succession to the Chinese throne, romantic heroism, and other feudal values. Though outnumbered, the men of Liu Bei's army succeeded in driving back the forces of Cao Cao, who, however, recovered his power by an alliance with Sun Quan. Liu Bei set up his own small kingdom in Sichuan, while Cao Cao seized the capital and throne of the Han Dynasty. Cao Cao died in A.D. 220, but his son Cao Pei, who was as bold as his father, took over the empire.

Cao Pei became the first ruler of the Wei Dynasty, which controlled most of North China from its capital at Luoyang. Cao was still threatened by Liu Bei, the last legitimate survivor of the Han family. Liu Bei, however, wasted his energies attacking Sun Quan instead of Cao, the man who had usurped the throne of his ancestors. Liu held Sun Quan responsible for the death of one of his trusted lieutenants. Eventually, his allies were killed in battle against Sun Quan. After a defeat in A.D. 223, Liu Bei himself perished.

Now China entered another quasi-feudalistic period. The many contending dynastic houses proved weak and ineffectual. After the Western Qin (A.D. 265—317) united, nomads invaded the Eastern Qin (A.D. 317—420). Thus China tended to be an armed camp. The real power was held by the landed gentry, who commanded private armies. These armies used codes of chivalry to bind soldiers to duty. The gentry, meanwhile, lived in walled fortresses apart from the towns, spending their time in Confucian studies or running the government. In addition to collecting the official taxes (often pocketing the lion's share), they loaned money to the poor farmers on their estates, charging high rates of interest. To show their disdain for manual labor they grew long fingernails and wore elaborate, heavy robes which impeded their movements.

Many aristocrats spent their leisure cultivating their artistic talents. They perfected the art of brush painting, as well as brush writing, called calligraphy. The most famous calligrapher of this period, Wang Xizhi (A.D. 321—379), wrote a script said to be "light as floating clouds, vigorous as a startled dragon." Wealthy landlords and literati thus made the Chinese language an intricate, esoteric medium of expression. They had the time, money, and desire desire to master it, but ordinary citizens found it mysterious.

A conquered nation. For three hundred years, China lay wide open to invasions by tribes from Mongolia, Central Asia, and Tibet. The invaders began to establish small kingdoms along the frontier, but seldom did they penetrate south of the Yangzi River.

In the north and northwest, nomadic tribes of Turkish-speaking peoples seized lands well within the Great Wall. One group, the Toba Turks, gained control in the north and established the Northern Wei Dynasty. Like many other conquerors of China, these Turks began to absorb Chinese civilization and so discarded the ways of their ancestors of the steppes. They mixed freely with the Chinese, giving rise to a vigorous new culture while allowing the Chinese literati to run the government. Ultimately, they also gave fresh stimulus to religious life in North China.

Isolated from Confucianism by the literati, the masses of common people turned to Buddhism for consolation. Buddhism offered a *personal* answer to the sorrow and misery of the times, a hope for release from suffering which Confucian ethics, with all of the abstractions that the literati had purposely built into them, did not afford. While Confucianism declined sharply in North China, Buddhism made millions of converts there under the patronage of the Northern Wei Dynasty (A.D. 386—534). By the end of the fifth century A.D,, nine-tenths of the population of the northwest had were Buddhists. Vivid evidence of Buddhism's success in this region has been preserved over the centuries in cave temples at Yungang

During the Sui Dynasty, Buddhist art was in its early development.

and Longmen. In South China Wudi helped Buddhism to flourish, especially at Nanjing.

During the rise of Buddhism, not even the Chinese who adopted the Indian religion abandoned the ancient ways of their own country. Most Confucians never doubted that they could be loyal to their own beliefs as well as to Buddhism. Some followers of Daoism were converted, too. Mostly, though, that faith, with its mystical, often superstitious overtones, remained strong among the peasants. Searching for an elixir or life, just as medieval alchemists did in Europe, some learned Daoists became noted scientists. The most scholarly of them are credited with the discovery of medicinal herbs, the magnetic compass, and the invention of gunpowder.

THE SUI DYNASTY (A.D. 589—618)

Toward the end of the Six Dynasties Period, civil wars shattered the power of the Toba Turks. In North China, by A.D. 535, this had the effect of crippling the government, causing it to split into rival states. The rift lasted for over a half century, until a general named Yang Jiang led his troops against Nanjing. He conquered it in A.D. 589. Thus, at last reunited after more than three hundred years of division, China saw a light dawning, signaling the end of its long period of chaos.

Yang Jian, taking the name Wendi, quickly formed an empire

called the Sui Dynasty. Under this powerful ruler, the nation once more enjoyed peace and a high level of culture. Wendi's government allowed merchants to travel; it encouraged writers, artists, and scholars. Re-establishing the Confucian examination system, it gave honest and efficient public officials authority over corrupt ones.

All of this changed, however, as Wendi grew older. Growing lazy and crafty, he allowed his high standards of government to slip. At length one of his sons, Guang, murdered him.

Reign of Yangdi. Chinese historians consider Guang, or Yangdi, the name he assumed after he seized the throne, one of the most intriguing characters ever to rule China. Whenever he wanted, he would build an elegant palace and fill it with concubines. Before long, he would tire of domestic pleasures and march off to battle the Turks. Then, returning from his campaigns, he would resume some of the public works projects begun by his father. Yangdi forced a million laborers to dig a canal from his palace in Luoyang to the Yangzi River. Perhaps an equal number were made to repair the Great Wall.

The efforts to preserve the wall were symptoms of a fear shared by both Wendi and his son Yangdi—invasion from the north. A new adversary, the so-called "Eastern Turks," had seized lands northwest of the wall. Their empire, under its ruler, the *Kaghan* (Great Khan), had come to that point from Persia and the steppes of Russia. Soon they pressed on to conquer the Sui Dynasty. Chinese armies resisted desperately, while the government raised taxes and conscripted hundreds of thousands of fresh soldiers.

Yangdi found his problems compounded after the failure of his campaign against the Koreans in A.D. 612. The Koreans repulsed three successive waves of Chinese armies. The emperor's defeats crippled his authority and his own morale. After barely escaping the Eastern Turks during a battle in A.D. 615, he retired to one of his palaces on the lower Long River. In A.D. 618, members of his bodyguard became the instruments of a conspiracy that had been whispered throughout the land. They burst into his chambers, assassinated his son, and then murdered him.

THE TANG DYNASTY (A.D. 618—890)

Following the collapse of the Sui Dynasty, rival generals fought over the pieces of the crushed empire. The struggle, however, soon was brought to an end by the Duke of Tang. He was Li Yuan, an officer whose ancestors were part Turkish. After the assassination of Yangdi, Li Yuan mustered a new army and threw back the nomadic tribes at the Great Wall. Then he turned his soldiers to the task of subduing the bandits and rival chieftains inside China. Through the brilliant diplomacy of his second son, Li Shimin, he became emperor soon after the murder of Yangdi.

Li Yuan worked for nine years to unite China under the House of Tang. Meanwhile, Li Shimin was eliminating brothers whose rights to the throne preceded his. He was popular among the sixty thousand troops in his father's army. A man of unique courage, he tested himself against the Turks while his father was still emperor. At the head of only a hundred horsemen, he rode up to a huge Turkish army encamped outside the gates of the capital and shouted: "The Tang Dynasty owes nothing to the Turks. Why then do you invade our realms? I am ready to try my strength against your Khan." His challenge won him the respect of the enemy, who dismounted and saluted him. The Turks refused to leave, but his army soon dispersed them.

Li Shimin became emperor in A.D. 626, when he was only thirty, apparently after forcing his father to resign. Known posthumously as *Taizong*, or "Grand Ancestor," he opened a brilliant period, marked by both peaceful achievements and military conquests.

Li Shimin formed a large standing army, supplementing a militia of farmers who could answer his call during emergencies. Farmers gave the state a month of military service, as well as a month of civilian forced labor every year. With the huge force thus gathered, China managed to beat back repeated assaults by the Turks, who were finally conquered in the east and, by A.D. 648, in the west as far as the Tarim Basin.

Li Shimin next turned his attention to the internal development of the country. The Sui Dynasty had restored the Confucian examination system, but Li Shimin improved on it and so drew abler people into public office. Whenever a landowner died the state took over 75 per cent of his holdings, leaving the rest to his heirs.

The Grand Canal, begun during the Sui Dynasty, was extended over the centuries, until it became the longest of artificial waterways.

The emperor gave the state lands to officials, whom he taxed heavily to finance the government.

The Tang Dynasty's realm extended from India to Russia to Mongolia, covering more territory than ever before in China's history. It was as broad and as powerful in Asia as the Roman empire had been in Europe. But when Li Shimin died in A.D. 649 all Tang lands fell under the control of one of the most notorious women in history—Wu Zhao, daughter of a minor public official. She had caught Li Shimin's eye when she was only fourteen, and he brought her into the court. Later he sent her to a Buddhist nunnery, but when he died his son and successor, Gaozong, brought her back to the court. After arranging for the murder of Gaozong's wife, Wu Zhao became empress—perhaps the most ruthless and powerful woman China has ever known.

RELIGIOUS DEVELOPMENTS: THE FURTHER GROWTH OF BUDDHISM

The Empress Wu, a devout Buddhist, gave land to the monks in the western capital of Changan and elsewhere, and she financed the construction of many monasteries and temples. Her dedication greatly increased the spread of Buddhism in China. One famous monk, Xuanzang, had gone to India during the reign of Li Shimin. There, he studied languages and philosophy, and on his return he translated Buddhist works into Chinese. Texts produced by Xuanzang streamed into schools established by the empress.

Chinese schools of Buddhism were indebted to India for their essential ideas. Yet each was more or less influenced by Chinese thought, particularly Daoism. The Confucianists, meanwhile, scorned Buddhists for advocating withdrawal from the family and society. They denounced the Buddhist monks as "useless drones who, not devoting themselves to farming, pay no ground rent or tax to the Son of Heaven (the Emperor) . . . [nor do they] give birth to soldiers for the Imperial Majesty's armies. . . ."

Of the many Buddhist sects in China, only Chan Buddhism (which in Japan and the United States is known as Zen Buddhism) won the tolerance of the Confucianists. Chan Buddhists advocated the way of meditation, which they believed may lead to Sudden Enlightenment. Possessing no costly lands or buildings, they threatened no one. They were philosophical rather than religious, even opposing the use of clergy for rituals.

The simplicity of Chan Buddhism was no threat to the more social principles of Confucianism. In fact, many Confucianists became Chan Buddhists while remaining loyal to Chinese traditions. One famous commentary on this group suggested that they could be "Confucianists in office and Buddhists at home," yet suffer no inner conflict. While Confucianism gave them the social control and sense of a Chinese past that they needed, Buddhism, particularly of the Chan Sect, satisfied their spiritual needs.

Among the many other schools of Buddhism that were developed in China, two became solidly established. One was the Tiantai Sect, which attracted many scholars when it came to favor the idea of the Buddha rather than to worship his images. Members of this sect preached from the Lotus Sutra, an Indian text which predicted that all animal life would one day achieve salvation. One of their main goals was to classify all ideas by relative importance, and so they appealed to the Chinese love of learning.

China's third important school of Buddhism was called the Pure Land, or Paradise Sect. Because it made no demands but absolute faith, this sect gained tens of thousands of Chinese adherents. In worship, it required of them only that worshippers repeat the name of the Buddha or of a holy man. In exchange, it offered them the full compassion of Buddhism.

Arts and letters. The Tang Period was remarkable for literary and artistic achievements. Tang scholars founded an Academy of Letters (Hanlin). Sculptors, painters, and potters gained lasting fame. They produced realistic terra-cotta horses and camels that seem fresh and vital even today. The greatness of Tang poetry may be sampled from these melancholy lines by Li Bo (A.D. 705—762):

> *Life is a journey,*
> *Death is a return to the earth,*
> *The universe is like an inn,*
> *The passing years are like dust. . . .*

Another brilliant and sensitive poet of the time was Du Fu (A.D. 712—770), who wrote brilliantly of war:

> *If I had known how bad is the fate of boys,*
> *I would have had all of my children girls. . . .*
> *Boys are born only to be buried beneath tall grass,*
> *Still the bones of the war-dead of long ago are*
> *Beside the blue sea when you pass.*

FINAL STAGE OF THE TANG: GLORY AND DECLINE

The Tang era reached its height under the Empress Wu's successor, Xuanzong, the "Bright Emperor," (A.D. 713-756). At this time, China was in close contact with Japan, where it was known as the

"Country of Tang," and its growing commerce fostered a sophisticated and powerful culture.

When he was sixty-one years old, however, the emperor took a dangerous step when he moved a beautiful young concubine, Yang Guifei, into his court. His administration weakened increasingly as she demanded all of his attentions. Sensing this weakness, An Lushan, a Turkish general in the pay of the Tang, led a rebellion in the northwest and proclaimed himself emperor. He soon gained control of most of the land north of the Yellow River, forcing the court to flee from the capital at Changan to mountainous Sichuan. On route, the imperial guards, embittered by what Yang Guifei had done to their ruler and to China, strangled her. A Tang army managed to quell An Lushan's rebellion in A.D. 763, but could do so only with the help of nomadic mercenaries.

There followed a long decline of Tang power, one caused by problems of the dynasty's own making. As so often in China's past, the government had allowed wealthy landowners to gain an authority superior to its own. A peasant could buy exemption from military service or taxation by bribing his landlord. Government, too, bribed the landlords, giving just a few of the wealthiest special tax benefits and property rights which put vast areas under their control. Peasants, forced to shoulder a larger share of the tax burden, soon became hostile both to the government and the gentry. The mighty Tang Dynasty hovered on the edge of collapse.

An anti-Buddhist campaign was symptomatic of the social unrest of the times. Led by a Confucian zealot named Han Yu (A.D. 768–824), it gained popularity even after he was exiled in A.D. 819. By A.D. 845, the bigotry that he fanned burst into open persecution of Buddhists. Other religious minorities, including Daoists and Nestorian Christians, suffered, too. As the govenment weakened, it neglected public works and was unable to enforce laws. Epidemics, floods, and famines added to the misery. The great House of Tang was to endure for another 150 years, but its powers ebbed away to local officials, who, as in ancient Rome, began to set up their own governments.

Toward the end of the ninth century, Huangchao, a demagogue who had failed his civil service examinations, gathered an army to overthrow the government. His rebellion became a revolution when his armies captured the royal cities of Changan and Luoyang. There, Huangchao put foreigners and members of religious minorities to death. His followers, in an effort to cripple the government, also destroyed thousands of mulberry trees and so ruined the once profitable silk industry.

Powerless, the Tang ruler, the Emperor Xizong (A.D. 874—888), followed the same course chosen by the last emperors of Rome. He called on a foreign general to help him defeat the rebels. Riding at the head of a column of black-clad horsemen called the "crows," a Turkish leader named Li Keyong accepted the invitation, galloping into China to overwhelm Huangchao's army. Then the emperor tried to buy off both the Turks and the leader who succeeded Huangchao, an officer named Zhu Wen. But Zhu Wen murdered the emperor. He set himself up as regent over the deposed ruler's thirteen-year-old son and became emperor himself after less than a year.

Thus the glorious Tang Dynasty came to a miserable end. Like the Roman Empire, which fell to the German tribes that had been permitted to enter Italy, it could not survive its barbarous allies.

Five Chinese generals carved up Tang lands. They dominated most of North China, each founding a minor dynasty. These dynasties are known as the Later Tang, Later Jin, Later Han, and Later Zhou. The first of them survived sixteen years, the others just five to ten years.

Throughout the last days of the Tang Empire and of its successors, China developed its commerce more vigorously than ever before. This was partly due to a rising market in Japan, which looked to China for the many goods it had not yet learned to make, and to its own increasing population. The porcelain industry, for example, added thousands of workers. Printing had become widespread and made books popular.

But the corrupt government of the time meddled with commerce, seeking to control and profit from it. Officials set up monopolies for the salt and tea industries and allied themselves with the larger merchants, causing the smaller ones to suffer. In North China the government further placed itself in commerce by

Artists of the Tang Period were increasingly interested in creating delicate forms, especially of animals, as shown in these scrolls.

increasing its use of paper money, which was first distributed during the Tang Dynasty.

At last, under the Later Zhou Dynasty, an army led by Zhao Kuangyin attacked the barbarian tribes of the north. The expedition was camping after a long march one night when some of the soldiers entered the general's tent. They carried with them their swords and the yellow robe that symbolized the power of the emperor of China. As Zhao awakened, his troops crossed swords, put the brilliant robe over his shoulders, and proclaimed him emperor. Zhao Kuangyin accepted the emperor's mantle. Then he marched his troops back to the capital, where he quickly deposed the young prince.

THE SONG DYNASTY (A.D. 960—1279)

Zhao Kuangyin, founder of the great Song Dynasty, immediately began the task of unifying China. In a series of well-planned campaigns, he subdued the northern provinces first. Rejecting vengeance, he offered pardons to the generals he defeated and even brought them into his government. Zhao cultivated patriotism among the people and allowed civilians rather than soldiers to hold high government positions. He garrisoned the best soldiers at the capital rather than in the provinces and so deprived the outlying lords of the power to rebel.

The civil service. During his fifteen-year reign this great emperor, called Taizu, or "Grand Progenitor," promoted the highest Confucian standards of education and the most loyal of civil servants. In keeping with his policy of centralizing China, he replaced the old bureaucracy with young men whom he made independent of wealthy landlords. He ranked them above all other government officials, including the military; and so they won the highest esteem of the people.

The Song Dynasty continued the examination system that had been developed over the centuries, but in a new form which seemed fairer to all. Even the poor could win jobs in the civil service. Every three years, whoever applied could take a series of tests, offered by local schools in many fields, including rituals, classics, law, history, and composition. The few applicants who passed these tests were examined again the the capital, and the winners there were screened again by panels of judges. It quickly became clear that the Song Dynasty welcomed people of merit, rather than just of wealth, into its government.

Thus China gained an honest and well-educated bureaucracy which kept a close check on all levels of its life. The emperor appointed a cabinet to run the army, finances, public works, the courts, and many other parts of government. With the exception of the modern one, perhaps no other Chinese government has been so intricate. There were so many agencies that a Bureau of Policy Criticism had to be created to oversee them. The effect of these controls, however, was to change the relationship between the government and the people. The Song government's methods were to endure, despite the complexities. From its time onward, the civil service stood between malcontents and the emperor.

The "Grand Founder" died in A.D. 976, but he had managed to restore the greatness of the Chinese Empire. He insured that there would be no quarrel over the succession by willing the throne to his brother, Taizong, instead of to his son, whom he regarded as too young to rule.

Meanwhile, danger still threatened in the northern regions which were occupied by barbarian tribes. The new emperor inherited this troubled situation. The north was historically Chinese— the site of the future provinces of Shanxi and Hebei and the present capital of the People's Republic of China, Beijing (Peking). Taizong launched strong assaults to recapture the northern territories, but they failed. At the same time, hostile Tibetan tribes were strengthening their position in the northwestern mountains, where they created a kingdom called "Xixia." To the northeast, the Manchurians had also developed a powerful kingdom, known as Liao, and were demanding homage from China. These problems had important consequences. Chinese administrators had to look for ways to strengthen the economy at home instead of seeking foreign conquests.

THE ECONOMIC REFORM MOVEMENT

During the Song Dynasty Period the son of a poor civil servant, Wang Anshi (A.D. 1021—1086), led the economic reform movement. Wang, though much noted for his bold ideas and disdain for formal dress and etiquette, rose to become a minor official in the court bureaucracy. He first suggested a change in the ancient practice by which learned Confucian scholars gained government jobs far too easily. Even under the Song, who worked steadily to improve the civil service, office-seekers often won government positions simply by buying or asking for them. The administration had become too complicated for such men to be effective, Wang argued. It seemed to him that a more efficient government would result from the appointment of some well-trained, well-paid specialists.

The emperor Shenzong, the sixth ruler of the Song Dynasty, agreed with Wang Anshi. In A.D. 1069, the year after he took power, he made Wang a special court adviser. Wang's greatest innovation was to build government granaries for the storage of grains collected as taxes. He used these granaries to control prices, distributing from them when there was a scarcity and collecting for them when there was a surplus. (Similar "ever-normal granaries" had been tried by the earlier reformer, Wang Mang, without success.)

Wang Anshi deepened his reforms by distributing both grain and loans to the poor. Under Wang, the state charged only 20 per cent interest on the loans. By contrast, the landlords normally charged 50 per cent. To relieve farmers of forced labor, Wang put through legislation called the "Public Services Act," which required the government to pay for their services in construction projects.

Wang Anshih (A.D. 1021—1036)

Wang financed his projects through new taxes, compelling both the rich and the poor to pay their fair share. To equalize taxation he brought the old register of lands up to date, surveying almost all of China's estates. The completion of this enormous task made it possible for him to gather taxes and to plan the national economy more efficiently. No longer could the large landowners escape the relentless tax agents and so threaten the government's authority. In general, Wang Anshi anticipated modern income taxes by more than eight centuries.

Wang Anshi's economic program affected many other sectors of

Chinese life. To improve both the budget and the army, he reduced the number of troops on the payroll from 1,600,000 to 600,000. He replaced the huge standing force with a militia of loyal farmers whom he trained to ride and fight. Wang tended to trust the peasant class from which he had sprung, saying, "If anyone has a poor harvest, I will give him all the grain I possess so that he has something to live on."

This philosophy, coupled with his efforts to rewrite many Confucian texts for use in schools, enraged the literati. Led by the noted historian, Sima Guang (A.D. 1018-1086), the conservatives had previously been aroused by Wang Anshi's efforts to base the civil service on merit rather than on Confucian scholarship. Sima Guang now declared that to help the common people through loans and grain would only make them lazy. His followers pressured many officials into disobeying Wang's orders, and when the emperor died they wasted no time in stripping Wang of his powers.

Wang Anshi's reforms might have wrought a permanent change in the character of China if they had been permitted to endure even a short time. His policy of encouraging merchants and industrialists by giving them tax benefits, his sponsorship of wider trading through the use of paper currency, and his willingness to help merchants to develop their trade associations, all encouraged the rise of a strong mercantile class. Such a class might have challenged the power of the gentry who traditionally ruled China through their ownership of land in an essentially agrarian economy. As in the Western nations and in Japan, this could have given rise to a more dynamic and modern society. But the merchants failed to win much political influence.

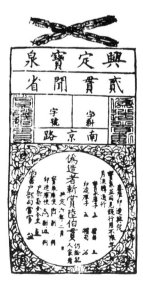

Paper money, created during the Six Dynasties Period, was suspended from belts on twine.

Despite the triumph of conservatives over Wang Anshi, Song China continued the commercial expansion begun during the Tang Dynasty. The forces of Islam, active to the west of China, had opened a lively new trade. The Song Chinese founded prosperous new cities, especially in ports which could accommodate ships from India. Merchants broke down the walls surrounding their commercial centers and lined whole streets with their shops. Their associations formed natural monopolies which were financed by banks that had begun to issue their own paper currency. Scholars formed major academies in the larger cities and created thriving centers of more vigorous Chinese thought.

THE FLOWERING OF SONG ART

The Chinese raised painting, ceramics, and other fine arts to new heights during the Song era. The greatest art patron of this age was the emperor Huizong ("Excellent Ancestor"), who took power in A.D. 1100. Huizong was a talented painter and Daoist who told admirers that his works were inspired by mystical visions.

The emperor, like other Song artists, made the human form small and humble, a speck in the vast expanse of nature. The lines of a Chinese painting do not draw the eye toward a single point in distant space, making the viewer larger and so more significant than the image. Unlike most Western paintings, they present waves of serene horizontals which make the viewer part of the scene. Such paintings seem to unfold slowly, harmoniously, presenting what is known as the "Asian perspective."

The Chinese developed the art of landscape painting more intensively than any other people. Painters expressed whole philosophies through their works of art. Chan Buddhists, who believed in "Sudden Enlightenment," often painted rapidly, without regard for detail. They hoped to capture the essence of their subjects in this way. They and the Daoists often painted mountains that seemed to be floating in the air. This technique demonstrated their belief that all life is fleeting. By painting mist over land, they expressed spirituality. They made humans small parts of vast natural images, as if to say that people, though part of the world, are less powerful than many imagine. Confucian artists, in contrast to the Buddhists or Daoists, were more likly to be interested in the form of their paintings than in the ideas.

Chinese artists won even wider fame for their pottery—so much so that porcelain itself became known as "china." They made it from a secret formula, using a fine clay called *kaolin*, which they mined in the Shan mountains. After shaping this material into realistic figures, delicate vases, or plates, they painted subtle colors, often azures and roses, on its surfaces. Their work has smooth, lustrous qualities which have been unsurpassed before or since. To protect the large pottery industry and share in its profits, the Song government established a state monopoly over it. At the same time, Chinese artists were advancing the arts of lacquer-working, bronze-molding, and jade-carving.

The government also assisted in the development of a fine paper made from gelatin—a secret Arabs later carried to Europe. The Chinese used this fine-textured paper not only for painting, but also for printing. The Chinese invented moveable type at this time. Often they made individual type pieces from terra-cotta, but more often from carved blocks. They printed with a kind of ink made from lampblack—the so-called India ink. These improved processes enabled a large Chinese industry to produce thousands of books and, according to some historians, eventually gave rise to the invention of printing in Europe.

In addition to splendid landscapes, artists of the Song Period depicted the rising power of China. Here Uigurs, a northern people, are shown paying tribute to a Song ruler. The painting includes calligraphy.

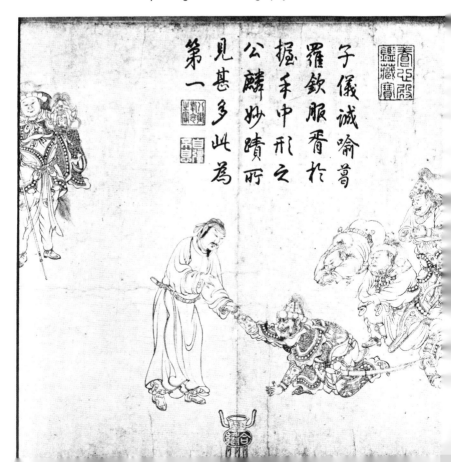

Chinese Philosophy: The Neo-Confucian Synthesis

Since the collapse of the Han empire, the Chinese people, having lost faith in political (Confucian) theories, had turned increasingly to the more personal doctrines of Buddhism and Daoism. Then the tides of religious ideas turned: anti-foreign sentiment, provoked by the threat of barbarian invasions, aroused hostility towards Buddhism as a foreign doctrine. The successes of strong, centralized governments under the Tang and Song dynasties revived the appeal of Confucian thought. Both Buddhism and Daoism declined as a great "Confucian Revival" began.

Yet far from abandoning either Buddhism or Daoism, the "Neo-Confucian" scholars of this period simply blended those faiths with their own beliefs. Many of them had been Buddhists or Daoists before embracing Confucianism. The appeal of Chan Buddhism was especially strong to them. Thus they had the basic problem of reconciling Buddhism's and Daoism's essentially personal, apolitical ideas with Confucianism's generally impersonal, ethical, and social doctrines. They tried to solve this problem by looking back to

the authority of the Five Classics, hoping to apply the wisdom of Confucius to the conditions of their own day.

Many schools flourished, but the one led by Zhu Xi (A.D. 1130—1200) was among the most influential. He tried to synthesize the three philosophies, and it was Zhu Xi who finally resolved the conflicting ideas of Confucianism, Buddhism, and Daoism for Chinese intellectuals. His principles became the Neo-Confucian orthodoxy which lasted until modern times.

Zhu Xi held that every natural object had an essence, or *li*, which was an aspect of a Supreme Ultimate. He thought that this Ultimate was present in all things, but that objects themselves were composed of elements of *qi*, that is, of matter. All material things, he said, pass through a cycle of creation and decay. Thus the Daoist concepts of *yin* and *yang* also entered into this system of belief.

But it was in the field of ethics that Zhu Xi's work had its greatest effect. As noted in Chapter 2, there was a disagreement between the two great disciples of Confucius—Mencius and Xunzi—over human nature. The former held it innately good, the latter, innately evil. Following Mencius, Zhu Xi held that the human li, or essence, was intrinsically good. He recommended formal education to bring out this innate goodness. Self-education, he thought, would lead to enlightenment and peace of mind (as in Buddhism). Thus he re-emphasized the paramount importance of education in Chinese society. Zhu Xi also reaffirmed the importance of the family and the "five basic relationships." Moreover, following Mencius, he again stressed that the state was an extension of the family, with its ruler the enlightened, benevolent father of his people. The widespread acceptance of Zhu Xi's commentaries did much to promote China's remarkable social stability during the next eight hundred years.

Downfall of the Song. The danger from the north persisted. During his reign, the Song Emperor Huizong launched an attack on the Khitans, the Turkish-speaking people who ruled the kingdom of Liao from what later became Beijing. Knowing that his armies could not defeat the Khitans without help, Huizong sought an alliance. At last he was able to make one with the Ruzhens. another nomadic tribe which lived in the far north, near the Amur River. The Ruzhens defeated the Khitans in A.D. 1124., then turned the conquered province surrounding Beijing over to China as promised. However, they rejected Huizong's claim to other northern provinces, and the two former allies went to war. Fierce Ruzhen tribesmen streamed southward into the valley of the Yellow River and laid siege to Huizong's capital. Forcing him to surrender, in A.D. 1127 they imprisoned him and most of his court.

The Chinese general, Yue Fei, finally rallied his forces and drove the Ruzhen northward. However, the Song Dynasty was shattered. A son of Huizong succeeded his father, but he lost hope after the enemy captured and executed Yue Fei. He agreed to let the Ruzhens keep all of the land north of the river Huai. Then he established a new Song capital at Hangzhou, where the Southern Song Dynasty continued until A.D. 1279. In the end, neither the Ruzhens nor the Chinese profited from the chaos. The real victor was a Mongol named Temuchin, better known as Jenghis Khan.

CHAPTER 5

THE MONGOL EMPIRE (1269—1368) AND
THE MING DYNASTY (1268—1644)

Jenghis Khan (A.D. 1162?—1227) founded a vast empire stretching from Asia's Pacific shore to the Danube River in Europe. The "Great Khan" began his career as the leader of a small tribe that inhabited the region along the border presently separating China from Mongolia. His subjects were mostly shepherds; but these hardy nomads could fight, shoot, ride, and endure pain better than their enemies. From their Mongolian stronghold they dominated Central Asia and were within striking distance of the rest of the known world.

RISE OF THE MONGOL EMPIRE

The Mongols made North China their first victim. They conquered it in this way: After seizing the kingdom of Xixia, in what later became Shaanxi Province, the Great Khan sent his archers into the rich lands of North China. There, behind the Great Wall, the Ruzhens fought for two years. Both sides suffered hundreds of thousands of casualties, but the tough little Mongol horsemen prevailed. They stormed down the Yellow River Valley to the sea. In A.D. 1215, they entered Beijing, previously bypassed because of fierce resistance. They massacred the inhabitants of the city and burned it to the ground. These nomads cared nothing for the capital's art treasures and put torches to them.

Victorious in his eastern campaigns, Jenghis Khan then moved westward over the mountains of Afghanistan into Persia. While a smaller Mongol force pursued the retreating Ruzhens in China, the Great Khan led his main army across southern Russia to the shores of the Persian Gulf. In succeeding years, the Mongols conquered vast areas in Russia and southern Europe, penetrating as far as Germany and Hungary. Then, in A.D. 1226 Jenghis Khan, a veteran of many campaigns, suffered a fatal injury when his horse stumbled and fell in northeast China. He died in A.D. 1227. In the same year his forces overwhelmed and massacred most of the survivors in the kingdom of the Xixia.

Jenghis Khan knew little of the gentler arts of civilization, but

In this duel, as drawn by a Persian, the Mongolians displayed the skills of riding and fighting that helped Jenghis Khan to seize Asia.

his willingness to learn softened his brutality. One of his chief advisers, a Khitan named Yelu Chucai, was versed in Chinese philosophy. Jenghis Khan admired this man and absorbed from him some Chinese concepts of government. "You have conquered the empire on horseback, but you cannot rule it on horseback," he told the Great Khan, echoing a Han Period precept.

Ogatai, Jenghis Khan's third son and successor, completed the task of subjugating the Ruzhens, who had fled south of the Yellow River. He captured their stronghold at Kaifeng in A.D. 1233 and made Yelu Chucai one of his chief ministers. Yelu Chucai divided North China into ten tax districts and established governments for these regions. He also founded schools in which Mongol students learned Chinese and so helped to begin the process by which Chinese culture absorbed its new conquerors.

Ogatai next allied himself with the Song Dynasty, which still ruled South China from its court at Hangzhou. Now, however, the Chinese rulers repeated the mistake made earlier when they allied themselves with the Ruzhens against the Khitans. The Song lords demanded that their ally (in this case the Mongols) cede them conquered territory. Angered because his troops, more than the Chinese, had suffered to gain the lands, Ogatai swept into South China. He died during the course of this invasion, but the new Khan, Mangu, continued the advance.

REIGN OF KUBLAI KHAN

Shortly afterward, Mangu put the Mongol campaigns in China in the hands of his younger brother, Kublai, who at forty-three was a man of culture with his grandfather's fierce temper. Kublai had both led armies and ruled a province; he excelled equally in combat and administration. After four years he resumed the campaigns in South China, using new siege engines that had been invented for use in the Crusades. His armies armies captured Hangzhou in 1276, but he mercifully spared the last of the Song emperors, a boy of six, sending him to a Buddhist monastery. By 1279, all China had fallen.

After this victory, the Mongols tried twice to invade Japan. They failed because of strong Japanese resistance and typhoons which wrecked their fleets. They were also repulsed in Southeast Asia because their horsemen knew much less about jungle warfare than their Vietnamese enemies there. Yet from the China Sea to the Mediterranean, the Mongols were supreme. At the end of Jenghis Khan's life they had the power to storm across Africa and into Europe, but voluntarily refrained, withdrawing in order to attend his funeral.

Kublai Khan, grandson of Jenghis, inherited the Mongol Empire. He moved his capital to modern Beijing.

In East Asia, the presence of the Mongols created an exciting and colorful period. The rough tribesmen from Central Asia mingled with Chinese merchants and peasants, turning cities into noisy bazaars. Products of the vast empire were hawked to buyers in every town. Mongols and Chinese lived side by side, learning from each other.

Kublai Khan, like his fellow Mongols, enjoyed contact with China's brilliant civilization. Nevertheless, all Mongols feared that Chinese customs and ways of thought would absorb and obliterate their own culture. They restricted their relationships with the Chinese and forbade intermarriage. The Great Khan hired many foreigners in his government, but few of them were Confucian scholars.

Under Kublai Khan, the Mongol Empire shifted its center towards China, reaching its height. He rebuilt the city of Beijing, which Jenghis Khan's armies had burned to the ground. New, magnificent palaces and public buildings rose there and formed his capital, which he moved from the ancestral Mongolian stronghold at Karakorum. The Khan had used relays of fast horses to carry mail in Mongolia. After settling in China, he extended this mail service to all parts of the empire, gathering two hundred thousand horses to do so.

During Kublai's reign, the population of Beijing grew so rapidly that the surrounding regions could no longer supply the city with enough food to meet its needs. The Great Khan solved the problem of food distribution by extending the Grand Canal between Beijing and the southern city of Hangzhou. He began a vast program of public works, supporting hundreds of thousands of needy persons by it. His government strongly favored Lamaism, a Tibetan Buddhist sect, but it tolerated Daoism and Christianity.

Stimulated by Mongol thought, the Chinese developed new art forms. The newcomers introduced techniques of knotting cord to make carpeting. The Chinese, whose carpets were previously made of felt, quickly perfected a remarkable carpet-knotting style of their own. The Mongols also brought cobalt blue pigments from the hills of Iran and made this vivid color a famous hallmark of Chinese ceramics. Literature, too, took a different direction under Mongol rule. Because of the collapse of the civil service examination system, many men of letters became jobless. Usually writing under pseudonyms, they produced many dramas, particularly for the opera stage. Their stories won widespread favor among the peasants; the presentations were exciting and were written in plain rather than scholarly language. *The Story of the Lute* and *The Story of the Western Chamber* are outstanding examples of this style.

The journey of Marco Polo. Reports of the Khan's fantastic wealth lured foreign adventurers to his court. They were delivered by Crusaders who, returning to Europe from the Holy Land, told tales of the incredibly rich lands that lay further to the east. In the mid-thirteenth century, Louis IX of France had sent emissaries to Central Asia to investigate. Soon after, rumors of spices and silks, of gold and jewels beyond calculation, spurred Niccolo and Maffeo Polo, two merchants of Venice, to make a voyage to Constantinople and thence across the Black Sea to southern Russia. Marco Polo, Niccolo's seventeen-year-old son, accompanied them on their second voyage. Carrying costly wares, this daring party, in A.D. 1260,

After spending his young
manhood in China,
Marco Polo returned to Italy
and reported on his travels.

joined a caravan bound for the Volga River region, land of the dreaded Tartars.

Temporarily stranded in Central Asia, the Polos remained with the Western Tartars, making friends, learning the language, and engaging in trade. One day, they accepted an invitation to join a diplomatic mission from the Khan of the Levant to the court of Kublai Khan in Beijing. With two monks, Marco Polo, his father and uncle joined this caravan moving eastward over the Silk Road. The Polos' excitement was enormous. As explorers, they felt the thrill of seeing the fabled riches of the Far East. They were the first Latins to do so. They remained in Asia for twenty years.

Marco Polo's record of his journey is an amazing epic. Written in simple, fluent style, it describes the Polos' arrival at the summer palace of the Great Khan and their reception at the even more splendid court at Beijing. The scope of the Khan's wealth dazzled young Marco, who described the royal palace in this way:

The palace itself has a very high roof. Inside, the walls of the halls and chambers are all covered with gold and silver and decorated with pictures of dragons and birds and horsemen and various breeds of beasts and scenes of battles. The ceiling is similarly adorned, so that there is nothing to be seen anywhere but gold and pictures. The hall is so vast and so wide that a meal might be served there for more than six thousand men. The number of chambers is quite bewildering. The whole building is at once so immense and so well constructed that no man in the world, granted that he had the power to effect it, could imagine any improvement in design or execution. The roof is all ablaze with scarlet and green and blue and yellow and all the colors that are so brilliantly varnished that it glitters like crystal, and the sparkle of it can be seen from far away. And the roof is so strong and so stoutly built as to last for many long year.

Marco Polo gave China the name Cathay, which sounded like the name of the local subjects of the Mongols, the Khitans. Marco Polo described the Great Khan as a wise and tolerant ruler, but full of force and passion. The Khan's glittering court retained symbols of barbaric power: a huge lion was led into the presence of the Great Khan, young Polo wrote, and "as soon as it sees him, it flings itself down prostrate before him with every appearance of deep humility and seems to acknowledge him as lord."

Besides his account of Kublai Khan's court, Marco also described life in Bengal, India, and the regions surrounding the Arabian Sea—all of which he visited on his return journey to Europe. On this trip he was accompanied, part of the way, by a princess that the Great Khan was sending to marry a Persian. Marco Polo finally reached Venice in 1295. Years after his return, while reminiscing on his deathbed about his youthful adventures, he is supposed to have remarked that he could have written twice as much about his travels to Cathay. His tale is part of the history of the West rather than of China, but it drastically altered China's future by awakening the world's interest in the Far East.

Decline of the Mongol power in China. Kublai Khan died in A.D. 1294 at the age of seventy-seven. Even during the most glorious days of his reign, there were signs of decay in the empire. Kublai Khan had allowed unrestricted printing of paper money. This led to inflation by forcing up the prices of food and land beyond the ability of small farmers to pay. Muslim moneylenders came from the Middle East to exploit the people, often holding whole families of debtors hostage. Eventually, there were rebellions. During this period there were severe floods; the Grand Canal fell into disrepair; and epidemics ravaged South China. The Mandate, it appeared, was shifting.

THE MING DYNASTY (A.D. 1368—1644)

One of the Chinese who led revolts against the Mongol government was a peasant named Zhu Yuanzhang. Most of his family had starved to death during the hard times of the 1340's. Zhu Yuanzhang became a Buddhist monk, but the rioting farmers destroyed the monastery that he joined. At the age of twenty-five he organized rebellious peasants in the south. By 1356 he had mustered an army strong enough to seize Nanjing. With the support of wealthy Chinese merchants and rivals whom he had brought under control, Zhu Yuanzhang in 1367 led an assault on the Mongols, who fled before him. They withdrew to their ancient capital at Karakorum in Mongolia, but the Chinese pursued them northward. In 1368 Zhu Yuanzhang destroyed Karakorum. He then declared himself the first emperor of the Ming Dynasty.

Zhu Yuanzhang was forty years old when he took command of China. He united the north and south under one government, setting up fifteen provinces under civilian administrators. Defending the country by means of a national guard, he worked to revive ancient traditions that had been weakened by the long Mongol rule. Zhu restored Confucian scholars and old noble families to power. At the same time he encouraged the Buddhist faith, which he had practiced as a boy.

Zhu became more tyrannical as he grew older. Nevertheless, he is honored even today as the warrior who liberated China from the Mongol yoke.

Reign of Yongle. Zhu Yuanzhang's fourth son and the third ruler of the dynasty, Yongle, advanced China's power and influence far beyond the areas surveyed by his father. His reign (A.D. 1403—1424) recalled the glories of the past. From his capital at Beijing he sent China's large standing army into Mongolia, which it conquered. He also struck southward into Annan, in the future Vietnam. China built a large merchant fleet during this period; the sea was an alternative to the Silk Road, which was infested by brigands. Chinese ships called on ports in Annan, Cambodia, Siam, Java, Sumatra, India, Ceylon, Arabia, and East Africa, carrying on trade with distant Arab and Indian merchants.

A court eunuch named Zheng He became the most famous Chi-

Yongle (A.D. 1403—1424) extended the Ming realm from Mongolia on the north to Annan on the south.

nese admiral of the day. Between 1404 and 1431 he visited ports in Southeast Asia, India, and Africa decades ahead of the Portuguese explorers in those regions. The Ming rulers revealed their weaknesses by failing to take advantage of Zheng He's successes: his exploits scarcely created a ripple in China. Far from applauding him, powerful Confucians tried to cut off his financing because they preferred domestic to overseas trade.

The Ming government had trained its officials to take this narrow view of the world. It had restored the traditional civil service examination and with it discouraged creative thinking in China. Under the rules of the test, a candidate had to use exactly seven hundred characters and was denied a job if he used more or less. The basis of the examination, the "Eight-legged Essay," contained eight sections that dealt entirely with Confucian thought, ignoring new ideas.

Conservative in government, the Ming rulers were lavish when spending funds on their own glorification. At Beijing, the brilliant and energetic Emperor Yongle built a palace of magnificent marble, surrounded by broad gardens and huge temples. He called the palace grounds the "Imperial City." One part of the grounds, known as the "Forbidden City," contained a series of marble courts crossed by a stream originating outside of Beijing. At intervals throughout the gardens there were brightly painted pagodas with upturned tiled roofs which jutted out over wide pavilions.

Ming literature. The Ming Period produced talented writers, and they developed the novel. This literary form had previously been suppressed by Confucian scholars, who valued ancient philosophy over works of imagination. Increasing literacy during the Ming Period overcame this bias and encouraged writers of fiction.

The novels of the time were mostly historical, but some also described contemporary life. They were published under pseudonyms because most of the authors were Confucian scholars who wanted to hide any interest in fiction from their colleagues. Published for ordinary people rather than for scholars, they contained everyday language. The most influential of these books, which are still being read, was *The Golden Lotus (Jin Pingmi)*. The first novel consciously created by one man, even now it is considered one of the most realistic works of its kind. Another popular work, *The Romance of the Three Kingdoms*, told the story of Chinese heroism during the fall of the Han Dynasty (See page 44.) It was republished to inspire idealism. Also famous was *The Western Journey*, a satire on religious sects which described animals acting out parts in a mythical story. *The Peony Pavilion* and *The Four Dreams* dealt with romantic notions.

Western merchants and missionaries. One of the most momentous events in world history, the opening of trade between China and Europe, took place during the Ming period. Previously, this trade had been in the hands of Arab merchants and occasional visitors such as Marco Polo. In A.D. 1516 a Portuguese merchant ship entered the Zhu (Pearl) River and docked at Guangzhou (Canton). This port remained open to Westerners. After a long struggle with Chinese authorities, the Portuguese in 1557 won the right to set up a trading post at Macao, in the Guangzhou area. As in India and Japan, the Portuguese merchants brought missionaries with them. China barred the leading Jesuit, Francis Xavier, who had made converts in Japan. However, it permitted another priest, Matteo Ricci, to live in Beijing from 1681 until 1610, when he died. Ricci failed to make many converts, but he developed a system for learning the Chinese language and translated important Western texts, both religious and secular, into Chinese. Like many other Jesuits he helped to bring Western science to China.

The seventeenth-century conflict between Catholics and Protestants in Europe spread as far as China. Dutch Protestants attacked the Portuguese colony at Macao in A.D. 1622, but were repulsed. The British, too, worked to undermine Portugal's Catholic colonizers, as well as their Dutch Protestant commercial rivals. China reacted to this warfare by refusing to allow Western merchants to enter the country at all. In time they relented, but confined trade to the port at Guangzhou.

The Japanese invasion of Korea. Late in the sixteenth century, China encountered a more urgent threat than the European traders. Japanese pirates had long harassed its coast. In A.D. 1592 Japan launched a full-scale invasion with an army of more than two hundred thousand men. Led by the feudal shogun Hideyoshi, the Japanese overran China's vassal state, Korea. After appeals from the Koreans, five thousand Chinese troops were rushed to the

The spring monsoons brought Western ships crowding into the port of Guangzhou. In the fall, winds from the northeast carried them home.

peninsula, but the Japanese quickly overwhelmed this token force. Luckily for the Chinese, the Koreans cut Japanese supply lines and prevented an enemy advance. Hampered, the Japanese finally signed a truce with the Chinese, and when Hideyoshi died in 1598 they withdrew from Korea.

The Chinese economy, however, had been weakened by Japan's invasion and by internal corruption. Impoverished farmers began to form private armies which turned to banditry and insurrection. In 1644, as a rebel army entered his capital, the despairing Ming emperor hanged himself. Then a general named Sangui took an historic step. He formed an alliance with the Manchus, a semi-barbaric tribe in the northeast. His intention was to suppress bandit uprisings and to liberate Beijing for the Ming ruler. The results proved much more far-reaching.

CHAPTER 6

THE AGE OF THE MANCHUS: THE QING
DYNASTY (1644—1911)

NORTH OF CHINA, in the cold forest of Manchuria, lived the tribe called the Manchus. They were the descendants of the Ruzhen nomads who had briefly occupied northern China in the twelfth century before they were subjugated by Jenghis Khan. In the sixteenth century, under the chieftain Nurhachu (1559—1612), the power of the Manchus rose, and this ruler began to copy Chinese forms of government.

The Manchus were allowed to enter China by the general Wu Sangui, the very man whose assignment had been to guard the Great Wall against them. Wu Sangui was infuriated at the murder of his father (as well as a favorite concubine) by Li Zicheng, the leader of the peasant revolt against the Mings. Seeking revenge, Wu joined forces with the Manchus. Their combined army destroyed Li Zicheng's peasant force and in 1644, after taking Beijing, the Manchus refused to withdraw beyond the Great Wall. The Qing Dynasty was established.

The survivors of the Ming Dynasty fled to Nanjing in the south. In 1645 the Manchus sent an army against this city. The Ming forces were routed, and the Manchus completed the conquest of China. The last of the Mings were supported by the Portuguese at Macao, where the Jesuits had converted many Chinese to Catholicism. One Ming loyalist, Zheng Chenggong, who was called "Koxinga," launched futile attacks from the port of Amoy against the Manchus at Nanjing. This bold sailor succeeded in capturing Formosa from the Dutch; he moved his base of operations to that island and held out against the Qing, much the same as the Nationalist Chinese today.

Meanwhile, the Manchus consolidated their empire. During the conquest of China, their leader, Abahai, son of Nurhachu, had died in Mukden, the Manchu capital. The ruling nobles established a regency, placing a helpless seven-year-old boy named Shun Zhi on the throne. Seven years later, to the surprise of the court, Shun Zhi seized full control. A good description of this boy comes from an account of a Jesuit missionary, Father Adam Schall, who became the young emperor's friend and court astronomer. Schall related

Nurhachu (1559—1612) led the Manchus from the northern forests into China. There, he established the Qing Dynasty.

how the emperor, in grief over the death of a woman he loved, died at an early age.

The older Manchu lords seized the opportunity to set up another regency. Their choice this time was another boy of seven, Kangxi (1622—1722). During his regency the Manchus broke the power of the Chinese warlords of the outlying provinces, replacing them with their own generals and governors. Traditionally, these officials were selected from among scholars who had passed the ancient civil service examination based upon Confucianism. But while the Chinese had to take extremely difficult tests, the Manchus were given passing grades after merely writing a graceful literary composition. The Manchus, by denying the Chinese equal treatment and prohibiting intermarriage, caused strong resentment.

The Manchus were determined to preserve their own ethnic identity while they occupied China. Knowing that previous conquerors of the Chinese had succumbed to the ways of the defeated people, they insisted on separating their Chinese subjects from themselves. As a mark of distinction, they forced the Chinese to wear their hair bound behind them in a pigtail, or queue. In social life, too, they tried to demean the Chinese and to elevate themselves. While Chinese soldiers were poorly equipped and trained, the Manchus poured funds into the maintenance of their own armies. Their troops rode behind Manchu banners brought from the homeland.

Under the Manchus there were two governments in China—one for the conquerors and one for the vanquished. They divided the country into eighteen provinces, each governed by an official appointed by the emperor and garrisoned with troops. The province was sub-divided into prefectures and then into *xian*. Guided by the results of the civil service examination, which the Manchus controlled, the central government would appoint officials to serve under the provincial governor. He himself was responsible to a viceroy, an overseer of several provinces who reported directly to the emperor.

While the Chinese government was permitted to concern itself only with the solution of minor problems, the Manchu authorities took control of the country's general development. Manchu officials were the most powerful men in China; their rank in government was symbolized by splendid costumes and in rules of behavior. They were a professional group, assigned to their posts the way that soldiers would be. To avoid corruption, the government reassigned them, and all other officials, every three years.

The emperor Kangxi, who, like his predecessor, threw off a regency and ruled in his own right, greatly extended the empire. Kangxi conducted a series of brilliant campaigns. All Mongolia fell to him, and later Tibet did, too. He supported his fighting horsemen with artillery; the Jesuits of Beijing, who had won his favor for

One of the most successful Jesuits in China, Father Adam Schall, was also the official court astronomer.

their knowledge of science and warfare, had assisted in the development of the cannon. During this period, the government permitted Catholic missionaries to work freely in China. Then, in 1715, the Pope condemned Confucianism as a pagan religion. Shortly thereafter, the emperor retaliated by reinstating an edict that forbade the missionaries to preach. Kangxi's son and successor, Yongzheng (1723—1735), ordered most of the Western missionaries out of China.

Reign of Qianlong. Qianlong, a grandson of Kangxi, ruled for sixty years (1736—1796). Like his father, he was a man of great learning and culture. He once told an English diplomat in his court that, by contrast to China, England was a nation of savages. Qianlong presided over an able government that regained control over the nation's outlying districts. He won popularity by redistributing lands previously held by the gentry and by placing higher taxes on wealthy families.

The emperor was keenly interested in literature and the arts. He assigned more than three hundred scholars to a great project— collecting and indexing the ancient literary works of China. This period also produced a fine novelist, Cao Xueqin, whose *Dream of the Red Chamber* has been admired ever since. It is at the same time a love story and an account of the fortunes of a large family in a period of social decay.

Despite these cultural attainments, the Manchu government was rotting from within. In the Beijing palaces, in the chambers and gardens of the "Forbidden City," wily officials and eunuchs schemed to defraud the government. Meanwhile, the nations of Europe, fully awakened from the Middle Ages, were pressing at China's gates. They demanded trading rights, but Chinese officials had become too self-satisfied or corrupt to respond.

At length, the government appointed a few powerful merchants to carry on trade and diplomatic negotiations with the Westerners. Their activities were confined to the port of Guangzhou. The haughty Manchus insisted that no Western trader could leave that port, even to visit the court at Beijing, without the permission of the emperor. The Chinese merchants, collectively called the Co-Hong, often had to pay tribute to the corrupt government officials. Trade in the port city of Guangzhou increased rapidly. At one point it was so successful that Chinese rivals of the Co-Hong merchants forced the government to close the port and to end foreign trade.

RELATIONS WITH THE WEST

Soon after 1800, China was drawn violently into closer relations with the West. This process began in 1816 when a British emissary arrived to negotiate a trade agreement with the Manchu government. The Manchu officials demanded that the envoy perform the "kow-tow" (bowing three times in three series while on hands and knees) prior to his audience with the emperor. The British envoy indignantly refused. He returned home without an agreement, but with an undying hatred for China.

This disturbing incident was one of a series that led to war between Great Britain and the Manchu Empire. At the time, the British insisted that military action was necessary to protect Western traders and missionaries in China. They and other Westerners wanted their own laws, rather than Chinese ones, to be applied to their nationals inside the Manchu domain.

The Chinese, on the other hand, declared that the British provoked the war in order to expand their trade in opium. The East India Company had been selling this drug in China. There it was valued both for medicinal purposes and as a means of inducing trances. The British imported opium in large quantities from the Bengal region of India, where it was made from poppies.

British merchants made fortunes in the opium trade. Before they began it, China had been able to sell more than she bought. Heavy purchasing of opium by Chinese reversed this favorable balance of trade. Large numbers of Chinese became addicted to this drug. China's currency became inflated and less important as more silver was sent to Britain from China. Responding to this social and economic threat, the Manchus banned the importation of opium in 1829. This ban was ignored: many Chinese officials and merchants connived with the British to perpetuate the sale of opium.

In 1839, the Manchu official in charge of the port of Guangzhou, Lin Zexu, took steps to cut off the traffic in opium. The British responded by declaring war. In this "Opium War" (First Anglo-Chinese War) British troops easily defeated the Manchu Empire's ill-organized armies. By terms of the subsequent treaty, signed at Nanjing in 1842, the British gained the rocky island of Hong Kong, near the Chinese port of Guangzhou. Britain planned to use the island as a trading post which would be free from interference by

The "Opium War" was ended by the Treaty of Nanjing, signed by the British and Chinese aboard the British ship *Cornwallis* in 1842.

Celebrating their defeat of China in the struggle of 1856-60, British and French troops paraded through the gates of Beijing in full uniform.

the Chinese authorities.

Through this same treaty the British wrenched an imposing list of commercial advantages from the Manchus. First, they gained the right to appoint consuls and conduct trade in five major ports: Shanghai, Guangzhou (Canton), Xiamen (Amoy), Fuzhou (Foochow), and Ningbo (Ningpo). Next, they forced the Manchus to limit tariffs on British goods to 5 per cent. Finally, under a "most-favored-nation" clause they gained the same privileges which the Manchus might later grant to other nations.

This agreement was signed in October, 1843. The following July, the United States instructed Caleb Cushing, its special commissioner to China, to sign a treaty which gained for it substantially the same rights. By 1844 France, too, had received the privileges granted to the British; Portugal, Belgium, Norway, and Sweden followed suit in varying degrees. Thus, although Britain did the fighting and led the negotiating, all of the West profited from its foreign policy.

However, Britain, with its base off the coast of China, enjoyed a trade advantage over its rivals. It had also gained the right of "extraterritoriality." Under this rule the British government was able to apply its own laws and ignore those of China in specified sections within ports. The United States later claimed the same right, as did other Western nations.

China suffered humiliation, but the Manchus readily accepted each new agreement. They permitted the foreign powers to create the famous International Settlement, outside the walls of Shanghai, as a port of entry for their goods.

Foreign treaty negotiators, especially those of the United States, France, and Great Britain, also insisted upon their right to protect missionaries in China after 1844. Within the century that followed, Protestant missionaries in China, who had begun coming with the arrival of Robert Morrison, a Briton, in 1807, numbered almost six thousand and had converted more than 750,000 Chinese to their faith. Roman Catholic missionaries were arriving in China during the Ming period but made little enduring progress until the right of extraterritoriality was extended to them in the 1840's. Their number rose to more than four thousand, and their conversions increased to more than three million within the following century.

When China would not grant more concessions, the British again attacked (1856-60). British and French troops invaded Beijing and forced more concessions. Western traders thereafter ranged freely throughout the interior of China. Traditional cultural values were affected by this abrupt exposure to Western ideas. In Shanghai, Guangzhou, and in all of the other treaty ports, Chinese customs and institutions were gradually modified by the ideas brought by sailors and merchants from Europe and America. The appeal of Confucianism to the Chinese mercantile class was weakened. The vast majority of Chinese still believed in the universality of Confucianism, even though a few Confucian scholars began to offer rationalizations. Confucian "self-strengtheners" attempted to justify the acceptance of Western materialism as a means of ultimately driving foreigners from Chinese soil.

THE TAIPING REBELLION

The pressures of inflation and rising taxes, as well as resentment against foreign intervention, all combined to bring a great popular upheaval. The rebellion flared first in South China and spread to the Yangzi River Basin. Its leader was Hong Xiuquan, a mystic. Hong knew Protestant missionaries and claimed that God had told him to throw out the Manchus and install a popular government. The "Taiping" (Great Peace) Rebellion, as this struggle was called, was at first successful. Hong led his army of peasants to victories in a number of important cities. However, his peasant soldiers had no administrative experience. The prolonged warfare aroused the opposition of many landholders who therefore supported the Manchus. These landholders feared that the rebels, once in power, might break up their estates.

A deep-seated anger motivated the Taipings. As peasants, they were disturbed by the growing concentration of land in the hands of a few members of the gentry-official class. China's population had been rising steadily, doubling to about 300 million during the previous hundred years. The Taipings demanded the redistribution of land in order to alleviate widespread starvation and unemployment.

Many other economic pressures forced the Taiping rebels into

Westerners helped the Manchus to defeat patriots under Hong Xiuquan, leader of the Taipings.

action. Under the lazy and arrogant Manchus, China was suffering from a lack of public works. Floods, droughts, and epidemics ravaged the land. Bandits preyed on defenseless villages. With more foreign merchandise being brought into China, the market for native handicraft goods was shrinking. At the same time, the prices of all things were rising because of the success of the foreign traders, and the Manchu taxes were being applied to more and more commodities.

The Taipings blamed their lot on ancient Chinese values. They reasoned that China could compete with foreigners if it overthrew Confucianism and adopted Western ways of thinking. With this in mind, whenever possible they abolished concubinage, arranged marriages, opium smoking, and footbinding. They were contemptuous of Chinese painting and calligraphy, both of which they identified with the gentry. While previous rebellions often were influenced by native religions, the Taiping Rebellion was associated with a foreign one, Christianity. This symbolized the desire of the rebels to rid China of its ancient ways.

But the Taiping peasant leaders refused to join forces with the numerous secret societies that had been organized in the cities as anti-Manchu movements. Without allies and never fully united, they faced the Qing and the Westerners who helped the Manchus. The imperial government was at last able to put down the uprising in 1864. It had the help of an army composed of Chinese soldiers and foreign officers such as Frederick Townsend Ward, an American, and Charles "Chinese" Gordon, a Briton. Together the Manchus and Westerners crushed the Taipings, but earned the enduring

hatred of millions of peasants who wanted basic reforms. They beat
down five other rebellions during this period.

The Manchu government by this time was desperate. Though it
had defeated the Taipings, it had literally sold itself to the foreign
commercial interests. To win the war, the Manchus had helplessly
ceded more trading rights to Westerners. Eventually, it even gave
the British the right to sell opium to the Chinese. In exchange, it
accepted munitions.

For about ten years after the defeat of the Taipings, the Manchu
government's concessions stabilized the economy. Then came a sudden economic decline which caused many foreigners to suspect that
China could easily be beaten in warfare. In 1872, the Japanese
struck the first of a series of deadly blows by seizing the Ryukyu
Islands. In 1875 and again in 1876, Japan sent a fleet to Korea,
which it frightened into opening two ports, in addition to Pusan, to
Japanese vessels.

These military successes encouraged the Japanese to advance
further in Korea in 1876. The Manchus warned them to retreat; but
Japan recognized the threats as empty of force and provoked the
Sino-Japanese War (1894—1895). Winning easily, it took Taiwan
and declared Korea a "free state"—that is, a puppet of Japan.
Japan also demanded the Liaodong Peninsula with its important
harbor, Port Arthur. But the Western powers prevented the final
transfer.

When the war ended, the European powers refused to help
China restore its strength in order to resist further Japanese aggression. Instead, they demanded more trade concessions, called
"spheres of interest." By forcing these agreements on China they
gained economic monopolies in certain regions. The British took
their sphere of interest in the Yangzi River valley, the Germans in
Shandong Province, the French north of Indochina, the Russians in
Manchuria, as well as in the Liaodong Peninsula. Seeing Chinese
markets divided by the European powers, Japan joined in "cutting
the Chinese melon," as these actions were called. It took a sphere of
interest in Fujian Province, across from the seized territories of
Taiwan and the Ryukyu Islands. The powers compelled China to
let them build major projects within the separate spheres. The
Chinese even paid for the construction through high interest on
loans which the powers made to the Manchu government. The
major Western powers also developed offices, warehouses, and
hotels in their spheres by hiring Chinese laborers at low wages.

Thus within fifty years China lost most of its ancient power and sovereignty. The "Middle Kingdom" had become nothing more than a Western province. The guns of foreigners dominated its major ports. Western goods, imported under low tariffs which the Westerners controlled, flooded Chinese marketplaces. In many villages less than a quarter of the manufactured goods for sale had been made in China.

The United States, with limited interests in China, began to fear that the Europeans might close Chinese ports to its goods. They could have done so by favoring their own merchants with special harbor and railroad rates. To protect American interests, U.S. Secretary of State John Hay negotiated the famous "Open Door Policy" with the Europeans in 1900. He won a guarantee that all nations would receive equal trading rights in China, that no unjust harbor rates would be charged, and that the weak Manchu government would continue to rule China. The term "open door" proved deceptive. It became a way for foreign countries to keep China's door open to trade, but not to China's advantage. It encouraged a new and desperate race among Westerners for China's markets.

As Western influence in China increased, educated Chinese (like their Japanese counterparts of this period) sought ways to adopt some Western institutions. They hoped both to strengthen their country and to resist foreigners. One leader among the Chinese reformers was Kang Yuwei. Born in Guangdong Province in 1858, Kang became a Confucian scholar-official. He believed that ancient Confucian doctrines, though corrupted by conservatives, offered a basis for radical reforms. Among other things, he advocated the downgrading of the family, urging that children be cared for in public institutions. He also proposed the popular election of officials.

The ideas of Kang Yuwei impressed the young Manchu emperor, Guangxu. On this man's advice, in the summer of 1898 the emperor attempted to carry out a sweeping reform program—later called the "Hundred Days of Reform." Between June and mid-September of 1898, he issued edicts creating a new school system and established an imperial university with a curriculum which included Western scientific and technical subjects. Kang Yuwei promoted railroad building, reforms in the army and navy, and major changes the civil service examinations. He also established an official translation bureau.

But opposition to these decrees mounted rapidly. The old Empress Dowager, Cixi, led the conservative court faction. Later in September, the conservatives carried out a coup d'etat. They seized and imprisoned the Emperor Guangxu. Then the Empress Dowager immediately restored the regency and repealed the emperor's reforms. The conservatives forced Guangxu and his associate, Liang Qichao, to flee the country, and they arrested and executed many other reformers. The rising conservative reaction against Western-style reforms and foreign influence ended in the Rebellion of 1900.

THE BOXER REBELLION

Among the many secret societies formed to drive the Western powers from China was an organization called "Righteous and Harmonious Fists." Westerners renamed the group the "Boxers." This society was not only anti-foreign but anti-Christian. Its members reasoned that this alien faith had powerfully contributed to China's decline. In 1871, members of various secret societies massacred Western and Chinese Christians in the city of Tienjin. Sporadic riots followed. Finally, in 1900, another uprising took place in which more Chinese Christians were slaughtered.

Meanwhile, the "Boxers" gained the support of the Manchu government in order to throw the "barbarians" out of China. After contingents of "Boxers" had attacked the foreign legations in Beijing, the Manchus declared war on the West. The United States, Great Britain, other European powers, and also Japan sent troops to crush the uprising. Americans helped to conquer and occupy Beijing and to force China to pay $333 million for damages inflicted by the rebels. The United States later voluntarily returned

After attacking foreigners and their properties in China, the "Boxers" and their allies in the Manchu government were crushed by Western troops.

The sight of starvation and disease in the streets stirred young Chinese to thoughts of revolution.

$22.4 million of its indemnity, however, when it discovered that the reparations far exceeded the damages. The United States allowed China to use the funds to build a college near Beijing and to send some of its students to American universities. For this act, the United States gained the gratitude of many Chinese.

Once again humiliated, the Manchu rulers at last agreed to very limited internal reforms that might strengthen the nation. They abolished the antiquated civil service examination system and considered a new constitution resembling the one in Japan.

Sun Yixian: early career. The collapse of the Boxer Rebellion and the slow progress of the moderate reformers helped prepare the way for more radical revolutionists. The man destined to lead the Chinese nationalist movement was Sun Yixian.

Born in 1866 on a farm in Guangzhou Province, Sun Yixian was exposed to Western ideas from an early age. At thirteen, he was sent to Hawaii to live with an older brother who had emigrated there. In Honolulu, he attended an Anglican school and was won over to Christianity. After returning home, he later moved to Hong Kong, where he met Sir James Cantlie, a British missionary and doctor. Sir James furthered Sun's Christian education, baptizing him in 1892 and also inspiring him to study medicine. After earning a medical diploma Sun started a practice in the Portuguese colony of Macao.

In Macao, and later in Guangdong, Sun organized local political movements against the Manchus. He petitioned the government to set up agricultural schools, a request that was denied. Subsequently, Sun was forced to flee to Hong Kong and thence to Japan. In the following years, he traveled extensively, visiting many Asian countries and also Britain and the United States. Sun Yixian became the leader of a worldwide movement of overseas Chinese who wished to overthrow the Manchus and establish a republic. Thousands joined his movement, which later became the Guomindong (Kuomintang)—the "Nationalist People's Party."

CHAPTER 7

THE DECLINE OF CONFUCIANISM:
THE EVE OF REVOLUTION

As the Manchu Dynasty lost its ability to control the country, the Chinese people began to question many of their oldest beliefs. Situated between the Pacific Ocean and arid or mountainous regions, they had been relatively isolated for thousands of years. They had become accustomed to thinking of themselves as the "Middle Kingdom"—as the society at the center or heart of civilization. But the arrival of the Western powers gave them reasons to compare their achievements with those of other nations. The ability of the invaders to subdue China made them aware of the world beyond Asia, a world in which no one nation could be regarded as superior to others. When they were defeated by people they had thought inferior, the Chinese were compelled to reassess the effectiveness of their social ideas.

China had given the world many important inventions: cartography, seismography, deep-drilling techniques, mechanical clocks, paper, printing, chemical explosives, and canal locks were among them. It was plain, however, that the nation had no *organized* science or industry, while the West had both. The West had been building its technology for hundreds of years, since its Renaissance. During this same period China developed but did not basically change its agricultural economy. While other countries had concentrated on increasing production, which brought them greater power in the world, China had spent its energies creating an internal social order. To understand the reasons for the decline of this order, the events and beliefs of these rebellious times must be summarized and examined in greater detail.

THE NATURE OF CONFUCIANISM

For centuries Chinese culture taught its people to lead a stable rather than a dynamic way of life. One cause of China's search for stability was the Confucian philosophy under which the nation lived for more than 2,500 years. Confucius had described a social order in which all things and all people were assigned places. Their behavior was controlled by a structure of manners. A person knew

84

his place in this structure by referring to the Confucian "bonds" or social relationships. "Let a ruler be a ruler and a subject a subject," Confucius said. "Let a father be a father and a son a son." Some of the most important bonds governed the relationships between ruler and subject, father and son, and husband and wife.

The bonds described relationships between relatives and relatives, but they chiefly affected people who were not social equals. Thus a hierarchy was created in which the lesser member of any pair was obligated to accept his or her superior. The superior was "mandated" to govern the person or group beneath him. The social system gave Chinese emperors, officials, and heads of clans and families justification for their exercise of power. Rulers could execute or dismember a subject without trial. A father could sell his child. A family could force a girl into an early marriage with a man two or three times her age.

Mencius (371—289 B.C.), a great apostle of Confucius (See Chapter 2), suggested that the "Mandate of Heaven" provided an important limit to these powers. There were times, in fact, when Confucians wanted a ruler to be deposed. Mencius said that if the monarch were in accord with "Heaven" (an abstract force not at all like the Christian God) he would correctly serve his people. Heaven could express its unhappiness. Natural events, such as an eclipse or epidemic, were taken as signs that the "Mandate" had been withdrawn. As each dynasty weakened and came to an end, superstitious people would look for these signs. Whoever was rising to power would point to them, claiming that the "Mandate" had been given to him instead of the ruler.

The idea that there is a universal order, existing apart from and above humans, has recurred in Chinese thought since ancient times. The Chinese have seen themselves as an agricultural people, as part of nature and subject to natural changes rather than in control of them. The oldest Chinese classic, *The Book of Changes*, suggests that good or bad luck is determined by a fate beyond the power of humans to influence. In Confucian thought Heaven was the supreme ruler and moral judge which determined the fate of humans. Heaven caused all events in the universe, including those of each person on earth. Ideally the relationship between Heaven and humans was harmonious: the seasons changed; new crops were planted and harvested.

But there were times when humans upset the order. Heaven responded with warnings or punishment—a flood, drought, or even a popular rebellion. These signs were taken to mean that it was time for a change.

It was as if Heaven were saying: "Mend your ways. I am displeased."

There were many more expressions of this belief in Chinese art, literature, and social life. Chinese paintings and stories present people as small parts of the whole landscape, powerless before the elements. China's scholars rejected the concept, so prevalent in the West, that people themselves may be the cause of their own fates. The Chinese land and climate, with their alternating extremes, have encouraged this way of thinking, as has China's remoteness from other cultures.

Developed during the Warring States period, Confucianism molded the legendary ideals of China into a promise of peace. It suggested that people live in harmony with nature, rather than in resistance to it. This program for order brought enduring power to some groups and servitude to others. The Confucian system favored males, especially the aged and the educated ones. It rewarded those who had mastered the rules of conduct—the so-called *gentry* or *literati* and deprived those who had no time to learn manners. Confucianism saw more value in the past than in the present or the future, and so it made the aged superior to the young. While glorifying the "Superior Man" *(junzi)*, it held women, manual workers, the poor, and children in lower esteem.

THE EFFECTS OF CONFUCIANISM

Confucianism was combined in China with another powerful national characteristic—the desire for a strong central government. Except for a few periods of transition, the Chinese people have experienced unified rule from the Qin Dynasty onward. The

Members of the gentry class often employed private armies of well-equipped guards and couriers.

emperor often was unable to control local despots, but the Chinese were commanded by their traditions to acknowledge his authority.

The special nature of China's terrain and culture fostered this growth of centralized power. Beginning with settlements near the rivers of the northeast, the Chinese spread southward and westward and quickly developed needs for large-scale projects—dams, levees, irrigation systems, and public health measures. These goals could only be accomplished by a government with the power to rule all of China.

When the theory of Confucianism was applied to government problems, the enduring Chinese bureaucracy was developed. The gentry class took control of this hierarchy and of government itself. From the Han Dynasty onward it set up an elaborate system of agencies which, by the Tang Dynasty, fell into six ministries: civil appointments, punishment, revenue, public works, and ceremonies. The military and censorate, through which the emperor spied on local officials, were separate agencies.

By the time of the Manchus there were nine ranks of civil servants, each with two grades. These administrators were supplemented by others who were associated with the emperor—the Grand Secretariat, the Imperial Academy of Literature, the Review Court, the Royal Stable, and the Banquet and Sacrificial Worship. The officials divided China's eighteen provinces into circuits, prefectures, departments, and *xian* (counties).

The gentry usually lived in market towns, often in compounds surrounded by high walls. Some who owned land in outlying villages kept their residences in walled garrison cities. Centers of government were situated there. Because the emperor could not run the country personally he had to rely on members of the gentry, called magistrates, to administer areas far from their homes. They were responsible for collecting taxes, running the courts, and keeping order.

Unwilling to trust local government employees and inhabitants of the unfamiliar areas, many bureaucrats hired guards to protect them. To the local residents, therefore, the arriving officials took on the appearance of an enemy force that had come to impose its will. The officials, meanwhile, were caused by circumstances to look upon the common people as a source of personal as well as public revenue. The emperor did not pay his officials well. The expenses of office usually exceeded the salaries paid to the magistrates. To help pay these costs the officials were expected to keep some of the taxes for themselves. As a result, government employees often harassed the peasants, extorting funds from them mercilessly. This practice led to widespread corruption and, when the emperor was deprived

The gentry were distinguished from ordinary Chinese by their long black gowns. Their manner suggested that they were above physical labor.

of needed taxes by his own officials, to the collapse of dynasties.

Tension invariably developed between the emperor and his bureaucracy. On the one hand a magistrate was appointed by and was responsible to the emperor, who had the power to remove him from office. On the other hand, each bureaucrat had such personal interests as a desire for power, money, and a high place among his peers in the gentry.

Once inside the remote villages, the bureaucrat had to depend on local leaders for help. But these men also had to look after their own welfare and had less loyalty to their ruler than to their overseers. Thus the bureaucrats were often caught between the conflicting needs of the emperor and the local leaders. Hemmed in on all sides, they tended to serve themselves and their class rather than the people and the government.

Structure of society. Unlike Western countries, China did not divide itself into lower, middle, and upper classes; it gained its large merchant and industrial groups only in recent times. In the West these classes grew out of the feudal period. But China had no comparable feudal period. Its social structure grew out of Confucian doctrine and produced two major classes—the gentry and the peasants.

The gentry (who were also called mandarins or literati) were distinguished first by their appearance. Long-sleeved gowns, silk hats, and untrimmed, curving fingernails were badges of their position. Emblems, insignia, bright feathers, precious buttons, and long titles with pompous forms of address were part of each office. The symbols were designed to show that the bearers did not no manual labor, which in Confucian China was considered unworthy of the "Superior Man."

The gentry managed almost all of China's government activities, arts, and charities. They founded and controlled the schools and religious institutions. Some members of the gentry supported themselves through the ownership of land or by lending money, but most were in the pay of the civil service. Many, of course, inherited money. It was not necessary to be wealthy to be a member of the gentry. A peasant might obtain a degree by passing a civil service examination, by purchase, or by the recommendation of a sponsor. But it was unlikely that a poor man could spare the time needed to pass the examination. Rarely could one earn enough to buy into the gentry class or win the attention of a sponsor. When China's population was well over 300 million in the 1840's there were only about 250,000 gentry. Less than 10 per cent of this relatively small group was able to pass higher level examinations leading to the more important civil service appointments. Begun during the Zhou Dynasty and developed during the Han, this examination was so complicated that aspiring civil servants began to study for it in childhood.

The test chiefly covered Chinese language and literature. The mastery of these subjects took enormous time and concentration. The Chinese language has no alphabet in the Western sense. It is

One of the last Manchu emperors arranged to have his portrait painted while practicing calligraphy.

made up of more than 40,000 characters which are pronounced with only 400 syllables. Thus many words sound alike and can only be distinguished by special tonal inflections, or, when written, by difficult brush strokes. To pass the examination the Confucian scholar had to master the writing of at least 10,000 characters. The civil service candidates were also expected to memorize the Five Classics—the *Book of Changes, Book of Odes, Book of History, Book of Ceremonies and Proper Conduct,* and *Spring and Autumn Annals.* This process began for some children before they could read or understand the works they were endlessly forced to repeat. Throughout their lives they were expected to practice the Five Confucian Virtues: *ren* (humanitarianism), *I* (righteousness), *li* (propriety), *zhi* (wisdom) and *xin* (faithfulness).

These words do not mean what they do in the West. The Chinese considered them to be a means of guiding social behavior, rather than a code of personal conduct. Whether dealing with superiors, peers, or subordinates, a person was enabled by the Confucian Virtues to know his or her place and how to behave in it.

Life of the peasants. The poor accepted the Confucian faith as readily as the rich. Out of this commitment grew attitudes which, to the rest of the world, seemed to characterize the millions of Chinese peasants: patience, respect for authority, and the ability to endure hardship. The world's perception of the Chinese was only partly correct. However, it was true that Confucianism obliged Chinese peasants to accept humble positions imposed upon them by their rulers. Their struggle for life was not a competitive one. Rather, as members of a class which was thoroughly controlled, they worked to distribute limited material wealth among as many people as possible. Farming with few tools, they were forced to work together to survive. These facts tended to make them more tolerant and cooperative than their Western counterparts, who were becoming more aggressive and individualistic.

The attitudes which developed among Chinese peasants discouraged the spirit of exploration. Chinese farmers did not often press into new lands, unless forced to by population growth or invaders from the north. Instead, they poured more and more labor into the acreage available to them. This tendency was reinforced by the ancient system of inheritance in China: when a father died, property was divided equally among the sons rather than given to the eldest son. The birth of each new son in China meant a further division of the land. Originated by the great Emperor Wu (140—87 B.C.) to break the power of Han Dynasty nobles, the custom persisted long after its original purpose had disappeared.

By 1800 China's population had risen to more than 275 million, probably because of domestic peace. Increasing food supplies, caused by the introduction of sweet potatoes and corn from Latin America, also contributed to the population increases. But Chinese farmers were still not able to improve their standard of living. Farms were divided into smaller and smaller parcels, and the total arable land was being divided among more and more people. By the time of the Republic, most parcels were no larger than two acres, or about a third of an acre per person. Yet the families living on them had to produce more than a ton of rice a year. The average family was made up of six members, each of whom would eat between one and two pounds of rice a day. Today, with the same levels of consumption, most individual peasants have about a quarter of an acre to farm.

Clustering near sources of water and transportation, the peasants built thousands of villages over China's valleys and foothills. Their houses were made of mud and straw or of stone or bamboo, with windows made of oiled paper. The typical peasant house contained four room section. At the center of one room was a *kang*, or bed. It was a raised platform of brick, heated by an interior stove or connected by a flue to a fire in another room. The platform was covered with a straw mattress. Here, particularly in the winter, families would spend much of their leisure time. They ate, slept, and played together.

A village included about seventy-five houses and was surrounded by small farms. Every major region contained a collection of villages radiating from a market town with approximately 1,500 households; the villages and towns were connected by footpaths. The major public functions took place in the market area, which was the scene of festivals, plays, military drafts, and tax collections.

A village often contained most of the members of a group of families, or clan. Loyalty within this group was intense. The older, more influential members of the clan sometimes were gentry, but more often they were simply natural leaders. The leader of a clan bore the same relationship to the whole village that a father did to a nuclear family. He would guide the group so that no one was without food, medical care, housing, or clothing. Depending on his own social position, he might influence public officials or members of the gentry. It was, after all, his duty to protect the clan and to help any individual in trouble, and they honored and protected him.

The help given by the clan leader might be emotional, but more often it was economic. In China's Confucian society, one of every five peasants owned no land, but paid up to half of his crop to a landlord. Emergencies, caused by illness, floods, or droughts, plagued him. Unable to save for these emergencies, he would almost always turned to his clan leader, who had the power to rally the community to the aid of its stricken member.

Civil rights in Confucian China. The law in Confucian China was never uniform. Though a legal code was assembled during the Qing Dynasty, the Chinese never gave up the idea that proper behavior should flow from a knowledge of Confucius rather than from specific precedents. The laws, therefore, were often contadictory. China had no legal profession to represent defendants; the Confucian ideal did not provide for the rights of individuals. Instead, it urged individuals to modify their desires in order to take an appropriate place in society.

"If I am not to be a man among men," Confucius said, "what am I to be?" His follower, Mencius, said: "Between father and son there should be affection; between sovereign and minister, righteousness; between husband and wife, attention to their separate functions; between old and young, a proper order; and between friends, fidelity."

Ideas of this kind, drawn from respected figures of the past, guided judges in the performance of their duty. A defendant could present his position to the judge, but he could have no way of knowing whether he had broken a law. If convicted he could appeal his case to a higher court. However, people feared the courts, which often used torture to gain confessions. Therefore, most convicted defendants would submit to one of the five punishments: beating with the light bamboo, beating with the heavy bamboo, penal servitude, exile, or death.

The courts served males in general and the male members of the gentry class above all. They favored those groups by pronouncing different sentences for the same crimes. A father who beat his son to death might receive forty lashes of bamboo whip, a punishment traditionally called the "Hundred Lashes"; a son who hit his father, even accidentally, probably would be executed. A woman who struck her husband might receive the "Hundred Lashes"; a man who beat his wife, however, might receive no punishment at all.

CONFUCIANISM UNDER CHALLENGE

Loyalty to the Confucian tradition prevented the Chinese people from accepting protest movements readily. To win popular support, rebels had to show that they had gained the "Mandate of Heaven." While the incompetence of the Manchus shook the people's faith in government, the Manchus did not crumble under the first attacks made against them. The rebels were unable to prove that they had gained the "Mandate." The White Lotus Rebellion of 1796—1804 was led by Buddhists who could not inspire many Confucians to follow them. The Taiping Rebellion of 1856 was led by a mystic who claimed to be the son of the Christian God. It, too, was crushed, but not before it came close to succeeding. This uprising, which capitalized on local discontent resulting from corruption and economic problems, caused the Manchu ruler to make concessions to local authorities and to Western powers. However, Confucianism continued to bind the country together.

At last, a new and irresistible social force arose in China: the growing resentment against the West, which produced increasing nationalism. The Boxer Rebellion of 1900 was in part a reaction against poverty, but it was also based on an older charge, uttered by the Taiping rebels, that imperialists were trampling on China's ancient glory.

The Chinese people, with a strong pride in their own culture, had long feared or resented Westerners. Their language reflects their concern. Westerners were called "foreign devils" *(yang guizi)*. The word "yang" (meaning foreign), was applied to anything that came from abroad, including people, products, or ideas. Strangers were not thought to be individuals with differences of their own. They were all alike, simply "people of the Western ocean." Nor were Western ideas readily accepted. Superstitious peasants invented frightening stories, including one that Westerners ate Chinese children. Peasants mainly rejected the work of Christian churches, whose members tried to help them with food, medicine, and education in exchange for conversion.

Nevertheless, Western activities did produce change in China. The work of the missionaries stirred a desire for greater personal independence than the Confucian code permitted. The presence of Western goods and businesses fanned desires for personal gain. At

Under the tribute system foreigners could gain the emperor's cooperation only after acknowledging the cultural achievements of China and its court.

the same time, the presence of Western soldiers in their midst caused many Chinese to think more of patriotism.

As the nationalist movement grew, the loss of Chinese territories became one of its major concerns. China had been defeated in three wars with the British and the French between 1842 and 1860. The Japanese and the Russians, as well as the British and the French, had forced China to sign what have since been called "unequal treaties"—treaties forced upon a weak nation by the victors. During the twenty-five years before the second Boxer Rebellion, Japan took several Chinese islands, and Russia annexed borderlands in Central Asia. Meanwhile the French seized Annan (in the present Vietnam, called Annam there), creating French Indochina in the Chinese sphere of influence, and the British invaded Burma. Korea began to trade with the West. After defeating China in 1895, Japan demanded and received many commercial privileges.

These treaties proved costly to China. They further alienated the Chinese people from the West. While the Chinese regarded the Westerners as menacing "barbarians," representatives of the West established eighty treaty ports in which they promoted their own culture and economies. Chinese were treated as inferiors within their own country. Western nations enforced China's economic concessions with gunboats. The opium trade, in which both the British and Americans were involved, suggested that the Westerners had little regard for Chinese welfare.

The Manchu government resisted the foreigners only sporadically. Officially it supported a rebellion against the British. Its efforts were weak, crippled by the many bureaucrats who were paid by the British. The Manchus seemed unconcerned by the growing unpopularity of the Westerners in China. They often cooperated with Western officials and sought their advice on government problem. In time, the foreigners were able to win almost any advantage they wanted.

The failure of reform. Japanese victories on the mainland, plus the ease with which the Western concessionaries "carved the Chinese melon," produced a deep sense of shame among the Chinese people. In an effort to reassert the nation's pride, young people surged forward with ideas for reform. They gained the support of the Manchu Emperor, Guangxu, who was his twenties; but members of the gentry persuaded the Empress Dowager Cixi to come out of retirement, imprison her nephew, and restore the traditional government. Thus in 1898 the chance for fundamental reform was lost.

The minor reforms that did take place merely encouraged

Situated well above centers of life, as if to symbolize the remoteness of religion from common concerns, this Daoist temple served relatively few.

nationalism, which only heightened the popular dislike for the Manchu Dynasty. At last, this resentment caused the fall of the Manchus. It was brought about, for example, because there were not enough schools in a country where education had always been revered. Then, under the pressure of the reformers, new schools, with both classical and modern curriculums, were established. The missionaries taught startling new ideas. Responding to cries that China must learn from abroad, the government sent increasing numbers of students to foreign schools. These students chiefly went to Japan, but also to the United States and Britain. When they returned to their homeland, they carried strange and appealing philosophies with them.

Confucianism had taught these students to honor their country and to work for a new government in the event that the old one lost the "Mandate of Heaven." Having lived in other countries, the students knew that the government had lost its mandate. They could no longer tolerate rulers who did nothing to prevent famines, floods, disease, starvation, bribery, domination by foreigners, early deaths, high taxes, female slavery, footbinding, opium smoking, and the control of millions of people by a few members of the gentry.

Many other groups were ready to accept the ideas introduced by the students. One was a new class of merchants which had been fostered by Western business activity and wanted lower taxes. Another was a new group of factory workers which also had arisen because of Western investments. These workers, for the first time, were being paid for what they produced and resented the special privileges granted to gentry who produced nothing. In all of China, hardly anyone approved of Western attitudes.

Thus the students found many allies. The pressure for change swelled from below.

Sun Yixian: leader of Chinese reform. As head of the Nationalist People's Party, Sun Yixian considered every available ally to attack the Manchus. The new dissidents inside of China might be organized, he thought. Risking his life, he disguised himself as a coolie peddler or a Japanese merchant and returned to his homeland. There, he organized a secret society whose members swore a blood oath never to reveal each other's names. On nine separate occasions the society attacked the Manchus, hoping each time to be joined by millions of discontented Chinese. But the rebels got little help, and many of them were executed. Then by a sudden turn of events, it became clear that Sun Yixian, the hunted and often lonely rebel, was expressing the urgent needs of millions of people.

Sun Yixian managed to smuggle a note to Dr. James Cantlie, his close friend in England, when, as a young medical student, he was kidnapped in London.

CHAPTER 8

THE CHINESE REPUBLIC (1912—1949)

DURING THE QING DYNASTY PERIOD, China's food production was decreasing while its population rose from about one hundred million to three hundred million. Crop failures and epidemics, as well as high taxes and foreign exploitation, plagued the country. The suffering prompted growing support for the republican movement led by Sun Yixian, whose followers fatally weakened the Manchu power. Dissident students began to bomb railroad stations and other public buildings. Then, on October 10, 1911, a revolt broke out in Hangzhou, marking the start of the Chinese Revolution. Risings followed in other cities, and early in the next year the Manchu government capitulated.

On January 3, 1912, the triumphant rebels proclaimed the Chinese Republic. Sun Yixian was chosen first president of China. The celebrations, however, were premature. After less than seven weeks of struggling to set up a government at Nanjing, Sun Yixian was compelled to turn the presidency over to a general, Yuan Shikai, who had control of Beijing. Foreign commercial interests saw advantages in supporting this northern warlord. Yuan Shikai formed his government at Beijing and soon after ousted the Nationalist element from the parliament. The remaining members of the parliament became a "rubber stamp" government under the dictatorial rule of Yuan Shikai.

In 1915, Yuan made plans to have himself declared emperor. However, opposition was so strong that he gave up the idea. He died in early June. Immediately, other northern warlords seized power in Beijing and formed cliques in an attempt to keep control of China. Meantime, World War I had begun in Europe. Japan had joined the Allies, hoping to seize German bases in China at Qingdao and elsewhere throughout Shandong Province. Japan's action led China to also declare war on Germany—in order to gain a voice in the future peace settlement. But although Japan and China were technically allies in the fight against Germany, the two countries did not cooperate.

In 1915, while Yuan Shikai was still in power, Japan made its famous "Twenty-one Demands" on China. If granted, the demands would have made China a Japanese protectorate. Having seized

German bases in Shandong, Japan now wanted to control Chinese mines and ports, exclusive trading privileges, and the right to set up Japanese schools in China. The Japanese would have dominated China's diplomacy, trade, police, arsenals, and much of its land. The demands were made in secret, but Yuan gave out news of them to the country. The Chinese people, led by students, reacted by boycotting Japanese goods and services.

The Nationalist Party under Sun Yixian, unable to wrest control of Beijing from the warlords, declared a republic in South China. However, the warlords maintained foreign recognition of their Beijing regime by selling their services and key areas in North China to Western interests. The extent of foreign investment and control was staggering: more than one half of the railroads, more than 90 per cent of the iron and coal industries, and over 16,000 square miles of rich farmland, were in the hands of foreign investors. A foreigner could travel anywhere in China without coming under Chinese jurisdiction; he could not be taxed or deported. Such was the power of the foreign concerns that their combined revenues exceeded those of the Chinese government.

THE POST-WORLD-WAR-I PERIOD

China assumed that by joining the Allies against Germany it could regain the former German possessions in North China. But in 1919, at Versailles, the Allied governments drawing up the peace settlement with Germany refused to recognize these claims. Chinese students rioted in protest.

Under the leadership of Chen Duxiu, a professor at Beijing University, Chinese students began questioning the country's traditional values. For the first time, the intellectuals went to the people with their grievances. They blamed the country's problems on its social and economic systems, its education, family life, and even language. Thousands of students shifted their loyalties from their immediate families to action groups. The mood of the country was radically altered. At this time, the government of Beijing was controlled by a succession of warlords, one of whom was said to have paid fifteen million dollars for the presidency. These warlords often sent troops to crush the rioting students, but they were unable to extinguish the rebellious spirit of the Chinese youths.

The political theories of Sun Yixian. In 1924 Sun Yixian announced his program, known as the "Three People's Principles." The nationalists would adopt three major goals, he said. The first, Nationalism, aimed at driving the foreigners from China and wresting control of commerce and industry from foreign concerns.

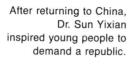
After returning to China,
Dr. Sun Yixian
inspired young people to
demand a republic.

The second, Democracy, would train the Chinese people in parliamentary procedures during a three-stage period, in the last of which there would be a general election. The third, People's Livelihood, called for a more equitable distribution of wealth, the creation of nationally owned basic industries and a small-scale private ownership.

An important part of Sun's program was his plan for a "Five-Power Government." Three of these branches would make up the executive, the legislature, and the judiciary—as under the system used by the United States. However, drawing upon Chinese traditions of government, Sun planned to incorporate two other organs—a supervisory body, or Censorate, which would keep a rein upon officials, and an independent civil service. In later practice, this five-fold system, unique to China, served increasingly to divide and weaken critics of the executive.

Sun always favored strong leadership and executive control. He thought that the primary task was to secure the "liberty of the nation" rather than individual liberty. His belief in the need for a governing elite was elaborated in his theories of "Party Tutelage" and "One-party Government." During the early stages of national liberation, Sun held, the party in power needed to tutor, or guide the people along the right path. A population accustomed to an absolute monarchy, he thought, could not adapt to democracy overnight. In time, as the Chinese Republic faced ever greater challenges from within and without, this theory of "guided democracy" came to be increasingly stressed. Sun Yixian's successor, Jiang Jieshi (Chiang Kai-shek), was to uphold the concept of "Party Tutelage" as the basis of his policy of strong governmental control. Later Asian leaders such as the Indonesian, Sukarno, were also to practice a form of "guided democracy."

Sun Yixian hoped to win recognition from the Western nations because of his parliamentary aims. However, the European powers were in no mood to help him during their recovery from the devastation of World War I. Sun Yixian then turned to the revolutionary government of the Soviet Union. The Russians agreed to give up their special privileges in China and to send military and economic advisers to the republic. Though Sun Yixian did not embrace communism, he accepted the Russian offer of assistance. He formed what was then called the "popular front" with the Chinese Communist Party, which had been established by professors Chen Duxiu and Li Dazhao. Following this development, many Chinese merchants, who had originally supported Sun Yixian, began to fear that Russian influence would touch off strikes and other attacks against private property. Thus they came to oppose Sun's leadership in the Nationalist Party. The merchants and Western-oriented liberals sought an alliance with the conservatives within the Nationalist Party to counteract the influence of the Communists and left-wing radicals. With the death of Sun Yixian in 1925, the policy of cooperation between the Chinese Communists and the Nationalists faltered.

The rise of Jiang Jieshi. Born in 1887, Jiang Jieshi had been educated in Tokyo and was an early supporter and close friend of Sun Yixian. Later he went to the Soviet Union to study military tactics. When he returned from Moscow he took command of the newly established Huangpu Military Academy, which Sun Yixian had founded with the aid of the Soviet Union. After Sun Yixian died he allied himself with a group of wealthy landlords, merchants, and bankers. Through a marriage with Meiling Soong, one of the three daughters of the wealthy Shanghai merchant, James Soong, Jiang Jieshi soon gained the support of financiers. (James Soong's eldest daughter, Qingling, had earlier been married to Sun Yixian.) Jiang Jieshi's mercantile contacts in Shanghai kept him in close touch with Western governments.

The gentry and commercial elements of the Nationalist Party dreaded the increasing influence of Communists within the government. They sought the destruction of the "popular front," or coalition of Communists and moderates, and chose as their spokesman young General Jiang Jieshi. In 1926, Jiang led a brilliantly successful Nationalist army into the north, and in 1927 moved it toward the strategic city of Shanghai. Communist elements had been busy in that treaty port, organizing the workers for a general strike to coincide with the arrival of Jiang's army. Unknown to the Communists, Jiang had already made a secret agreement with the Western powers. Upon his arrival in Shanghai, instead of attacking the Westerners, Jiang turned his army against the Communists and other radical elements. The Shanghai Incident of June 30, 1927, in which thousands of Communists and radicals were summarily executed, initiated Jiang's long struggle to annihilate the Chinese Communists. Pleased by this policy, the Western powers recognized Jiang's Nationalist government, which immediately granted them certain commercial concessions.

Jiang Jieshi was a young graduate of a military academy who won influential support through marriage.

From his capital in Nanjing, Jiang next made plans to attack the warlord government centered in Beijing. Successes against small armies of this adversary resulted in the rapid capitulation of the Beijing regime. Many warlords switched their support to Jiang, having been promised important positions in the new Nationalist Army. However, most former revolutionists, intellectuals, and students, who had supported Sun Yixian, considered Jiang's alliance with warlords and Western governments to be a betrayal of the ideals of the 1911 Revolution. Madam Sun, widow of the late leader, declared her brother-in-law Jiang an enemy of her husband's principles.

Chinese inflation became
so severe that stacks
of money were needed to
buy even simple needs.

Nevertheless, Jiang did make progress in reuniting and strengthening the Chinese nation. Some hostile warlords continued to control the mountainous provinces of the north until the 1930's. With the help of his brother-in-law, T.V. Soong, a shrewd banker, Jiang untangled some of China's budgeting, currency, and accounting problems. Jiang soon expanded the civil service. He also built new railroads and attacked such social problems as opium smoking and footbinding. On the other hand, Jiang, with the aid of his brilliant wife, introduced other highly conservative programs. His government insisted upon such traditional Confucian values as loyalty to the family and obedience to authority.

China was in desperate need of new industries that would supply jobs for its unemployed and restless farm workers. It might have gained them from a new tax policy. It could also have moved to break up the huge, unproductive landholdings. But Jiang's government lacked the skills or the desire to make basic changes in the economy. At a time when the nation's increasing population was overburdening the old economic framework, the government took little interest in reforms. Indeed, instead of encouraging new industries, the government taxed more heavily those already in existence. Public revenues were squandered to build a larger army. This drained funds which might have been spent on public works to increase employment. As the government spent more on arms, Chinese currency shrank in value. Riots occurred in the cities. Many farm tenants became indebted. Also, thousands of small independent farmers lost their lands to moneylenders. Private bankers charged dangerously high rates of interest on loans. The government, in turn, had to rely increasingly on foreigners to supply capital needed to fight the Chinese Communists.

Japan's aggression in Manchuria. In Manchuria, the Chinese state where the Manchus had originated, Japanese agents dynamited the South Manchurian Railway in 1931. The Japanese government then announced that it was dispatching troops to take over Manchuria in order to protect its economic interests and nationals there.

Disorganized and surprised, China failed to mount effective resistance. In 1932 the Japanese opened a second front in Shanghai, hoping to divert world attention from Manchuria. There, the Chinese resisted heroically, but they were no match for the thoroughly militant Japanese. International mediators persuaded Japan to withdraw from Shanghai in May, 1932. However, Japan continued its conquest of Manchuria. The Japanese renamed the province "Manchukuo" and placed the last ruler of the Manchu Dynasty, Henry Puyi, at its head.

Next, Japan defied the League of Nations and invaded the province of Jehol. When the League protested, Japan resigned from that organization. Finally, the Japanese accepted a truce in 1933. However, its government insisted upon keeping "Manchukuo" and played Puyi on its throne as "emperor"—its puppet.

Campaigns against the Communists. Between 1930 and 1934 Jiang Jieshi launched five campaigns against the Communists. In the first four he was unable to dislodge them from their mountain base. Despite numerous defeats, they regrouped into small guerrilla forces. In the fifth campaign, Jiang is said to have dispatched more than 750,000 troops, directed by such high German officers as General von Seeckt. His tactics were to employ blockades and economic strangulation.

By 1934, Jiang's forces had completely encircled Jiangxi Province and cut off all food shipments. Thereupon, one hundred thousand Communists, led by Mao Zedong and General Zhu De, began the famous "Long March." Entirely on foot and without detailed maps or extensive supplies, they broke through enemy lines in October 1934 and began an enormous journey. They were straffed by Nationalist planes, many flown by German pilots, and assaulted by Jiang's huge armies using American and British guns. Primitive tribes harrassed them in South China, but they fought their way into the northern mountains. "We were so tired, we strapped ourselves to trees, to our guns, we strung ourselves to each other. . . . We slept standing up, we slept walking. Long rows of us roped ourselves together so as to keep on the march. We called it 'sleep-flying," said one survivor later.

Suffering disease, starvation, and cold in mountains of Sichuan they struggled across the vast countryside. Primitive tribes, as well as the Nationalists, harassed them as they fought disease, starvation, and cold. At last, after covering more than 6,000 miles, they reached the province of Shaanxi, in the northwest.

Above: The Long March began on October 16, 1934 and followed an irregular course of 6,000 miles to the west and north. *Below:* When Mao Zedong's firm leadership during this year-long ordeal became known, millions of Chinese were persuaded that he was the patriot to lead them towards peace.

While Nationalist troops pursued the ragged Communist army, the Japanese continued their assault on undefended people, progressing steadily.

Of the 100,000 soldiers who had begun the march, only 20,000 survived. These men sought shelter in the caves of the Shaanxi mountains and there established a Communist government. Like Ulysses in the Greek tale, Mao Zedong later was to achieve an almost legendary status in China because of his epic journey.

The Xian Incident. Weakened and concerned about Japan's continuing threat to China, the Communists began to call for national unity again in 1936. But Jiang Jieshi could not forego one last chance to eradicate them. The Manchurian leader, Zhang Xueliang, was the son of a warlord whom the Japanese had murdered at the time of the bombing of the railroad. He had formed an alliance with Jiang to free Manchuria. When ordered to attack the Communists in the northern city of Xian, he announced that he preferred to fight Japanese rather than fellow Chinese.

On December 3, 1936, Jiang Jieshi flew to Xian to see Zhang. He hoped that his national reputation would enable him to persuade the general to obey orders. Nine days later, the Manchurian officer placed him under house arrest. Zhang demanded that the Nationalist leader unite with the Communists against Japan. But Jiang remained adamant. In disgust, while much of China clamored for the Nationalists to rescue Jiang by force if necessary, the Manchurians offered him to the Communists.

To the amazement of China and the interested world, the Chinese Communists declined to take Jiang prisoner. Instead, they called for national unity. Stunned, Zhang Xueliang released Jiang and returned with him to Nanjing to stand trial. Thus a great civil war was averted for the moment.

This conclusion of the so-called "Xian Incident" revealed much about the character of Jiang Jieshi's hated antagonist, Mao Zedong. He had survived the Shanghai Incident, the assaults on Jiangxi Province, and the Long March. Now in Xian as a Communist general, he had placed himself in the role of a patriot helping to unite his country. Meanwhile, of course, he was gaining time for his cause. Both the past and the fate of this charismatic leader, who eventually affected the entire world, are described in the next chapter.

JAPAN'S FURTHER INVASION AND WORLD WAR II

Meanwhile the Japanese, taking advantage of the civil war between the Nationalists and the Communists, were sending troops to probe North China. In 1937, fearful that the Nationalist Party might succeed in unifying China, the Japanese launched a full-scale attack upon China Proper. Advancing south from Manchukuo, they arrived outside the gates of Beijing. Jiang Jieshi was now caught in a dilemma. Should he accept Japanese offers of a united front against the Chinese Communists, or should he form a partnership with the Communists against the Japanese? On July 7, 1937, a clash occurred outside Beijing, at the Marco Polo Bridge, between Japanese and Nationalist troops. Efforts to localize the incident failed, and fighting soon spread to other parts of China.

Although obliged to ally himself with the Communists, Jiang never accepted them as trusted allies. He revived an ancient Chinese system of administration under which a number of families, in this case one hundred, constituted a self-governing unit. He organized the units, in turn, into villages, the villages into districts. Each district had a Nationalist Party official who reported directly to the central government controlled by Jiang. Fearful of Communist subversion, Jiang organized a strong and efficient secret police which carefully spied on teachers, journalists, and critics of his government.

Raised in the Confucian tradition, though he later became a Christian, Jiang believed in strong family ties and in what Confucius called "rectification of names." That is, he thought that all people should be compelled, if necessary, to respect the head of their family or state. The Communists, on the other hand, believed that people must be made to shift their loyalties if China were to be

Nationalist soldiers, on orders from Jiang Jieshi, executed their Communist prisoners. Fearing the victim's "evil eye," they usually fired from behind.

saved. They wanted a country in which political groups were respected more than families. The Communists insisted that everyone in their own group be dedicated to revolution. Whoever, within their ranks, seemed content with less was "re-educated."

The Chinese fought valiantly against the better equipped and well-trained Japanese. After North China fell to the enemy, they took a stand at the Yangzi River. Thousands of defenders died. The Japanese finally broke through the Chinese lines and occupied major cities.

As the undeclared war progressed, the Nationalists and the Communists worked behind the battle lines to achieve two purposes: to repel the Japanese and to prepare for the civil war which would inevitably come after the Japanese were defeated. The Communists formed hundreds of "anti-Japanese" clubs which were also anti-Nationalist cells. The Nationalists did not overlook these tactics. During the long war with the Japanese, tensions between the Nationalists and Communists ran high. In May 1941, Nationalist troops almost wiped out a Communist force while it was crossing a river to engage the Japanese. The Communists retaliated with similar strikes against their "brothers-in-arms."

Britain and France were fighting desperately against Germany and so were unable to offer much aid to China. The United States was sympathetic but not materially helpful; the Americans were debating whether or not to continue their historic policy of non-involvement in foreign disputes. Meanwhile, almost all of China's industries and ports fell under Japanese military control. While Japan dominated China's urban, industrial centers, Chinese soldiers could only defend their country's mountainous interior.

The Western nations suddenly found themselves allied with China. France fell to the Germans. The Japanese, becoming allies of Germany and Italy, stormed over the indefensible French colony of Indonesia. A year later, on December 7, 1941, Japan struck at Pearl Harbor, the United States military base in Hawaii. The British colony of Hong Kong fell soon after. Thus China no longer stood alone.

Japan's attack on the United States allowed China to gain badly needed time in combat. Meanwhile bombs rained continuously on the suffering Chinese people. The Nationalists' wartime capital, Chongqing became the city most bombed during World War II. The United States shipped food, military equipment, and later small contingents of service troops, to assist Jiang's government. It moved its supplies over the dangerous Burma Road, which follows the summits of mountains between Burma and China for 700 miles. The Japanese repeatedly attacked these caravans from the air. The only other method of shipping materials to China was by air from India over the peaks of North Burma and Western China. Fliers who followed this route called it the "Hump."

American policy planners faced a critical problem. Should the United States also send food and arms to the Chinese Communists, fighting from their mountain stronghold in northwest China? Diplomats, legislators, and two generals who had been sent to China, Joseph W. Stilwell and Albert C. Wedemeyer, all offered conflicting views. One group, which included General Stilwell, criticized the

The fall of Shanghai brought this outburst of pride from Japanese soldiers, who raised their "flag of the rising sun" over the key Chinese community.

Ill-equipped and poorly trained, Chinese guerrillas fought the Japanese as boldly as possible, sabotaging rail lines, roads, and ammunition depots.

government and war efforts of Jiang Jieshi. It argued that aid should be given to the Chinese Communists. However, the opposite view prevailed; only Jiang's Nationalists received American help.

This decision had its pitfalls. The Nationalist Party had become increasingly corrupt. Some of its members even sold American munitions to the Japanese. Jiang's armies seemed helpless against the enemy, while the highly disciplined Communist guerrillas continued to fight a determined guerrilla war. Many Chinese began to think that the Communists were their only defenders. They wondered whether the United States, despite its substantial aid, might not be supporting the widespread graft among Nationalist officials.

Further angering large elements in China, the Western powers refused to invite Mao Zedong to sit at international conference tables. In Cairo, Egypt, in 1943, it was Jiang Jieshi, unaccompanied by Mao, who met with President Roosevelt and Prime Minister Churchill. He pledged that Japan would be beaten and compelled to return all of the lands it had taken from China. This situation was not to last for long. As the Communists gained more and more territory from the Japanese, the West was forced to recognize their existence. The Western diplomats continued to ignore Mao Zedong, but they dealt with his fellow Communist leader, Joseph Stalin, Premier of the Soviet Union, when discussing the future of China.

At Yalta, in the Crimea, in 1945, Roosevelt and Churchill altered the agreement they had made at Cairo with Jiang Jieshi. They offered rewards if the Soviet Union would join in the war against Japan within six months after the defeat of Germany. Among the prizes they suggested were Outer Mongolia, railroads in Manchuria, and the naval base at Port Arthur. Thus they ratified the Soviet Union's historic claims to these lands, claims based on treaties which Czarist Russian had signed with the old Manchu govern-

President Roosevelt and Winston Churchill did not invite Mao Zedong to Cairo to discuss the peace. Instead, they clung to the failing Nationalist, Jiang.

ment. Responding promptly to the offer, the Soviet Union entered the war a few days before Japan's surrender. Soviet troops, in accordance with the Yalta Pact, moved into China.

Both the Soviet Union and the U.S. took sides in the civil war which followed Japan's surrender. Soviet troops turned over captured railroads, trucks, munitions, and food to the Chinese Communists. For their own benefit they stripped all Japanese factories in Manchuria, hauling captured machinery back to the Soviet Union. While withdrawing from China they turned over as much of the occupied areas as they could to the Chinese Communists. The United States and Great Britain, meanwhile, aided Jiang with money, supplies, and advice.

Throughout the postwar world, new alignments were taking form. The Allies had defeated their common enemies, Germany, Italy, and Japan, and now resumed their prewar quarrel. Communists and non-Communists everywhere opposed each other. For China, this contest had a special significance. The Chinese had lost 3.8 million soldiers in battle and 18 million civilians dead or wounded in some of the worst massacres the world has ever known. Their property losses were estimated at $120 billion.

Yet for them, this was not to be the end of massive death and destruction. The powers drew new battle lines in China. The United States and Great Britain, angered by Soviet actions in China, rallied behind Jiang Jieshi. They strongly supported the claims of the Nationalist government to China's seat on the Security Council of the United Nations, which had been formed in San Francisco in 1945. While the Soviets shipped munitions to the armies of Mao, the Western nations rushed supplies to the troops commanded by Jiang.

CHAPTER 9

COMMUNISM IN CHINA
THE COURSE OF IDEOLOGY (1949-69)

Soon AFTER THE SURRENDER of Japan in 1945, the Chinese Communists and Nationalists reopened their desperate struggle for control of China. The United States helped Jiang Jieshi by airlifting troops to vital cities in Central and North China. The Americans ordered Japanese garrisons to turn over their positions only to the Nationalist forces and to the Soviet army in Manchuria. U.S. Marines occupied several major Chinese cities and awaited the arrival of Nationalist forces. But Mao Zedong's Communist troops held large parts of rural China in the north. They had also captured Manchuria from the retreating Japanese.

The United States government tried at first to mediate the fierce dispute between the Nationalists and Communists. From 1944-46, U.S. Ambassador Patrick J. Hurley and U.S. General George Marshall tried to arrange a peaceful settlement between the two sides. The Americans urged that a coalition government be set up. This effort to end the conflict proved unsuccessful, however. Each side remained hostile and suspicious of the other. Marshall, in a famous report, finally said the two sides could not be reconciled. He urged Chinese moderates to come forward to lead their country.

Later in 1946, the civil war began again in earnest. Throughout 1947 the Nationalists kept the upper hand. They controlled most of the large cities, while the Communists increased their power in the rural Areas. But almost 85 per cent of the people were farmers, and the Communists were gaining wide support. The Nationalists had a force of more than three million men against a Communist army of one million, but they were steadily undermined by inflation and bureaucratic corruption. As the Communists moved unhampered through the countryside they promised to free the peasants from landlords and material shortages. Meanwhile the nationalists waited in the cities for the attackers to arrive.

At last the battle was joined about 100 miles north of Nanjing. Overruling his advisers, Jiang Jieshi sent more than one-quarter of his troops there in 1948. The Communists trapped this force. Then they surrounded a relief army of 120,000 Nationalist troops. Despite heavy aerial attacks, the Communists killed or wounded

Mao Zedong escaped
the assaults of the
Japanese and Nationalists
and led the Chinese
Communists to power.

more than half a million men in this battle and claimed that another 327,000 surrendered to them. At this point Mao Zedong moved his Communist army south, and in April 1949 this force entered Nanjing.

On October 1, 1949, Mao Zedong announced in Beijing that the "liberation" of mainland China had been completed. His Communist followers proceeded to organize a powerful new state, the People's Republic of China. Meanwhile, Jiang Jieshi formed a rival government of refugees on the island of Taiwan (which the Portuguese had called Formosa). Bringing the six million people of Taiwan under his authoritarian regime, Jiang established martial law and a strict censorship. He made his Nationalist Party the only legal political organization on the island, while Mao Zedong did the same on the mainland for his Communist Party.

THE COMMUNIST STRUCTURE OF GOVERNMENT

As the leader of the victorious Communist army, Mao Zedong won the esteem of millions of Chinese. Most of the entire population believed that he had enabled the country to recover its ancient glory. Not only had he freed them from foreign domination, but he promised to rid them of landlords as well. Therefore as Jiang Jieshi fled to Taiwan, they rallied behind Mao as if he were a new emperor who had won the Mandate of Heaven. They did not know it then, but Mao was to affect their lives, and world history, too, for the next twenty-five years.

The policies adopted by Mao differed from those of any of the national leaders who preceded him. Underlying them was the theory, at least, that the millions of Chinese peasants were basically wiser and more honest than the officials who usually held power over them. During Communist military campaigns he had insisted that his troops "be as fish in the sea"—that is, to move in harmony with the peasants among whom they lived. His standing regulations included three main rules and eight points that were circulated among his followers for many years. The rules were:

"(1) Obey orders in all actions; (2) Take not a single needle or piece of thread from the peasants; and (3) Turn in everything captured."

The points were:

(1) Speak politely; (2) Pay fairly for what you buy; (3) Return everything you borrow; (4) Pay for everything you damage; (5) Don't hit or swear at people; (6) Don't damage crops; (7) Don't take liberties with women; and (8) Don't ill treat captives.

The contrast between Mao's troops, known as the People's Liberation Army (PLA) and the Nationalists, who often had contempt for peasants, was one of the chief reasons for the Communist victory. When establishing China's first Communist government, Mao insisted that the policy of respect for peasants be continued. For the Chinese people, this was a stunning change from the days when they had to submit to landlords, moneylenders, and foreign invaders. The peasants repaid Mao's respect for them with esteem and even adoration. To the more than half a billion Chinese whose political independence he had helped to win, Mao was a hero. He appealed to them, in large part, because his personal struggles clearly resembled their own and those of the country itself.

The Life of Mao Zedong. Mao was born in 1893 in a clay-brick

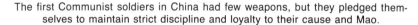

The first Communist soldiers in China had few weapons, but they pledged themselves to maintain strict discipline and loyalty to their cause and Mao.

farmhouse in rural Hunan Province, a region famed for the courage and vitality of its people. His grandfather had built the house of mud and straw, but lost it to a landlord to whom he was in debt. To recover the house and its half-acre of land, Mao's father joined the army at the age of sixteen. He saved every coin and scrap, and after years of toil at last paid off the family's debt.

Mao, eldest in a family which eventually included two brothers and a sister as well as his parents and himself, grew up under a stern father who lived in constant fear of a return to poverty. By the age of six, Mao was put to work planting seedlings in a rice field, picking beans, or collecting manure or wood for fertilizer and fuel. At school he often saw his fellow students beaten by a strict Confucian teacher for failing to memorize every passage of an ancient book. After these ordeals Mao comforted himself by reading such popular historic novels as *The Romance of the Three Kingdoms* and *Water Margin*, which described how Chinese heroes had rebelled against unjust conditions in the past.

During Mao's youth, China stood between the Opium War of 1840, when the British sent troops to compel China to buy its narcotics, and the revolution of 1911, when the forces of Dr. Sun Yixian were replacing the crumbling Qing (Manchu) Dynasty with a Chinese republic. The young Mao was determined to take part in movements which he hoped would liberate the Chinese people from economic and political oppression. Given a choice, he said later, he would have shared his father's grain with starving peasants.

By 1908, Mao's father was a small landowner who employed a worker or two for about a dollar a month, and he resented his son's attitudes. Hoping to change the boy, he forced Mao to marry a local girl at the age of fifteen. Mao, however, considered child marriage an offense both to bride and groom and simply walked away from the arrangement.

At last while still a young man, Mao was able to escape his father's harsh rule by enrolling in a distant school. There, he read constantly and began to teach at night, telling his students that ". . . it was the duty of all the people to save (the country.) Ten thousand years are too long," he declared. "Seize the day, the hour!" He called on young people to prepare both body and mind for a struggle that would end with a more just social and economic system. He himself became a successful athlete as well as scholar.

Thus Mao became a revolutionary rather than a reformer. He rejected the idea of a democracy along Western lines, pointing out that Western nations had misused China even while claiming to represent justice. Gaining a job in the library at Beijing University, he studied the ideas of Vladimir Ilyich Ulyanov, the leader of

Communist revolutionaries in Russia, who was known as Lenin. Mao began to call for a Communist state in China. On May 4, 1919, he became an active leader of the historic "May 4th Movement." This organization of students and intellectuals called on patriotic Chinese to reject the "Twenty-one Demands" that would have brought China under Japanese rule. After helping to organize China's first Communist Party, Mao went on to lead a growing Communist army among the peasants. It was Mao and his close friend, Zhu De, who led this force on its 6,000-mile "Long March" after its entrapment by the army of Jiang Jieshi in 1935 (See Chapter 8). Finally, it was Mao whom the Chinese people came to idolize after his army descended from its mountain strongholds and defeated Jiang's Nationalist troops in 1949.

THE SOVIET MODEL (1949-59)

When he was studying the Russian Revolution, Mao was struck by a theory advanced by Lenin, its principal thinker and tactician. In an essay called "Imperialism, the Highest Stage of Capitalism," Lenin had predicted that Western capitalism would collapse if deprived of its colonies. According to him, the economies of Western countries depended upon an ability to draw wealth from colonies, especially those in Asia. Lenin persuaded the Soviets to spread revolution throughout the world through an organization called the Communist International (Comintern).

Mao became convinced that it was China's destiny to share the aims of the Comintern. He was persuaded to accept this belief, in large part, by the history of the Communist Party which he himself led. It had been established in Shanghai in 1921 with fewer than sixty members. Within thirty years it had grown to almost six million members and had driven foreigners, as well as the Nationalists who enjoyed foreign support, from the entire mainland. It seemed to Mao that a tidal wave of communism was rising and would quickly engulf capitalist nations when they had been deprived of colonial riches.

To prepare for the struggle, Mao sought to reorganize Chinese society along collective lines. His aim, shared by most of his Communist associates at the time, was to create a new kind of individual. This individual would commit him- or herself more to the country than to personal gain. To achieve this far-reaching goal the Communists undertook changes in every part of the economy. They believed that the Chinese people, through constant effort, would change their basic way of thinking.

The cities. Mao's reasoning placed China's new government

Even the youngest members of the commune were taught to consider themselves part of the military forces.

firmly beside the Soviet Union in a worldwide struggle against capitalism. At the outset of Communist rule, Soviet advisers and equipment poured into China, and Soviet engineers, architects, and economists came to live in major Chinese cities. They encouraged the Chinese to establish the same kind of central planning agencies, with rigid controls over labor, materials, and equipment, that were used in their own country.

With Soviet help, the Chinese developed their first Five-Year Plan in 1953. It stressed the need for sacrifices by the people so that the nation could follow the Soviet example. The plan called for new heavy industries, such as steel- and machine-making, most of which were in the cities. Hundreds of thousands of officials entered into all phases of this plan. Their job was to manage totally the economic lives of a population that grew to about seven hundred million by the 1960's. After setting production goals through their five-year plans they allocated all materials, decided what should be produced, distributed all products, established all wages and prices, and organized large building projects.

The countryside. By combining threats and rewards, Mao's new government won the support of millions of small farmers. It began its rule by executing tens of thousands of people whom it regarded as incapable of learning the ways of communism. Merchants, land-

lords, moneylenders, and scholars, all suspected of capitalist ten-
dencies, became vulnerable. Squads of soldiers pulled "class
enemies" out of their homes and shot them.

In general, those accused lived in cities rather than on farms. To
most peasants the government offered fair treatment in exchange
for cooperation. It won widespread support by promising a gradual, rather than a violent transition to rural communism. No large
group was threatened by swift change, and none was stripped of its
wealth compared with others. The Communist Party established
associations called "lower" (first-stage) cooperatives which pooled
farm animals, equipment, and land. Whoever put land or equipment into these common pools was paid in amounts directly proportionate to the original contribution. This policy quickly
overcame fears that the Communists would seize land and property
without compensation. It brought about the rapid spread of farm
cooperatives. By 1956 the government was able to expand the policy, calling for "higher-level" cooperatives. Advancing towards a
program of communal labor on the farms, it began to pay the
members of these new cooperatives in work points rather than in
money. Farm workers were organized into "brigades" which were
told to work, plan, and be rewarded together.

During the mid-1950's, China experienced sharp agricultural
progress which will be detailed in the next chapter. This progress
probably convinced the country's leaders that the time had arrived
to organize the highest level of collectivization, the farm communes. Millions of workers, known as cadres, spread across farm-
lands to organize the communes, which combined the efforts of
about thirty-five to forty villages. In time, Communist China had

In China's first enthusiasm for communism, most farms became communes with
goals to reach. Today, more and more farmers are working individual plots.

more than 54,000 communes. The average commune had about 3,300 families and 14,000 people, but some had as many as 25,000 people.

The communes functioned on a social as well as an economic level. They established schools, hospitals, and training programs. Their own leaders helped them to meet the goals established by central planners, buying or selling equipment as needed. When officials notified them that a public effort was needed, commune members would stream out of their villages to build a road, dam, or power plant.

By the time it was celebrating the tenth anniversary of its revolution, the People's Republic of China was able to declare that its agricultural policy was a success. The Chinese people were not eating large or varied diets, but they were spared the massive starvation of pre-revolutionary times. Nor were they suffering from the high interest rates and lack of credit of the past. Under Mao, the government was their landlord, accountant, distributor, warehouser, marketer, and banker. It developed their water resources, energy supply, and roads. Relieved of many tasks, people suddenly began to produce more food, as the next chapter will show.

Still, the rate of growth in the food supply troubled China's leaders. They wondered whether even the commune system could produce enough food for a population which probably exceeded 750 million in 1959 and was growing rapidly.

Early political structure. Mao claimed no personal credit for the achievements of his government. He said that he was simply an instrument of the people and was following a "mass line." China was far from holding democratic elections. Still, Mao stated that its people controlled their government through the National People's Congress and the Congress of the Communist Party. He called these bodies "transmission belts" through which the nation could command officials and even depose of an unwanted leader if necessary.

However, delegates to the two congresses were not widely or freely chosen. Only members of the Communist Party, which included about 2 per cent of the population, could belong to either of them. The Party made contact with the people chiefly through political study groups which even non-Party members were forced to attend.

The People's Congress in those years included 1,200 delegates who were elected every five years or so. It was far too large to set directions for the country, and it was not always in session. China therefore was guided, not by its people, but by a Standing Committee. This small group of men was led by Mao, who had the title

Chairman.

Revolutionary leaders. Mao consulted chiefly with other members of the Standing Committee, which included Zhou Enlai, Zhou De, and a few others. Almost all of these men were in their sixties or seventies. Most had been drawn into revolutionary work because of the success of Sun Yixian in 1911, when they were in their twenties and thirties. Close friends, the majority of them had been founding members of the Communist "study groups" which Mao organized before World War II, or they had suffered the ordeals of the Long March together.

Zhou Enlai, for example, had formed an "Awakening Society" as a university student. He joined the May 4th Movement in 1919, when he was twenty-one. A writer and publisher of revolutionary materials, he went to France to continue his studies and helped to found the Communist Party there. On his return to China he lectured on military affairs, but later turned to more active roles. He led assaults on Nationalist police stations and developed strategies during and after the Long March. As Communist Party grew stronger he became its negotiator with both the Nationalists and the Americans, including General George C. Marshall.

All of the other members of the Standing Committee were early Communists who were reaching the last stages of their lives. Zhu De, a warlord during the disturbances following the 1911 Revolution, had been converted to Marxism, which he studied in Germany. Chen Yi, member of a scholarly family, had studied Marxism in France and directed study and assault groups in the struggle with the Japanese and Nationalists.

Thus the new rulers of China sprang directly out of the small group of young radicals who were inspired by Sun Yixian. They were chiefly scholars, thinkers, and fighters whose early training had been Confucian. All of them acknowledged the unshakeable leadership of Mao Zedong. They were dedicated Marxists, many of whom had studied in the Soviet Union, but were far from blind to the unique problems in their own country.

CHINA IN SEARCH OF ITSELF

After seven years of following the Soviet model, the Chinese discovered that dangerous cracks were appearing in their economy. Peasants were still producing less than the government hoped, partly because they saw the industries in cities being developed at their expense. The tension between rural and urban populations had begun to threaten national unity.

The peasants had no way to know when their sacrifices for city-dwellers would end. Their complaints seemed to be lost among the hundreds of thousands of officials who distributed goods and services under the First Five-Year Plan (1953-57). Though discouraged from speaking publicly of their disappointments, peasants privately yearned for shorter working days, for more bicycles, television sets, and refrigerators. Officials merely told them wait because the country needed more machinery.

The Soviet Union's faith in heavy industry sprang directly from its own experience. The Russian Revolution of 1917-18 had been essentially a movement of city dwellers. Believing that peasants stood in the way of progress, the Soviet government under Joseph Stalin moved ruthlessly to eliminate them. The Soviets had little hope that peasants could be taught to practice an entirely new economic system, let alone to join in a worldwide struggle against capitalism.

Chinese Communists were unable to accept this Soviet point of view. Mao honored peasants. He depicted them as "poor and blank"—meaning that they could be enriched and taught. He had depended on them to help carry out the Chinese Revolution. He knew, when building Chinese Communism, that he would need them again because they comprised all but 15 per cent of the population. While Mao and his followers remained ardent Communists, they disagreed sharply with their Soviet advisers on matters concerning the peasants.

Tension between China and the Soviet Union was also developing for historical reasons. China repeatedly asked the Soviet Union to return lands seized by Russia before the Soviet Revolution. According to the Chinese these lands, situated in what is now known as Soviet Central Asia, were gained by Imperial Russia only because a weak and corrupt foreign dynasty, the Qing (Manchu), had control of China at the time. Immediately after their own revolution the Russians had called on all nations to return lands taken through

As the Communists consolidated their power, tourism began to rise. Chinese travelers, other Asians, and Westerners began to stroll over the Great Wall.

"unequal treaties," but they refused to take this advice themselves.

Soon, these ideological and historical conflicts were to break the bonds which linked the two countries.

The Hundred Flowers. In 1957, Mao at last allowed some complaints about the new government to be expressed in public. "Let one hundred flowers bloom, let one hundred schools of thought contend," he declared. Mao was confident that his followers had overcome all opposition. As he himself remarked in two public speeches, more than eight hundred thousand "capitalist-roaders" had been executed during the first five years after the revolution. Mao became alarmed, therefore, when, in response to his invitation, many new critics came forward. Because of their sharp attacks he ended the "Hundred Flowers Period," in which he encouraged free speech in Communist China, after little more than one year. The government had restored its strict rules of censorship by 1958, and it punished those who spoke out.

The Great Leap Forward (1958). To respond to his critics, Mao decided to reduce the amount of central planning prescribed by the Soviets. He proposed instead to test one of his most cherished ideas. The Chinese peasants themselves, if encouraged to solve the nation's most urgent problems, would succeed where official planners had failed, he said. Mao believed that the peasants could reshape the economy, bringing about a "great leap forward," if permitted to use their own methods. He urged all Chinese to "walk on two legs." By this he meant, "Use your ancient technologies, along with modern ones, to make the whole country independent of foreigners."

The result of this summons stirred the whole population to begin that part of China's history now called the Great Leap Forward. In back yards, kitchens, and on small farms the Chinese people set up primitive furnaces, smelters, and mills. They struggled to produce everything from steel to machine parts. Women entered the work force on a scale much larger than ever before. The government urged communes to begin small industrial projects such as metalworking and milling.

Westerners ridiculed these makeshift enterprises, calling them primitive and useless. To the Chinese, however, they were part of Mao's vision of a country secure from imperialism, disease, and poverty. The Chinese hoped to solve the nation's most difficult problems through a more complete use of its greatest resource—the skill and ingenuity of its millions of peasants.

Mao had other reasons for urging the breakup of industry. He continued to believe that both the United States and the Soviet Union were planning to bomb Chinese cities and so wanted to reduce targets. At the same time, by shifting activities into the countryside he was able to contain the growth of massive cities which were developing extensive slums.

The Great Leap Forward had some positive effects in every part of Chinese society. It brought about a new, healthier relationship between men and women. It decentralized the government, forcing officials to place more trust in local authorities. It awakened millions of people to the need for education. Finally, it compelled Chinese leaders to reexamine their ideas about planning and technology and left the nation with a reorganized form of agriculture.

But on balance, most Chinese today see the Great Leap Forward as a failure—the romantic dream of a revolutionary leader who understood little about economics. It resulted in the waste of raw materials, land, and labor. It turned peasants to tasks about which they knew nothing. Their end-products, such as impure iron, often were unnecessary or lacking in quality. It may even have set back the economy. As shown in the next chapter, agricultural output decreased sharply as the nation poured its energies into the fulfillment of Mao's wishes.

Most Chinese leaders were less concerned with social change than with immediate economic results. Faced with the problems of China's huge and growing population, many became alarmed when they saw the net effects of the Great Leap Forward. Some brought Mao's policies under serious attack at the 1959 meeting of the Central Committee at Lushan. Disruptions caused by the Great Leap Forward forced the government to scale down its hopes to build larger industries and communes.

The Communist government sent dancers, singers, and acrobats into communes to remind people of their patriotic duty and of the government's benefits.

The immediate damage caused by the Great Leap For
outweighed the long-term benefits. More than any previou
ment, it brought about sharp divisions in the People's F
These divisions soon proved to be the most menacing ʂ
revolution itself.

The Soviet Reaction. Seeing the confusion among their Chinese
allies, the leaders of the Soviet Union took a bold step which had
severe consequences in China. These leaders were new to power in
Moscow, and their policies reversed those of the past. Led by Nikita
Khrushchev, they replaced Joseph Stalin, who had ruthlessly suppressed all opposition and isolated the country. Khrushchev condemned Stalin's harsh tactics and began to invite more outside
contacts. He concluded that cooperation between the Soviet Union
and the United States was necessary. Khrushchev hoped to avert
an atomic war or the economic chaos which would be caused by an
arms race.

The Soviet leader initiated this policy by opening cultural
exchanges with the United States. At the same time he called China's Great Leap Forward a major error in Communist tactics.
These actions and remarks infuriated Mao Zedong, who had
worked closely with Stalin and was wary of the new Soviet government. Mao was not prepared to accept any cooperation with Western powers and urged the Soviet Union to reject agreements with
the West. In fierce speeches, he charged that the Soviet Communists had become more capitalist and should change their ways.

Reacting to what he considered Mao's arrogance, Khrushchev
appeared before the Soviet Presidium in 1960 to declare that China
must be taught a lesson. He recalled advisers who were helping to
establish a nuclear capacity in China. Then he scornfully sought
new agreements with China's enemy, the United States. At that
point, all of the recent gains in China seemed to have been lost.

The strain between the two Communist countries became severe.
As they exchanged angry accusations, the Soviet Union abruptly cut
off all aid to China. Many Chinese factories were left without
operating blueprints or data. Mao, furious with what he called a
betrayal of communism, sent a delegation to Moscow the next year
to demand that the advisers be returned. But the 22nd Congress of
Communist Party, before which the Chinese diplomats appeared,
denounced both the Chinese and their allies, the Albanians.

Thus began an historic break between the world's largest Communist states— a break which soon was to lead to a realignment of
world power. Moreover, this break, along with Mao's domestic
policies, was quickly followed by a major upheaval inside of China.

The Cultural Revolution. The failure of the Great Leap For-

At the height of Mao's power almost everyone in China was expected to devote at least thirty minutes a day to group discussions of his "Little Red Book."

ward, the loss of Soviet support, and the suppression of Mao's critics stunned all of China. People were finding themselves drawn into a debate over whether Mao had chosen the correct path for them. Those who favored Mao, generally young and idealistic, insisted that the country cling to the purest Communist principles. The pro-Mao group hoped that China could develop a new, more moral kind of human being who could set an example for others throughout the world. Rejecting ideas of the past, they called upon the nation to leave its history behind. They demanded a new way of life, one based upon collectivism, whatever the cost.

Those who opposed Mao, on the other hand, insisted that China had no time for social experiments but must quickly develop its economy in order to survive. They pointed out that the Great Leap Forward had set China back many years and that China could not afford such errors. This anti-Mao faction hoped that China could become one of the world's leading powers by the end of the twentieth century.

The debate simmered for five years after the end of the Great Leap Forward in 1960. Mao's critics, however, were unable to speak openly for fear of repression. Then as Soviet aid was withdrawn and factories were closed, tensions increased. They forced the country into a change which Chinese leaders compare in importance to the Revolution of 1949. This change is known as China's Cultural Revolution.

The Cultural Revolution was the result of a difference in philosophy between Mao and one of his oldest friends, Liu Shaoqi. By the 1960's Mao had retired from an active role in government. He was still Chairman of the Communist Party, but Liu replaced him as the country's chief executive officer.

Then in 1965 Liu initiated a policy which so infuriated Mao that the long debate over policies at last broke out into violence. Massive food shortages and problems of organization moved Liu to try to stabilize the economy. He offered financial rewards, such as special bonuses, to workers who excelled in production. But Mao thought this was a step backward—a "capitalist restoration" which must be resisted at any cost.

This internal contest was sharpened when the United States began to bomb North Vietnam in 1965. The Chinese thought this might mean war because American bombers were coming closer to Chinese borders. In many of their villages, mobilization began. Some of the country highest officials repeated a traditional argument that all of Asia must be defended against the West. They called for the immediate support of North Vietnam.

A close friend of Mao Zedong, a general named Lin Biao, was among the strongest advocates of armed struggle. He rose to become minister of defense, replacing a general whom Mao had criticized after the failure of the Great Leap Forward. In an essay closely noted by Western diplomats, Lin Biao proclaimed, "Long Live the Victory of the People's War." This document predicted that the world's rural areas, such as China, would one day surround and destroy the world's urban countries such as the United States. The aggressive tone of Lin Biao's essay frightened both Chinese and Americans who yearned for peace.

When discussing the issue of war, however, China's leaders were restrained by their own lack of unity. Many of them feared that China was not yet strong enough for combat. The older leaders were particularly concerned that the revolution might not be "complete" and feared that under stress China might slide back into its ancient ways. They began to test each internal policy to see whether it should be regarded as Communist or as "bourgeois revisionism."

After consulting with the North Vietnamese, the Chinese leaders decided to build their defenses and await further developments in the war. This policy corresponded with Mao's view that any nation

To remind China's millions of the need for solidarity, officials sent tens of thousands of people into demonstrations. The sign called for patriotism.

can best resist its enemies through its own resources rather than through alliances. The discussion about how to make communism more effective inside of China, however, did not abate. In November 1965, an article entitled, "On the Play *Hai Rui Dismissed from Office*" attacked a playwright named Wu Han for having criticized Chairman Mao and for hinting at incompetence in government.

The article brought Mao's attention to the play. It was about a Ming Dynasty official who was dismissed for calling the emperor self-righteous and dictatorial. Mao, however, saw in the play a parallel with the case of Peng Dehuai, whom he had dismissed as Defense Minister in 1959. He asked the mayor of Beijing, Peng Zhen, to help investigate. When in 1966 Peng Zhen declared the play harmless, Mao angrily rejected Peng's conclusion. He stalked off to Shanghai while claiming that reactionary individuals were plotting against him.

Mao's rage brought about a struggle in the Communist Party of China, a struggle which he won. The Great Proletarian Cultural Revolution began soon afterwards. "Proletarian revolutionaries," Mao wrote, chiefly addressing students, "unite and seize power from the handful of party persons taking the capitalist road." He reminded them that "Revolution exists only in the state of being born" and called on them to purge the country. Mao spoke to almost a million of them one day in Tiananmen Square in Beijing. He urged them to "bombard" officials, whom he despised and compared to the ancient gentry.

Ever responsive to Mao, tens of thousands of Chinese students poured out of schools. They surged into public offices, challenging officials to adopt more revolutionary practices. Soon they began to call themselves the "Red Guards," as if they alone could defend communism against its enemies.

To the Red Guards Confucianism, with its emphasis on the family, the past, and well-defined human relationships, was the main reason for the decline of China. The Red Guards considered Confucianism to be a root cause of capitalism. They opposed all that it supported, including the family, historical relics, and traditional behavior. Racing through China, they attacked the "four olds"— old ideas, old culture, old customs, and old habits. Their first assault was on temples, art objects, books, and symbols of ancient beliefs, customs, and ceremonies. They smashed family altars and statues, tore down ancient walls such as the one around Beijing, and burned old clothing, housing, and pavilions. Students burst into and disrupted weddings, funerals, and festivals. They invaded temples, mosques, churches, museums, and libraries to ruin ancient calligraphy, jades, and images.

To replace the signs of antiquity, the students raised images of Mao Zedong, installing portraits and statues of him in every city. In their zeal to halt "capitalist revisionism" they quoted the works of Mao endlessly. Often they awakened foreigners late at night to read aloud from his "Little Red Book" of political advice. As Mao became the hero of the Cultural Revolution, the officials became the villains. Students cast aside and in some cases murdered those who tried to quiet them.

The Soviet Union, too, had compromised the revolution, the students said. Though there were no longer any Soviet advisers in China, the Red Guards identified those who had gone with capitalism. They scorned incentive programs, signs of rank in the army and government, and the development of class in society. Soon the Red Guards seized the government of Shanghai and eliminated all Soviet influence from it. They took similar action in China's other cities.

"Reform through labor!" the Red Guards shouted. This was not a new slogan in China, but they made it seem so. The Red Guards demanded the complete social equality of workers and intellectuals. They assigned students, as well as officials, to manual tasks in addition to regular duties in schools or behind desks. Following their orders, tens of thousands of students and teachers left schools to work beside the peasants, assist in communes, or serve as "barefoot doctors." Distinguished officials found themselves planting rice or harvesting wheat beside peasants.

These attacks paralyzed schools, laboratories, factories, and cultural institutions. After detecting any sign of the "four olds," the Red Guards imprisoned professors or public officials for months in dark closets, refusing to allow them even the slightest contact with relatives. The teaching of classical music or literature was considered reason enough to punish the members of school faculties.

Officials and students who cooperated with the Red Guards learned to live as the peasants did. Typically they arose at 6:30 a.m., washed and studied, then completed their farming chores until lunch at 1 p.m. In the evening they provided the commune's entertainment or the factory's instruction. At 8 p.m. they were given another hour to study, then a little time for personal matters until going to bed.

The officials were permitted to join the peasants only after publicly "confessing" to the crime of "revisionism." Many who were high in government, including Premier Zhou Enlai, made confessions in which they admitted having departed from Mao's communism. All of the confessions ended in a similar way: the "guilty" persons declared that because they were now aware of their

The image of Mao Zedong loomed over this conference of import-export traders. Such reminders became a major part of the campaign to create the "Maoist Man."

"crimes" they could work more effectively in behalf of the people.

It is difficult even today to know how many officials lost their posts or their lives during the Cultural Revolution. Some were murdered during the first onslaught of the Red Guards. One of these seems to have been Peng Zhen, the vice premier and mayor of Beijing who had told Mao that he found no evidence of an anti-Maoist plot. He, the deputy mayor, and the defense minister disappeared. Others, including the head of the Secretariat of the Communist Party, simply were stripped of authority. The Red Guards paraded most of their surviving victims through the streets, forcing them to wear dunce caps and signs proclaiming guilt.

In time, Mao was forced to ask the students to end their aggressive tactics. He is said to have wept at the destruction of the social order. The students, heeding him, returned to their classes and jobs. Mao's leading enemies in government, however, were deposed. The chief among them were his former comrade, Liu Shaoqi, who was popularly labeled a traitor to China, and Zhu De, founder of the Red Army, who was publicly humiliated. Power shifted, instead, to Mao's secretary, Chen Boda, and to Mao's wife, the former actress Jiang Qing.

The "Maoist Man." One effect of the Cultural Revolution was to raise Chairman Mao Zedong to a position more imposing than ever before. "One sun in the heavens, one ruler on earth," had long been a saying of the Chinese people. The work of the Red Guards enabled Mao to become China's "one ruler." His name, picture, and statements were seen throughout the country. His words were in the lessons of children, posters, paintings, music, newspapers, books, lectures, and daily conversations.

Mao used his authority to create a new way of life in China. Previously, China was less a country than a collection of families, clans, and associations. Government generally resembled a remote enemy more than a friend of the people. Chinese were loyal to their culture but often not to their nation. It was difficult, in this condition, to raise taxes, enforce honesty in official behavior, or gain the cooperation of the masses of people. The emperor often had difficulty in raising armies or taxes, but Mao Zedong had none. Children, in fact, yearned to become members of the People's Liberation Army. Many wanted to give their lives for the state. Millions volunteered to perform tasks for Mao and their country.

Any Chinese who accepted this nationalist way of life became known as a "Maoist Man." Through constant efforts called "re-education," the People's Republic struggled to create this "new man." He thought and acted differently from his father or grandfather. The past was almost completely erased in the conscious mind of the Maoist Man, except for constant reminders that China once was the prey of foreigners. The Maoist Man drew no pleasure from personal gain, but from the extent to which he could contribute to the state. He did not model himself on people who were passive, scholarly, or acquisitive, but on those who actively contributed to their communities through physical labor. Mao's theories called on him to demand constant vigilance so that new classes in society could never arise.

Mao, at this point, received much of the love and attention that previously had been granted to families and ancestors. Children were taught to praise him from the time they could speak. When at home they often heard quotations from his books read aloud. At Mao's command, hundreds of thousands of people would suddenly stream into Tiananmen Square in Beijing. There, they would march or hear Mao's speeches. Workers everywhere, on communes

Minority children, studying their own language in a remote school, were told to revere Mao Zedong. Communists hoped to shift loyalty away from families.

Ordinary people were shown proudly volunteering for public service. They did so in this subway train without pay.

and in factories, spent their free time repeating his words.

To create the "Maoist Man," all of the arts were turned to the purposes of the state. Sculptors poured images of Mao out of their workshops. They raised a thirty-foot high figure of him in Shangyang's Red Flag Circle. On either side of the Nanjing Bridge they raised ten giant-sized Chinese characters, each weighing four tons, which said: "Long Live Our Great Leader Mao Zedong." In bookshops they replaced the works of classic writers, poets, and playwrights with those of Mao. Only the few plays and operas approved by Mao's wife, Jiang Qing, were permitted on stages.

The object of this din of praise was to break down the will of individuals and replace it with the will of the state. But Mao was soon to learn that this task was larger than it seemed.

The End of an Era. At the height of his power Mao purged the government of leaders whom he thought were "capitalist roaders," including his old friend Liu Shaoqi. Mao took direct control of the Chinese government again. However, because he had hopes of retiring he shared this power with another comrade of revolutionary days, Defense Minister Lin Biao. Together Mao and Lin took the titles "Supreme and Deputy Supreme Commanders of the Whole Nation and the Whole Army." Mao was counting on Lin to become his successor.

Under Mao and Lin the military took control of the Communist

Party, and so they controlled the whole country. Army officers, warning that both the United States and the Soviet Union had become increasingly hostile to China, arranged for the entire nation to go on a wartime footing.

But tensions between China and the Soviet Union began to heighten. Rumors suddenly spread that Lin Biao, with the help of the Soviets, had been plotting to overthrow and replace Mao. Suddenly Lin and his family bolted from China. They left in a small plane, only to be shot down the Soviet border. They had been on route to Moscow.

A frenzy of activity followed. Everywhere the Chinese people dug air raid shelters and stocked them in case of an attack by the Soviet Union. The People's Liberation Army called more and more young men to active duty, swelling the numbers stationed at the borders with Vietnam and the Soviet Union. Hundreds of thousands of other students were ordered to report to farms to help increase the nation's food supplies.

Large numbers of people began to protest when confronted with these new hardships, which reminded them of the failures during the Great Leap Forward and Cultural Revolution. Some students became outlaws rather than accept longer military service. Others fled to Hong Kong. In some months as many as ten thousand swam or took small boats across the channel between the mainland and that island. As crime and other expressions of discontent spread, the government responded with mass trials and, often, with executions.

Mao was approaching his eightieth year, and people were questioning his ability govern much longer. As border clashes and tensions with the Soviet Union increased, the Chinese found themselves completely isolated and engulfed by conflicts. They wondered where to turn for help. Soon they received a surprising answer to this question. Under pressure, Mao permitted negotiations with the country he had long identified as "the greatest enemy"—the United States.

Mao's advisers at last persuaded him that China needed Western trade and other support to defend itself against the Soviet threat. Italy, Canada, and ten other Western countries took note of China's new attitudes by recognizing its Communist government. Then came the turn of the United States.

The relationship of the Americans and the Chinese Communists began with an exchange of ping-pong players, followed by cautious diplomatic moves. At last in 1972 Mao extended his hand to welcome President Richard M. Nixon, who had agreed to mutual recognition by the two countries. Both leaders had drastically changed their viewpoints. For the Chinese, diplomatic contacts had become possible because the Americans were slowly withdrawing from the war in Vietnam. For Nixon, who had long condemned Communist China as well as its sympathizers in the U.S., American losses in Vietnam meant that China's help would be needed against the Soviet Union.

New agreements with the United States signaled the end of Maoist power in China. After 1972, Mao's supporters rapidly broke into rival factions and quarreled among themselves. Civilian officials, usually more moderate than those of the military, gradually took control, both at home and in China's embassies abroad. Hundreds of bureaucrats who had been attacked as "capitalist roaders" suddenly reappeared in their old offices. Moreover, China witnessed the rebirth of organizations that had been suppressed during the purges of the Cultural Revolution, including the Women's Federation, the Trade Union Congress, and the Communist Youth League.

With his last energies, the aging Mao tried feebly to resist these changes and continue the struggle against capitalism in China. He still believed that a "perpetual revolution" was necessary to uproot thousands of years of capitalist behavior. Nevertheless, his efforts, based upon tirades against Lin, whom he called a traitor, were moderated by the diplomacy of Premier Zhou Enlai. Zhou, greatly revered as a stable influence in government, reduced China's support for worldwide revolutions. At home he turned the anger stirred by Mao into campaigns against Confucian behavior. At the same time he encouraged those officials who favored cooperation with the United States and other capitalist countries. The struggle must continue against capitalism, he said, but it must first attack "feudalism" in the Chinese economy.

Zhou died in January 1976. Mao died nine months later. Thus ended what has been compared to a modern dynasty in China. Together these two men had presided over what may have been the most tumultuous period in the long history of the most populous nation on earth.

Now the Mandate of Heaven passed to new leaders.

CHAPTER 10

THE PEOPLE'S REPUBLIC OF CHINA:
THE EMERGING NATION

Reviewing their situation after the death of Mao, China's new leaders saw that more than three decades of communism had produced mixed results. Foreign rulers were gone. Gone, too, was the hereditary class which refused to allow the bulk of the population to increase its standards of living. China had strong defenses and, despite its many factions, a unified government and economy. Vast public works projects had been completed, wrenched out of the land by a determined population guided by powerful ideals. There were important gains in the fields of public health, transportation, agriculture, science, and industry.

But communism had also imposed severe costs on the nation. At least forty million Chinese had perished. They died of persecution, unrest, or because the government had been unable to ameliorate sufficiently the effects of continuing droughts, floods, earthquakes, and epidemics. Thirty years after the country, aided by a single ally, had sealed itself off from the rest of the world, no Chinese was yet able to criticize the government freely. All but a small number of Chinese still labored in the fields, using primitive tools and earning only subsistence. Progress among industrial workers was greater than among the peasants, but still lagged far behind that of comparable workers in Western nations.

The flagging enthusiasm of the Chinese people for their leaders was one of the more damaging costs for the administration. The years since the revolution had brought neither freedom nor prosperity. Conflicts over ideology had forced an entire generation to grow up without skills. Dispirited, many Chinese were questioning the need to work as hard as before or to produce goods of quality. Most were tired of hearing officials nag them to invest more of their lives in the country. A growing desire for consumer goods was sweeping over China, just as it had swept over the rest of the world. Yet the government could not begin to satisfy it.

A solution to these problems would require keen thought and skillful organizing on the part of China's leaders. In countless meetings after Mao's death, the officials who managed to survive decided to make historic changes in the nation's economic and

133

social structure. In effect, they planned to modify communism to suit the needs of their own country. But first it was necessary for them to consolidate their power and to gain the support of the people. Only then could China's leaders move rapidly towards putting their plans into action.

Politics and Government. Almost immediately after Mao died, posters began to appear attacking his wife, Jiang Qing, and three others who claimed to have inherited his powers. Called the "Gang of Four," this group was said to have manipulated the old and dying leader in order to seize control of the government.

Accusers of the Gang of Four became bolder with every passing day. They claimed Jiang Qing and her associates had put close friends into high office. The four, it was widely believed, had strongly influenced Mao to bring about the disastrous Cultural Revolution. They were identified with the "puritans" or "idealists," who insisted that China hew to the Communist principles of Marx, Lenin, and Stalin. They were willing to risk everything gained since the revolution, but not to surrender their belief that the whole world must inevitably become Communist.

Popular anger with Mao and his wife had begun to arise immediately after the death of the revered prime minister, Zhou Enlai, in 1976. At that time, Mao had only nine months left to live, and apparently it was his wife who ordered the removal of funeral wreaths that had been placed near Zhou's tomb. Finding the wreaths gone when they came to pay tribute to Zhou, hundreds of Chinese began to demonstrate in Tiananmen Square, in Beijing. It seemed to them that Mao and Jiang Qing had shown profound disrespect for the dead leader. The angry crowd swelled to thousands, and its fury spread to other cities.

Then this anger became political. People who resented their continuing low pay and lack of consumer goods joined the protest. Zhou, they said, had been disgraced because of his moderate policies. "Down with Qin Shihuangdi!" they shouted, openly comparing Mao to an ancient tyrant, and "Down with the Empress Dowager!", a slogan which compared Jiang Qing to a hated ruler of the Qing (Manchu) Dynasty. Mao thus heard himself publicly reviled in China shortly before his death. His widow lived on and was to suffer the people's hostility for many years longer.

Mao, powerful even in his waning days, had made one final effort to shape the government. He ordered the arrest and dismissal of officials whom he said had provoked the riots. To head the new bureaucracy he appointed Hua Guofeng, an old and trusted friend. Mao, no doubt, died believing that Hua Guofeng would carry on his program of "perpetual revolution" to assure communism in

China. But Hua, instead, was replaced by a man whom Mao had recently ousted from office, Deng Xiaoping. The change was made because Deng, a former general, had the respect not only of the military, but of party leaders and the people, too. He seemed to be the only man who could unite the country.

This was the same Deng Xiaoping who, ironically, had been forced to wear a dunce cap and proclaim his "crimes against the state" during the Cultural Revolution. Soon he replaced Hua as head of the Standing Committee. From this position he was soon to introduce some of the most momentous changes in the history of the People's Republic.

As Hua gave way to Deng, the government sought to end forever the remaining influence of the Gang of Four. It put Jiang Qing and her three associates on trial. All four were found guilty of using her late husband's authority to conspire against the state. Defiant to the end, she declared in open court that Mao had empowered her to carry on his will and that the state had no right to try her. The judges, however, sentenced her to death, then suspended the sentence. She was allowed to live, but under arrest.

Millions of Chinese rejoiced at the conclusion of the Gang of Four trial. They considered themselves freed of the burdens that had been placed upon them. They gladly removed tens of thousands of Mao's pictures and statues everywhere in the country. But now it was time to respond to a new breed of officials—the "practical" Communists (or "pragmatists") led by Deng. He had urged that China follow more flexible policies than Mao had been willing to permit.

Deng Xiaoping invited foreign leaders to open the way to renewed commercial and cultural exchanges with China, and President Reagan cooperated fully.

THE GOVERNMENT OF THE PEOPLE'S REPUBLIC OF CHINA*

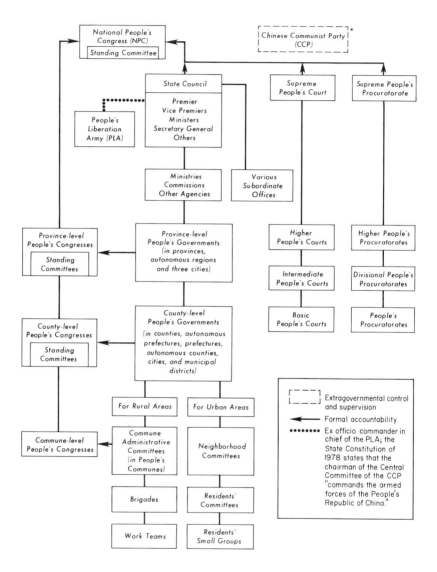

*Article Two of the Constitution of 1982 states: "The organs through which the people exercise state power are the National People's Congress and the local people's congresses at different levels. The people administer state affairs and manage economic, cultural, and social affairs through various channels and in various ways in accordance with the law."

In the field of government, Deng's first task was to sweep aside countless tired bureaucrats who tended to block official action. As always in China's history, this large group had assumed great power and privilege, doing little for substantial pay. Deng insisted that no bureaucrat be able to keep his job for life and dismissed tens of thousands of them in order to create a more efficient government. He called for legal guarantees so that no one person could ever again achieve Mao's enormous power. Finally, he prosecuted more than eighty high officials who had been discovered taking bribes.

The new government took much of the same basic form as the old one, but with less control from the top. As before, the chief administrative areas were the provinces, autonomous regions, and the large cities of Beijing, Shanghai, and Tianjin. Within the provinces, local officials governed China's districts and its cities. Under Deng, many of them were chosen by election of the people for the first time. Rural areas were still divided into counties, towns, villages, and teams. However, plans were made to allow some private ownership of small farms, thus reducing the spread of collective farming.

On the national level, the Communist Party, which by now included 3.8 per cent of the population, continued to dominate the country. Its chairman automatically became commander of the armed forces, and it alone had the power to summon the National People's Congress. Urged to do so by the party, the Congress could change the Constitution, pass laws, and choose the premier. He, in turn, helped the party to select twelve vice premiers and twenty-nine ministers who formed the State Council. In addition, he became one of the five members of the Standing Committee, which guided the Congress. Thus the Premier of the Standing Committee and the Chairman of the Communist Party remained the most powerful figures in a nation whose population had exceeded one billion.

Law. Most Asian legal systems differ greatly from those of Western countries which follow traditions begun in ancient Rome. In China, particularly, law is not a firm body of rules listing human rights and crimes. Nor is it a code which announces predetermined punishments for violations of law. Rather, the Chinese have always expected the members of their society to behave in ways acceptable to all. Those who fail to do so are sought out and made to pay for their failings, but not always, as in the West, by surrendering their freedom.

The Chinese try to define good and bad behavior by establishing models for action, rather than by proclaiming codes of law. A model originates with reference to novels, plays, and especially to histories. Yet often a definition of this kind may prove ambiguous, as it is among Americans who refer to George Washington's honesty. To clarify this ambiguity, the Chinese turn to a popular leader who most closely meets their ideals, then model themselves on him or her. Those who best follow the correct model may be widely praised, celebrated in speeches and holiday toasts, and perhaps even granted a state pension.

In this way, national standards are established. A woman in Beijing often is honored at state dinners and in publications because she recovered from what seemed to be an incurable illness. She is thought to have saved her own life by concentrating on, and so eliminating the illness from her body. The Chinese also prize individuals who, overcoming obstacles of poverty or the demands of society, teach themselves to write well, solve mathematical problems, or play musical instruments beautifully. Such people, as models of good behavior, are sometimes called "dragons," meaning that they are superior beings. The standards they set become an essential, though usually unwritten part of Chinese law.

In the same way, the Chinese agree on what they mean by criminal behavior and the price that must be paid for it. People know the criminals among them because photographs of convicts appear in most public places. The criminals, humiliated, become outcasts, and their families are shunned. Yet they do not necessarily go to jail; they may simply be paraded through the streets and forced to confess "error." Someone resembling the convicted person may become the villain in a local play, and his or her name may be mentioned scornfully on posters and in newspapers. After suffering in this way, the condemned person may go free on the general assumption that re-education has taken place. An environment of this kind is often called a "shame society."

This method of controlling human behavior is based upon the belief that people can and should be educated. It suggests that the community's standards are, after all, the right ones. Community standards, however, always change. The individual who wishes to express his own standards may be a hero or villain according to the times. Mao Zedong, for example, was widely believed to have won superhuman status after leading the Communists to victory in China. Millions of Chinese visited his birthplace, kept his photographs on their walls, and studied his "Little Red Book" of quotations. Today his post-revolutionary behavior is considered by many to have been criminal. Few speak of him. An opposite course was taken by Deng Xiaoping. At one point, when he was Mao's enemy during the Cultural Revolution, he was forced to declare himself a criminal. Later, as China's premier, it was Deng whose image was more often seen in China than Mao's. He became the current model for good behavior.

Confucianism played a major role in establishing this method of law in China. It pointed to the major heroes of the past and encouraged people of the present to model themselves accordingly. It declared a framework by which all Chinese could live together in harmony, showing just how all could behave with respect to relatives, friends, neighbors, and the world. Thus Confucianism does not accept the modern Communist idea of a worldwide struggle between economic classes. Instead of struggle, it advises its followers to accept their conditions.

Other Chinese philosophies also use models to promote peace and harmony in society. Daoism, for example, describes the "Way of the True Gentleman" (or "Good Man" or "Dragon"). Buddhism calls on people to live the purest kind of lives in order to teach others respect for all beings.

Despite the opposition of the Communist government to these philosophies, they remain embedded in Chinese life and law. They impart a sense of almost religious morality to Chinese ideas about both crime and punishment. For example, the Chinese believe that criminals simply have the wrong viewpoint about life. "Re-education through labor," a common slogan in the courts of China, suggests that people can be changed if only they can be made to work hard. Once convicted of a crime an inmate may be held for years, even if the offense was minor, until his or her attitude seems to have changed.

Near New Virtue Street in Beijing there is a labor camp called the Benevolent Forest. There, police confine up to one thousand young people each month for crimes as minor as loitering. The prisoners, most of whom were caught in the streets because they had no jobs, are called "hooligans." They are given strict tasks to perform until they can show eagerness to cooperate. Few of them will be able to find work in the overcrowded city, but no one will be released without a promise to try.

Such demands for conformism, whether or not it is possible, apply to people who criticize the government as well as to the unemployed or to criminals. In 1957, after inviting his critics to come forward in what became known as the "Hundred Flowers Period," Mao Zedong declared the government's right to imprison them for their opinions alone. His law has remained in force, though after the Cultural Revolution the Chinese people were assured that they would no longer be subject to arbitrary police action. Today, those who do not conform politically are called "counter-revolutionaries," "anti-socialists," or "troublemakers" and are subject to arrest. Many have been kept for months, perhaps years, without the freedom to defend themselves.

The effort to enforce conformism begins in the neighborhoods. People watch each other, insisting on law-abiding behavior. They have been known to stop and thrash thieves. But normally it is the police or agents of the Communist Party—the cadres—who initiate an accusation. Once accused, a defendant is almost certain to be punished. Police may bring him or her to a labor camp without trial. The law limits their right to do so to six months, but police are said often to ignore this law. Usually the facts in a case are given to a "procurator," a government investigator who decides whether or not to bring the case to trial. The office of the procurator was created to limit abuses by police.

A trial may also be held at the request of a judge or of a neighborhood group called a "People's Mediation Committee." It is through such committees that China's enormous population controls its individuals. Neighbors stir shame in lawbreakers, often ostracizing them. Many prisoners in China turned themselves in because they could not bear looking at others while knowing of their own crimes. They voluntarily confessed. Similarly, in the event of a trial a defendant's best chance for a light sentence is to confess and claim to have a changed attitude. There is little chance for an acquittal, for the judge assumes that the procurator has previously determined guilt.

This system of law differs broadly from those of the West. In contrast to the United States, China has few lawyers. There was no legal profession in China until the Revolution of 1911. Basically, the Chinese assumed that they could create a harmonious society through Confucianism rather than through litigation. While there are many lawyers in the U.S. Congress, there are almost none in the government of China. Beijing University rarely graduates more than seventy-five law students a year, compared with hundreds at every major law school in the United States.

Lawyers in China are expected chiefly to resolve business problems rather than to represent people in criminal or civil cases. There is no body of written law to which they could point to make their case. China has no Bill of Rights which is as rigorously followed as the American one. To decide guilt or innocence the judge, who probably has no legal training, represents the community and so depends on the common wisdom. A simple lecture may be the sole punishment for a lawbreaker who had good reasons to commit a crime. On the other hand, a long sentence may be in store for someone who refuses to admit guilt.

In at least small ways, China has been moving towards a legal system more like that in the United States. The Chinese have found it necessary to import lawyers from the West or from Hong Kong in order to build their international trade. Foreign investors and travelers in China have demanded legal protections which are slowly being extended to the Chinese It seems probable, as China ends its centuries-long isolation, that its laws will offer more protection to individual rights.

THE ECONOMY

Pressures for change. Immediately after Mao's death, the return of relative calm in the country enabled China's new leaders to study the economy carefully. They acknowledged that, by following the Soviet model accepted by Mao, China had been able to produce enough food to survive. It was also true that there had been some industrial expansion. However, the study revealed, major social problems were developing. These problems had been ignored in the glowing reports issued by Mao's government.

Essentially, the Communist economy required the Chinese to sacrifice most personal desires so that the whole nation could move forward. The state collected all of the profits from more than a million separate enterprises, then reinvested them. With few trading partners or allies, China depended on its vast population to

Propagandists under Mao boasted that this Beijing school for machinists was enrolling 2,500 students, but most Chinese machinery was obsolete and slow.

finance the expansion of heavy industry, national security, and the government itself. All of these expenses were being borne by laboring people, and officials could only hope that the growth of the economy would lessen the burden.

But the economy was not growing, and the Chinese people were becoming restless with their sacrifices. They were no longer suffering the mass starvation of pre-revolutionary times, but more than a hundred million of them were undernourished and at least twenty million were unemployed. They dreamed of owning more consumer goods but found few in the shops. By the 1980's, when most families were earning $3-400 a year, a bicycle cost $102, and another item much in demand, a wristwatch, cost $80. Beside these small items, people were pleading for electric fans, television sets, and refrigerators. Such larger appliances were either unavailable or far beyond the reach of the average worker.

The nation's new administrators found, in their study of the economy, that under existing conditions China was unlikely to break out of its cycle of poverty. Other countries were making lasting gains in such fields as electronics, communications, and transportation, while China was simply laboring to feed its people. In 1980, with its 1.2 billion people representing about 25 per cent of the population of the world, it had less than 7 per cent of the world's arable land. Expensive drainage and irrigation projects had enabled it to increase this percentage by about a third since the revolution, but the number of Chinese was increasing, too. China's collective farms, or communes, still chiefly used primitive tools and so bound more than 85 percent of the population to steady labor. In Europe, Japan, the United States, and even Israel less than 3 per cent of the population was able to feed the whole country, and often to export food, by using modern farming methods.

In the cities, matters were made much worse by a system which assured workers that they could not be fired. This policy often led to incompetence on the job. In 1982 the government estimated that more than two-thirds of all of China's senior technicians knew little about their work. During the Cultural Revolution, when most schools were closed and young people sent to labor among the peasants, few Chinese learned professions or skills. China's struggles over ideology had forced the country to pay a heavy price.

Finally, the government seemed to be doing badly with the little income that it did receive. A large part of its revenue went to pay for central planning. This activity was so inefficient that food often rotted because there was no transportation for it. At least a third of its budget was being used to hold down prices, for it was absorbing heavy losses in the sale of foods. Its subsidies permitted it to keep the cost of biscuits at 40 cents a pound, pork at 86 cents, vegetable oil at 27 cents for nine ounces, rice at 9 cents a pound, and salted fish as 25-50 cents a pound. People could afford these necessities, but neither the country nor its individuals had anything left over for expansion.

Under these policies, China began to suffer large budget deficits, unemployment, and shortages of capital. Lacking skills, enthusiasm, and equipment, its economic problems increased. Its dreams of assuming a place among the world's leading countries, which it hoped to achieve by the end of the century, were vanishing.

The "Four Modernizations." Deng Xiaoping proposed to overcome China's economic problems by means of an entirely new program. Calling his program the "Four Modernizations," he envisioned changes meant to revitalize agriculture, industry, technology, and national defense. After gathering power in 1978-9, he launched China upon a course of which Mao Zedong would certainly have disapproved.

The philosophies and methods of the two men were clearly illustrated by China's economic policies during their leadership. Under Mao, China announced six five-year plans which were shaped and administered by officials. Mao expected people to work for the love of country rather than for themselves. He encouraged them to seek equality among each other by pooling incomes. His administration struggled to assure equality by fixing wages and prices.

Deng, on the other hand, announced a ten-year plan which was essentially run by the managers of factories and farms. He allowed them to offer bonuses to workers who exceeded goals—a process which yielded inequality. Eventually, Deng hoped, prices and wages would be determined by the amount and the quality of goods and services, not by officials. Under Deng, the government still regulated enterprises but no longer managed them directly. Instead, individual plant managers and entrepeneurs controlled their own enterprises and gained or lost according to their successes or failures. Deng called this China's "responsibility system."

The operation of Deng's new policy was best shown in the few plants where his government first tried it out. One such plant produced steel in Sichuan, where it had been built in 1965 to create employment in a depressed region. The plant was closed during the Cultural Revolution, when Red Guards forced its skilled workers to labor beside peasants. Its machinery began to disintegrate, and even after it was reopened in 1975 it earned too little to buy the simplest tools for its workers. At this time the government was collecting all of the factory's income and paying for all losses, which often were severe.

Deng Xiaoping's first efforts to offer incentives to Chinese workers were in steel plants such as this. The effect was to raise production immediately.

In 1979, Deng offered the plant's managers 5 per cent of all profits if they met production goals and 20 per cent of whatever they produced above the goals. The managers were free to use this money for bonuses to workers or to finance improvements in the factory. This new policy quickly revitalized the plant. Production quadrupled in a single year. The factory began to pay much more in taxes as well as substantial bonuses to its workers. Moreover, the quality of its products steadily improved.

Successes of this kind encouraged Deng to offer incentive programs in many more factories. Soon, workers throughout China were able to earn additional wages for work well done. No longer could they be sure that they would keep their jobs even if they performed badly. In the past, the government had guaranteed them food, however well they worked, through a policy called the "Iron Rice Bowl." Suddenly, it turned out, the bowl handed them was made of something more breakable than iron, and it had no food for slackers.

As open markets were established, a new sense of risk and enthusiasm spread through the cities. Officials encouraged enterprising or unemployed workers to set up small shops and to take responsibility for their own success or failure. In Beijing's Qianmenwai district, a bazaar of these shops now unfolds under tents every morning. Its merchants sell a variety of inexpensive consumer goods, including pictures of film stars, candied crab apples, bright plastic tablecloths, and dishware.

The Four Modernizations Program encouraged merchants to set up small shops throughout China. This food stall in Beijing became a profitable business.

In the countryside, the introduction of the Four Modernizations produced an equally startling effect. The policy allowed peasant families to take over the work of production teams. In time, farmers were allowed to own and operate their own small farms, and the role of the communes in China's economy began to shrink. The new method gave the peasants the right to set goals through contracts with the government. Like people in the cities, they could keep large amounts of whatever they produced above the goals. These incentives resulted in the production of far more food. Some peasant families, particularly successful under the new incentive program, began to earn as much as $15,000 a year in a country where people rarely made more than $400 a year. Officials predicted that incentives granted to farmers would create 200 million wealthy peasants by the end of the century. They foresaw a huge group which would comprise a vast market for consumer goods.

In addition to these changes, Deng's government began to break down the fear of foreigners which had long existed in China. The Chinese began to exchange more information with outsiders through international conferences held in their own country and abroad. Under the Four Modernizations policy, Chinese firms were encouraged to invite foreign companies to cooperate with them in such highly technical fields as oil exploration, mining, and electronics. In dozens of coastal cities they offered special tax credits to international traders.

In sum, Deng's new policies suggested that China had reached an historic moment in its economic development. In many parts of the world observers wondered whether the People's Republic might not be leaving the Communist fold. This possibility was advanced after a stunning analysis was made in 1985 by the Beijing People's Daily. "Marx died 101 years ago," the authoritative newspaper reported. "There have been tremendous changes since his ideas were formed. One cannot expect the works of Marx and Lenin to solve all of today's problems."

China was not likely to desert its Communist ways completely. Yet certainly it was developing its own version of that economic and political philosophy. Communism, with its restrictive laws and strict moral outlook, generally pleased those Chinese who are still affected by Confucian traditions. The Confucian element in China has resented the growing forms of corruption that have inevitably appeared as the country rushes to establish free markets. On the island of Hainan, for example, officials were found to have pocketed millions of dollars by permitting smugglers to sell television sets, washing machines, and refrigerators freely in their jurisdiction. Pornographic films have become available in what has always been one of the most puritanical countries on earth. Drugs are being smuggled into the mainland from Hong Kong. There have been uncontrolled bank loans and inflation.

The Confucianists in China hope to preserve the country's ancient culture. They, along with the Communists, have been resisting the changes introduced with the Four Modernizations policy. The contest between these groups and those advocating open markets is certain to produce a new, distinctly Chinese system of government.

SCIENCE AND TECHNOLOGY

Despite political and economic turmoil, China astonished the world when it succeeded in exploding an atomic bomb in 1964. Its scientific and technical progress were such that, within six years afterward it was producing missiles capable of delivering atomic warheads. It followed this military effort immediately by launching of its first satellite into orbit. New Chinese satellites soared into space each year during the succeeding fifteen years. Then China also tested its first hydrogen bomb.

After the death of Mao Zedong, China's new leaders announced their desire to "bring up a mighty contingent of working-class intellectuals as fast as possible." They were able to sweep aside Mao's policy of forcing scientists to learn peasant ways. Instead, the government encouraged scholars to concentrate on their own work. Foreign teachers began to enter the country, and Chinese students went abroad to study. Scientific equipment never before seen in China suddenly appeared on Chinese docks, imported from Japan, Europe, and the United States.

The new policy produced rapid results. The Chinese satellite launched in 1984 required some of the world's most advanced rocket engines. From this evidence and from China's own announcements, Western military experts concluded that China had an arsenal of missiles capable of reaching other continents. The Chinese government declared that its weapons would be used for national defense only. Military research, meanwhile, spurred the development of new industries such as electronics and communications.

It was in the field of medicine, however, that the Chinese made their most startling progress. During the last days of the Republic millions of Chinese died of epidemics and plagues. Many people were seen in the streets, ridden with flies or fever or saddled with the habit of opium smoking. Today, there seems to be no one who cannot gain access to effective medical treatment. In all cases patients are free to visit clinics, hospitals, and private doctors. Often, though, the sick choose to be treated by folk doctors who sell herbs. Modern investigators have found that reviving the use of herbs to treat disease may sometimes have real and current value.

Chinese doctors also tend to favor another traditional form of

China began to press forward in the production of electronic equipment. In large factories it began to produce consumer goods, such as television sets.

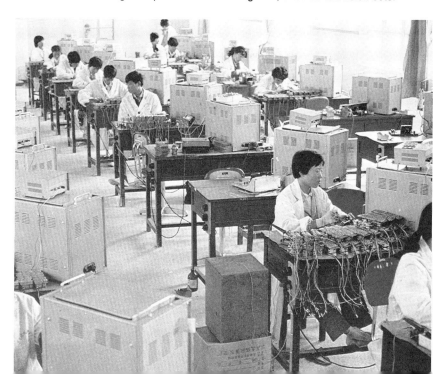

treatment called acupuncture. Said to be several thousand years old, acupuncture requires the use of various-sized stainless steel needles. The needles are inserted into parts of the body indicated by ancient charts said to describe subleties of the human nervous system. In some cases where they are meant to relieve pain, the needles are twirled; in others they are used to stimulate nerves. Many observers, including respected Western doctors, have seen the needles used and witnessed improvement in cases of childhood deafness or dumbness, arthritis, paralysis, rheumatism, heart palpitations, and nervous disorders. Many patients claim that acupuncture relieved them of headaches and even hangovers. Others have undergone surgery, such as the removal of tumors, the birth of a child, or the repair of the heart, with no other anesthetic but the needles. Researchers, both in China and the West, could find no reason for these effects, which the more skeptical therefore attributed either to chance or to the power of human belief. For whatever reason, the method produced at least limited success.

The Chinese dealt with some of their severest medical problems through public education. Many diseases grew out of the country's enormous population and so were more easily prevented than cured. Venereal diseases, for example, were reported to have stricken almost 10 per cent of the population—including 20 per cent of all soldiers—in 1949. (In contrast, these diseases are considered exceptionally high in the United States when they attack 3 per cent of the population.) These diseases were reduced to minor proportions by eliminating prostitution, offering broader medical care, and by promoting greater equality for women.

The government mounted its educational campaigns with the help of hundreds of thousands of volunteers. Medical care was made available to more people. Most communes put aside one yuan

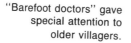

"Barefoot doctors" gave special attention to older villagers.

Classes for the barefoot doctors gave intensive training in the dispensing of both ancient and modern medicines, helping to control raging diseases.

per person in a separate fund every year. This money was used to buy all medical care except dental work and eyeglasses, which were inexpensive. Almost every commune put up a small building near places of work where both modern and traditional drugs were used. Communes employed "barefoot doctors," usually young people who treated patients when there were no highly trained doctors available. After six months of medical education these young men or women were able to deal with minor ailments. In major cases they called on physicians in medical centers for help.

By the 1980's there were 1.5 million "barefoot doctors" in China, but the number fell off because they were receiving little pay for an increasing amount of work. The growing population was placing great strains on the medical delivery system, causing long waits for treatment and, often, hasty diagnoses. People had to travel long distances because doctors working for the state were not permitted to make house calls. After the revolution in 1949 the new Chinese government was able to count only 12,000 doctors for a population of 500 million. Today, with more than a billion people, China has 1.35 million physicians, though about 10 per cent of them do not have advanced degrees. This was substantial progress, but it was not enough to provide rapid and effective medical treatment.

By the mid-1980's the government was introducing incentives in the practice of medicine, as it had in the rest of the economy. Under this new system, a typical private doctor might see about fifty patients a day and charge the equivalent of less than eight cents a visit. The doctor was permitted to keep about 80 per cent of his income, but paid the rest over to the local pharmacy to finance the purchase of medicines. He received a monthly pension equal to about $36, and with the money earned from patients was able to live comfortably in the present Chinese economy. The incentives also apply to "barefoot doctors," many of whom may take medical examinations and, if they pass, may set up private practices in the clinics.

The Chinese people seem pleased with their combination of public and private medicine. If they choose, they can draw an annual subsidy which now is high enough to cover the cost of private medical care. An increasing number of people have been turning to private doctors to avoid the crowds and delays in public clinics. Yet in many ways medical care in China is not as great a problem as in some Western countries. The Chinese, with their plain diets and avoidance of animal fats, sugars, and salts, are less prone to some of the most dangerous diseases in Europe and the United States.

Even as health care changes from a public to a semi-private system, the Chinese seem to take a special pride in how, when it was necessary just after their revolution, they worked together to produce an improved medical system. They also recall how, when it was urgent to do so, they greatly reduced the "four pests"— mosquitoes, rats, bedbugs, and flies, all of which were spreading dangerous diseases. Millions of Chinese responded to the government's call to kill ten of these pests a day. They soon reduced the "four pests" to relative harmlessness.

China's current public health problems are less easily solved, but community efforts are still the best tool to use against them. One of the most critical problems is caused by a parasite that embeds itself in snails that infest the human sewage on riverbanks. Along the crowded rivers children are exposed to a disease, schistosomiasis,

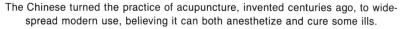

The Chinese turned the practice of acupuncture, invented centuries ago, to widespread modern use, believing it can both anesthetize and cure some ills.

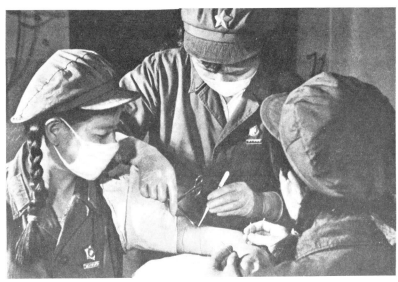

which often causes glandular disorders and even death. The government has attacked the disease by organizing thousands of young workers to kill the snails. Similar campaigns have been mounted against kala-azar, another disease caused by flies. Community efforts have greatly reduced such problems as cholera, typhoid, typhus, tuberculosis, malaria, hookworm, leprosy, and opium addiction.

CHINESE CULTURE TODAY

The arts. Throughout its past, China has regarded the arts as an important part of its educational system. Most Chinese writers produced historical materials and poetry until the nineteenth century, when foreign novels arrived and stirred interest in the modern art of fiction. Chinese calligraphy and painting required high artistic skills but were not intended to be inventive. Rather, they taught self-discipline, respect for the past, and awareness of nature. In the same way, music, dance, and the theater in China constantly emphasized the country's enduring values.

This attitude persuaded many Chinese rulers to insist that the arts be used to rally people to the support of their regimes. From the time of the Emperor Qin Shihuangdi (259—210 B.C.), who burned books that he disliked, Chinese governments have persecuted artists who advocated change. Censorship became customary, and in recent centuries many writers have been executed or imprisoned.

Of all Chinese governments, the modern Communist one has been one of the most rigid with respect to the arts. It has censored them severely, perhaps because it regards them as even more important and threatening than past administrations did. It organized artists' federations to review all works so that the Communist point of view, and no other, was represented. A single play, considered offensive by Mao Zedong, helped bring about the disastrous Cultural Revolution. During the Cultural Revolution itself, Beethoven, Shakespeare, and other great Western artists were banned in China. Even the dance was restricted to only two ballets, *The Red Detachment of Women* and *The White Haired Girl*. These ballets told stories of ordinary people who led heroic struggles against foreign and domestic enemies, and often they were performed by soldiers who toured villages to urge vigilance and patriotism. The popular Beijing Opera, which traditionally consisted of music, dance, and acrobatics, became a vehicle for the delivery of political messages.

Free speech, as well as uncensored writing, painting, and dancing, has been forbidden in China as in other Communist countries.

To a small extent, however, censorship has been lifted since the death of Mao Zedong and the imprisonment of his wife, Jiang Qing. Mao's successors ended the ban on Western artists and encouraged the production of more creative works. Impressive films, dances, and paintings began to appear, along with a revival of ancient handicrafts. They showed the desire of the Chinese people to renew their ancient culture. Many of these products were sent overseas. In keeping with this new policy of open relationships a Chinese Olympic team went to Los Angeles for the 1984 summer games, and it returned home with a number of medals.

Education. To a large degree, the Chinese government has replaced parents as the first teacher of young children. While parents are at their jobs in the cities, the state supplies teachers for children between the ages of three and five. About half of all children attend either nursery schools or kindergartens, though in rural areas the number probably is less. In the countryside production brigades managed primary schools until recently, but the brigades are disappearing as the responsibility system spreads. Some rural children live in their schools and may not see their parents until weekends, but most are transported to school every day.

By the age of five, the children have learned to sing patriotic songs and repeat some government slogans concerning China's relationships in the world. China in recent years has regarded both the Soviet Union and the United States as enemies. Even the youngest students were heard accusing them of aggression. Pupils were taught to lunge with bayonets while reciting accusations against foreigners. Today, the United States is considered friendly, and Chinese anger with past U.S. policies has abated. Students are taught to read and write Chinese and often English, too. They are exposed to music, dance, and games as well as self-discipline.

In elementary school, which begins at the age of six, Chinese

Village children give long hours to study, but also are expected to help parents.

The new burst of energy in China was accompanied by the introduction of many more operas and ballets than had been permitted during Mao Zedong's regime.

children gain substantial amounts of practical information. Studies generally include science, geography, history, mathematics, and music as well as politics and simple military tactics. There is special emphasis on language. By the end of their first year in school, students must know 850 Chinese characters, and by the end of their primary schooling 3,000. Under a recently adopted policy of the government, students learn a romanized script designed to help them pronounce Chinese as well as English words. This script, called *hanyu pinyin*, now is seen everywhere in China, even on street signs, but is not intended to replace traditional Chinese writing. Literacy in China now is so widespread that books are more popular there than television is in the United States. With less television available, they are likely to remain so.

After five years in elementary school, most Chinese students spend three more years in the lower middle and three in the upper middle schools. The high school curriculum stresses mathematics and science, which account for more than half the time in classes. Among the other subjects are Chinese language and literature, agricultural biology, musical instruments and the Beijing Opera, politics, and ideology. A school day consists of seven 45-minute periods, the last of which is usually a sports period. It is often held outdoors, where many schools maintain facilities for gymnastics or basketball.

In the past, politics took up to 10 to 20 per cent of the time spent in high schools. There were pictures of Mao Zedong in every classroom, along with political slogans such as "Heighten our vigilance and defend our motherland." This concentration on politics is greatly reduced today, although textbooks continue to present the government point of view. China's present leaders have called for more scientific training and recognize that scientists need not be political.

All Chinese children are educated free of charge through three years of secondary school. In exchange for this education they be called upon to work as well as to study. For example, some teachers and students spend time at manual labor, either inside or outside of their school. Typical jobs may involve the production of furniture or diodes for use in transistor radios. Other services to the state may take place during eight weeks of "vacation," during which students may undergo military or on-the-job training in factories and communes. Before the next semester begins there is a week for "summing up," during which the students are tested for the degree to which they have absorbed Communist principles.

Mao Zedong generally lowered college entrance standards in order to educate more peasants. The current government has concluded that this policy sharply lowered the quality of college education in China and has introduced strict entrance examinations. In keeping with the current effort to improve the quality of the college system, all applicants must pass an entrance examination. Even greater changes may be in store for the colleges. The government, concerned with China's lack of creative technicians and scientists, has hired an American professor to build a new university near Hong Kong. Of Chinese ancestry, he was authorized to design an American-style curriculum which could become a model for colleges throughout the country.

Dropping fear of Westerners, the Chinese began to study English and other languages.

CHAPTER 11

THE NEW CHINA

T OWARD THE END OF THE 1980's, the Chinese government published two lines of text that changed the history of the world. "The right to the use of land may be transferred in accordance with the law," it said. "...(T)he state permits the private sector of the economy to exist...."

For forty years, the Communists who ran China had been insisting on principles that they refused to compromise. Now, by amending Articles 10 and 11 of the Constitution (page 214), they not only did compromise, but allowed the country a whole new way of life.

Because they no longer demanded that the state own all major capital resources and land, China's leaders had transformed Chinese communism. Their new policy promised to affect environmental conditions everywhere on earth. They would not acknowledge the overwhelming force of their proclamation, but accompanied the change with declarations that they were not renouncing what they called "socialism." They rededicated China to social, political, and economic equality—a global revolution.

Meanwhile China took the first steps toward an economy shaped by markets instead of by the government's regulation. It surrendered its exclusive right to allocate labor and materials and allowed private businesses to respond to the public's needs. This guaranteed inequality in a state that continued to call itself Communist. In China's changed society, some people were certain to be wealthier and more powerful than others. "What's the point of equality," one official explained, "when living standards are low?"

The supporters of the new program comforted themselves with the slogan, "One country, two systems!", knowing that vast changes were coming. Deng Xiaoping also demonstrated his willingness to abandon ideology. In a typically Chinese remark, he said, "It doesn't matter if the cat is black or white, as long as it catches mice." Thus communism, or at least the Chinese form of it, was vanishing as the country's leaders at last accepted a different point of view.

China had compelling reasons to change its course. The most important of these was the size of its population. The government's strict policy of limiting each family to one child had greatly lowered the rate of growth. Even at its lesser growth rates, China had almost 1.2 billion people. Effective public health measures, coupled with a larger food supply, brought this about by increasing the life span. The average Chinese could be expected to live just 25 years in 1930. That figure soared to 45 years in 1950. Today, it is over 80.

Every year, China has been gaining the number of people in the state of Texas. Experts predicted that before the end of the decade, it would add the number in the whole of Japan. China had only slightly more land than the United States, but its population outnumbered Americans by more than 4.5 to 1. Unless it took drastic steps, China was almost certain to run out of food, housing, and medical facilities early in the next century.

Deng's ambitions provided other reasons to shape a new economy. He and other Chinese leaders were determined to see their country take its proper place in the world community. To accomplish this goal they needed more advanced technology. But technology would serve no purpose when only a third of all Chinese companies showed a profit. No state-run industry could have survived if forced to compete in global markets.

Thus Deng launched his program by necessity, not choice. He began his experiment in rural areas, giving farmers the right to own small plots of land. After he granted them the right to compete, many farmers soon earned enough to buy cars and television sets. They created new jobs. This so pleased the rural community that Deng extended economic incentives to the cities.

It was as if a dam were bursting—the dam of Communist regulations that had prevented the normally enterprising Chinese people from venturing into commerce. New business sprang up. Merchants lined the streets, and those who had saved a little money started shops. Most people, men, women, and children, worked overtime to buy more of the things they wanted. Every dawn, people began selling their services at curb-sides before going to their regular jobs. Barbers cut hair under streetlights; bicycle repairmen fixed gears in traffic, vendors sold persimmons, tomatoes, or peppers in doorways. Government studies show that the number of private businesses has been growing at the rate of 80-90 percent a year. By the mid-1990's these businesses registered capital investments between $4-5 billion.

This torrent of human energy quickly attracted foreigners. They sensed a chance for huge profits in China. Using loans and co-investments from overseas, the Chinese government began to build rapidly. New hydroelectric plants, television stations, luxury hotels, and restaurants appeared. Competing airlines and railroads replaced those formerly run under state monopolies. In cultural exchanges certain to promote mutual understanding, millions of foreign tourists arrived, and many Chinese scholars went overseas for work and study.

By the mid-1990's, the boom had become the largest in history. "Not even I can stop this now," said Deng. He had become China's most enthusiastic supporter of rapid expansion. Overruling advisers who, fearing inflation, called for annual growth of 8 to 9 percent, he set a goal of 10 to 13 percent. In 1994 his administration prepared to stop advocating public- over private-ownership. It turned 100 of the largest state-owned factories into corporations much like those in the United States, where managers must take responsibility for success or failure. It took the first steps toward joining the General Agreement on Tariffs and Trade (GATT). Under this treaty, the world's major producing nations are lowering their tariffs to promote trade. They require countries signing the agreement to have free currencies, controlled only by monetary and interest rate policies, not authoritarian edicts. China indicated a willingness to make this further capitalist move.

Then China announced a surprising experiment. If within three to five years the new corporations could become more efficient and profitable, it said, it would extend the program to all 11,000 of China's medium and large industries. Under this plan, the state would be a partner of each corporation rather than its master. It would no longer subsidize incompetent executives or finance the schools, hospitals, and welfare of more highly-paid workers.

With the help of foreign capital, China has sent its urban skylines soaring over apartment blocks the state built for workers long ago (foreground).

Thus China abandoned the idea, as old as communism itself, which said that social and economic justice were impossible unless the state owned the basic means of production. The country now allowed foreign investors to set up businesses and join boards of directors. Seeing this, capitalists streamed into the country from overseas. They expected to hire Chinese workers for a fraction of their labor costs at home. Besides, the Chinese government reduced or even eliminated all taxes on their profits. By 1994, with the help of these outsiders, China had the third largest economy in the world.

The government did not neglect the opportunity to note that many of the outsiders were of Chinese descent. To awaken their patriotism, it pointedly referred to them as citizens of "Greater China." It seemed true that sentiment, as well as potential profit, had attracted many investors, but knowledge of the Chinese language was also a major factor. Despite legal barriers, for example, wealthy Taiwanese came to increase their fortunes. They added as much as $10 billion to the Chinese economy. Investors from South Korea, another economic giant in the region, came to take advantage of the cheap labor costs. In 1993 alone, people from more than forty countries invested $100 billion in new industries and small businesses. In most cases they formed partnerships with the government or with local corporations.

Americans eagerly joined this process. Soon after landing in California, one Hong Kong businessman was able to sell $375 million worth of stocks within a few weeks. He was financing a new six-lane toll road between Hong Kong and the mainland. Other Americans put their money into factories which produced textiles, athletic shoes, and electronic goods. All of these products found ready markets overseas.

China's economy responded instantly to these moves. By 1994, its rate of expansion had reached 13 percent a year, more than four times the one in the United States. This was faster than in any other country on earth. Suddenly China, depressed for centuries, had the third largest economy in the world, and the effects on its people were immediate.

The cities. People who started new businesses in China rarely were disappointed. A tidal wave of buyers swept over their new fast-food restaurants and department or specialty stores. Consumers marched out of shops with goods, hoping to stuff new cameras, microwaves, television sets, or refrigerators into tiny apartments.

Other signs of impending capitalism also appeared. In the streets, restaurants, and hotels of every major city, young men made deals in meetings or over portable telephones. Many were calling the new Shanghai Stock Exchange, housed in what was once an Eastern Orthodox Church on New Happiness Road. Others were in touch with the suppliers of imported jewelry, perfumes, or cars who were based in coastal cities or in Hong Kong. They found a good market for those products among newly rich Chinese, some of whom had become millionaires.

Such risk-taking was impossible for the vast majority of Chinese. The average worker in China presently earns about 19 cents (10 yuan) an hour. This seems minuscule when compared with the average of about $8.50 in the United States. It is not small when compared with prices or salaries paid to Chinese before the revolution. Moreover, housing, medical care, and education cost little or nothing. The city worker pays a small rent to the government—three to four yuan a month. Nurseries, kindergartens, and recreational facilities are among the services supplied without charge. Women are given maternity leaves with full pay and in general are treated as the equals of men in the marketplace.

These tens of millions of laborers and housewives are seen each day struggling to survive in urban China. Endless numbers of them stream to jobs or markets on bicycles or foot, ignoring stoplights and snarling auto horns. Workers spend eight hours on each shift, with a lunch break and a half hour of rest. Most employees spend six days a week at their jobs. They have no vacations but enjoy seven holidays every year. A couple may take a three-day vacation to be married. When workers retire—usually at the age of 55 for men and 50 for women—they continue to receive 70 percent of their normal salaries.

In the recent past, life was uniform and gray in Chinese cities. People wore drab clothing as an expression of the powerful movement to encourage hard work and equality. The most popular style among men, women, and children, was a light-blue or olive cotton tunic and pants.

All of this changed as the Four Modernizations program advanced. More Chinese men began to wear Western business suits. Women took an interest in the bright silks, woolens, and floral print dresses shown in department stores. The American T-shirt, imprinted with any words in English of whatever meaning, became the most popular article of clothing in Beijing. Young people started discos and started practicing styles once popular in the United States, such as the fox trot, jitterbug, and waltz. Even the elderly began to enjoy slow dancing in Beijing's parks every morning.

The Chinese have been getting their concept of modern luxuries from television programs and publications that originate overseas.

In coastal cities they can see lavish productions originating in Hong Kong or Taiwan. Glossy fashion magazines trumpet the idea of individualism in fashion. At least one model who poses for them earns hundreds of thousands of dollars a year giving testimonials and seminars on beauty. In Guangdong Province alone, more than 18,000 women sell cosmetics from door-to-door. Foreign tourists and investors have resumed their travels to China and also provide the Chinese with new ideas and designs. In 1993, the number of tourists and merchants landing in Beijing passed two million for the first time.

These events signaled an end to the puritanical idealism that prevailed until recently. Many students now shun Beijing University, the country's most respected school. They think they would have little chance of getting a job if they were to graduate from an institution with a reputation for democratic ideas. China's intellectuals, including its students, once chiefly hoped to go into public service. They considered commercial activities beneath them, as did almost all Confucians, who favored education over money. Today, almost all of China's students want to go into business. One study showed they held government jobs eighth on their list.

Like the students, few others in the new China have time for ideals. The rising classes do all that they can to succeed. Meanwhile the laboring classes do all that they can to survive. For entertainment people enjoy the same simple pleasures that the majority of Americans do. They drop in on family or friends, walk, converse, play board games, see movies, fly kites, work puzzles, involve themselves in sports, and ride public transportation. Visiting the Beijing Subway is one of their favorite pastimes; about 60,000 people do this every day. The subway, pride of all China, was built by soldiers and revolutionary cadres over a period of four years. After installing 16 stations and 15 miles of track, the government began planning further extensions to serve the huge population in China's largest city.

The countryside. Farm communes, with their hundreds of millions of peasant families, became the nation's new social centers during the "Great Leap Forward." They offered nurseries, schools, homes for the aged, recreational centers, and hospitals to most of the Chinese population. In time, the communes tried to govern their members completely, regulating their work, recreation, and even their thoughts. They "educated" children in nurseries while their mothers worked in the commune's fields or handicraft factories. The commune's officials, who were always members of the Communist Party, helped to set up monthly schedules for educational, cultural, and political events.

In rural China, many village homes consist of little more than a single room occupied by three or four people. This woman is cooking rice and greens.

From the outset of this system, many of the demands made by China's Communist theorists proved too severe. Initially, for example, they assigned different tasks to people from the same family and so caused much distress. The government also housed families in dormitories with common eating facilities so that there would be more time to work, once again dividing relatives. But China's tradition of family life would not die. Families demanded their own houses and insisted on eating together.

The tradition of strong family life eventually prevailed over the idea of communes, especially after the introduction of the Four Modernizations program. In rural China the typical family includes from five to ten people who live together in a well-kept two-room house on about a quarter of an acre of land. Most families have all of the meat, fish, grain, and vegetables they want, but few luxuries. Beds are likely to be above a brick oven, on straw mattresses. People bring in water from a well and keep it in a jar. Each of their two rooms is lit by a single electric bulb.

But not all rural families are poor. Some have been particularly successful under the new incentive program and have been able to save large sums. The communes have been phased out, but some of their practices remain. Many farmers still pool labor and funds to buy heavy equipment, implements, and land. Whole villages may join forces to finance an airplane for spraying crops. They also cooperate in the administration of rural schools, hospitals, and recreational programs.

Chinese farmers are unlikely to give up the self-government they have enjoyed under the commune system for so many years. Commune members selected members of Revolutionary

Committees which, until private farming became widespread in the 1980's, handled local economic planning. Similar committees still concern themselves with projects that take large amounts of capital or labor, such as road-building, irrigation, or the milling and storing of large amounts of grain.

Today, villagers take new pride in their communities, cleaning and whitewashing them, sweeping their stone streets and court-yards spotless. But farm labor goes on as it has for centuries, chiefly with the help of water buffaloes and a few tools. Millions of men, women, and children still stoop over flooded soil to plant rice seedlings as Chinese have done for centuries. Village children still care for pigs and ducks and carry burdens on poles braced across their shoulders.

Rural China is basically returning to the social conditions that existed before the revolution. As before, some farmers are growing richer than others. The government still owns most of the good farmland, but its new laws hint that it will sell off more of it soon. Thus China has tested a thoroughly communal theory and found it wanting. Now, while creating a new society, it is mingling ancient customs with modern ones as it spreads its economic reforms.

Civil rights. On June 4, 1989, a hail of bullets, fired from semi-automatic rifles by Chinese soldiers at Chinese people, stripped a mask from the government of China. Officials ordered troops to clear Tiananmen Square, at the center of Beijing. Hundreds of thousands of unarmed students had gathered there to petition their rulers. The students called for freedom of speech and a greater voice in their own affairs, as guaranteed by the Constitution. (*See* Article 35, page 217). Their Democracy Movement protested official corruption which had, in effect, created a new dynasty by grasping power tightly within a small group. Within hours after the troops arrived, hundreds of students lay dead. Tanks crushed their bodies, which the People's Liberation Army doused with kerosene and burned. Stunned, millions of Chinese suddenly realized that the time had come to fear their government.

The complaints of the students gave voice to a cry that was rising throughout China. In sum, they were that a vast government bureaucracy had silenced the people and was seizing advantages from Deng Xiaoping's economic reforms. What began as a government dedicated to absolute equality had, in effect, become a new dynasty. China's rulers were refusing to share power with the people. According to the students and millions who supported them, all but a few public officials were enriching themselves and their children. The officials sought favors and gifts for the right to take almost any action in a tightly-regulated society.

After slaughtering hundreds of unarmed students in Tiananmen Square on June 4, 1989, Chinese soldiers quickly burned the bodies and retreated.

Moreover, the rapid and uneven development of different parts of the country was pitting region against region, cities against the countryside. Throughout the country inflation, ranging from 20-30 percent, was making life increasingly difficult for all but the small group that had bribed its way to success. These complaints were not confined to a relatively few students, as shown by the outbreak of simultaneous demonstrations and riots in other cities, including Shanghai and Chengdu. But the government crushed all who protested, shedding much blood.

In many countries, but especially in China, the brutal suppression of a peaceful demonstration raised memories of China's cruel past. In recent years, millions of Chinese died because of the Great Leap Forward and the Cultural Revolution. For centuries China has wavered violently between two of its most ancient, yet still vital philosophies, Legalism and Mohism. Hanfeizi, the originator of Legalism, demanded strict obedience to law. He was a burner of books who inspired the most ruthless of China's emperors. Mozi, founder of Mohism, trusted the people and urged respect for them. (*See* page 33.)

Until June 4, 1989, most observers of China believed that modern China was moving away from the harsh demands of its early Communist government. They hoped that it had shifted away from Legalism and was accepting more of its Mohist tradition. Such a change would have echoed ideas that evolved in other formerly authoritarian states, such as Russia, and that have long been established in Western democracies. After June 4, there was no turning back. The People's Republic of China had committed itself to a long period of stern Legalist behavior.

Secret police, hidden cameras, and the registration of almost every Chinese citizen unquestionably enabled China's government to persist in this course. The students who called for more democracy were either been executed, imprisoned, or dispersed. The few who escaped to other countries mostly pledged themselves to rebellion, but the promise will be difficult to keep as long as their government keeps its massive powers.

Religious freedoms. China claims to leave people legally free to practice religion, meanwhile discouraging it. The extent of freedom is shown by the recent history of Chinese Buddhists, one of the country's largest religious groups. Soon after the Communist victory in 1949, the new government ordered Buddhist priests to work at more practical jobs. It left Buddhist temples largely undisturbed. Then, during the Cultural Revolution, waves of Red Guards swept through Buddhist centers such as the one at Mount Wutai, a group of five peaks soaring to 10,000 feet in Shanxi Province.

Young Communists beat and dispersed the 1,500 monks, lamas, and nuns who occupied temples on those peaks. Then they destroyed most of the images within the buildings. They set out to eliminate religion, which they identified as one of the "four olds"—old ideas, old culture, old customs, and old habits.

Today, with the ideas of the Red Guards discredited, Buddhists are returning to Mount Wutai. Beginning in distant homes, teenaged boys often walk for days to become novices on the mountaintop. The government has improved the dirt roads which lead to the reviving Buddhist community. It hopes to make a tourist center out of Mount Wutai, one which will attract badly needed capital from abroad. Buddhism is also reviving in remote places like Mongolia, where China executed Buddhist monks in recent years.

The government takes a less tolerant view of Daoism, which it regards as a superstition and has tried to stamp out. This sharp difference in treatment demonstrates that religion in China may be free at some times but not at others. Whether or not a religious minority is persecuted depends on the political winds.

The government's treatment of Muslims gives evidence of how it may grant a special position to an influential minority. Muslims form one of the largest groups in Asia, and so the Chinese Communists chiefly allow them to worship as they please. The government takes a less tolerant view of Christianity, which it regards as an arm of the Western countries that tried to exploit China in the past. Nevertheless, unwilling to offend major trading partners, it permits small groups to practice Christianity again.

As their small businesses flourished, many Chinese restored the same kind of sprawling, crowded bazaars their country knew in previous times.

THE PRICE OF SUCCESS

"May you get what you want," says an ancient Chinese curse. Now it is possible that China itself will be cursed for getting what it wants—material wealth equal to that of the world's most prosperous countries.

If China continues growing at its present rate, it will overtake Japan within ten years and out-produce the United States within twenty. Its able, hard-working people have been striving for their own private advancement as passionately as they recently did for the public welfare. But what if they succeed? Some problems are growing in scope even faster than the economy. Along with soaring growth, China had begun to suffer large trade imbalances, soaring inflation, and discontent because of injustices.

Corruption. Throughout its long history, enormous bureaucracies have governed China's vast, widespread, and diverse populations. Today, bureaucrats still run the country as part of a far-reaching Communist system. Under the present government's supervision, ordinary citizens need permits to make most basic changes in their lives. They must apply to an official to have a baby, get a passport, change jobs, start a business, gain an apartment, get a bank loan, or connect utilities to a residence.

The power to grant these permits tempts China's millions of officials to sell their services rather than to treat them as responsibilities. Many ask for bribes, and buying *guanxi* (pronounced goo-*ahn*-she, meaning influence) has become commonplace in the new China. Officials who sell guanxi often justify themselves on grounds that their salaries are low. Many earn less than 100 yuan a month, but some have collected enough illegal money to buy fine cars, houses, and vacations overseas.

So massive had corruption become that in 1993, the government discovered three men who managed to swindle $80 million from the Bank of China. Corruption is not limited to major crimes by public officials. It penetrates all areas of Chinese society. One of the best public schools, for example, only enrolls students in exchange for bribes. Recently the employees of a sweater factory had to pay $4,000 to officials of the school, plus a cashmere sweater for each member of the faculty. Only with these gifts would the school accept ten of the workers' children as students. Countless similar cases occur every day.

When it punishes such crimes, applying fines, jail sentences, or even execution, the government seems to be taking steps to cure the problem. Yet studies show that it has not reduced corruption much. About a third of China's 103 million bureaucrats have full or part-time jobs on the side. In China's metaphor for starting a private business, they "leap into the sea." But these people make the leap with an advantage over ordinary people. They can issue permits to each other or even to themselves. A 31-year-old mid-level official in the city of Yantai did this to start a part-time business that brings him more than $1 million a year.

Like most other corrupt officials, this man kept his government job. Without one, he would lose his guanxi and an excellent apartment. He knows that officials in China are rarely fired, even for neglect or incompetence. Therefore he spends almost all of his time making money for himself, ignoring public responsibilities. In the same way, millions of other Chinese who "leap into the sea" ignore their tasks as policemen, professors, factory managers, or students.

Obsessed with the desire for private gain, many non-official Chinese have been infected by corruption, too. A walk through the streets of any Chinese city may arouse money-changers, prostitutes, pickpockets, and confidence men. These eager wealth-seekers press themselves on people who look wealthy, especially tourists. Shopkeepers, often grabbing passersby off sidewalks, routinely double or triple prices for anyone who seems uninformed or eager to buy. Shrewdly they watch the shopper's eye light on an object or dilate with interest. Then, while complimenting the customer for good taste, they bring over the object and announce its great, if fictitious value. Thievery and even banditry also are spreading. Thousands of cars, stolen each year in wealthy Hong Kong, turn up in Chinese cities. In at least one case thugs stopped a train to rob passengers.

All of this is taking place in a country where, in the 1950's, people could rightly boast that the Chinese were far too honest to steal. Merchants would run after customers to deliver neglected change. Even today, the principle of honesty prevails among the vast majority of people. "You should have stopped the whole bus," said an indignant woman sympathetically to the victim of a pickpocket during a ride in Xian. "You should have had police search everyone on the bus!" Still, the drive for individual success has caused more than a few Chinese to abandon such old Confucian ethics as they seek their share of the bonanza.

The revival of classes. Once they have power, officials often set up relatives, particularly their sons, in business. Those people in turn endow their relatives and friends with money and businesses. In the same way, people who acquire large land, stores, enterprises, and investment fortunes pass them on to their children.

Thus China has again planted the seeds of the class structure against which it rebelled in the 1940's. As before, the people of rural areas comprise the bulk of the lower classes. China's millions of peasants find themselves lagging far behind people in cities. To match their incomes with rising costs, they stream toward Beijing, Shanghai, or Guandong, begging for jobs. Tens of millions of these rootless people surge through every train station. When they can settle in one place, they head for the outskirts of the major cities. There, they set up tents or scraps of wooden huts. Of China's 580 million peasants, as many as 160 million now live in urban areas. Another 130 million are trying to find places in cities, and still the rural population, which grows at 20 million a year, can send more.

In contrast, not far from the shacks of the poor, owners of tall buildings are inviting investors to buy apartments with swimming pools, security systems, and golf courses. Investors are promised returns of 15 percent on their capital and the right to mortgage property at 60 percent of value, especially in Beijing and Shanghai.

Increasing unrest. Boatloads of Chinese emigrants have been intercepted near the coasts of the United States. Hundreds of Chinese, dreading political suppression and lacking the opportunities of the privileged class, have fled their homeland despite the growing wealth of their country. Often they pay over a year's income for the hazardous trans-Pacific journey.

To escape, these sea-going refugees suffer for weeks or months in the hold of an unstable ship. The risks they took were comparable, though longer-lasting, than those taken by the increasing number of people hijacking planes in China. In 1993 alone, hijackers diverted ten commercial flights from China to Taiwan. The fugitives in these cases were not ordinary criminals. Often they were students, intellectuals, or moderately well-to-do families who could not endure life in China.

Such incidents are only symptoms of the profound problems developing beneath the surface of the rising economy. A feeling of chaos has been growing in China. The country has insufficient supplies of raw materials, transportation, and energy to keep up with the demand for goods. The price of everything, as a result, has been rising as spendable income increases. Each year the boom proceeds, vital steel and oil may cost 40 percent more than the year before. The managers of state-owned factories, overwhelmed by inefficiencies, find themselves insolvent, unable to pay their work-force. That compels many to reduce their production. It guarantees that prices will rise further as supplies decline. It also weakens the central government's control over outlying areas, where people turn increasingly to local authorities for support.

Speculators assume the price of everything will rise under the pressures of rising spendable incomes. Seeing the government in frenzied construction of new office towers or casinos, they snap up land, driving prices higher. The price of space in China now may exceed the one in the U.S. Even a less desirable apartment in Beijing may cost $500,000. These and other pressures on costs have forced people with long memories to reflect on inflation in the past (*See* page 102). They see prices now rising by as much as 20 percent a year. To prepare for the worst, many now are hoarding gold, which is normally more stable than currency.

Thus China could literally choke on its own growth. Some officials acknowledge this but fear the wrath of Deng Xiaoping and his supporters, who urge even faster growth. To quiet the unrest, the Central Committee of the Communist Party issued a secret document (No. 6) in 1993. It canceled some useless projects and reduced some of the credit that has fueled speculation and public debt. Still, when it tried to call back loans it managed to recover only a third of the $38 billion that regional banks loaned to factories, developers, and speculators.

A major obstacle to the control of credit has been the almost complete lack of effective records. In the past, the government simply directed its banks to lend money to state-owned enterprises, ignoring the consequences. No one, and no company or institution, has had responsibility for bad loans. The government may have increased this problem when, in 1994, it opened the Chinese market to Western banks, setting the stage for even more credit.

Under the impact of these aspects of the boom, social institutions have been disintegrating. The government cannot finance them as easily as before because its tax revenues have been shrinking. In Western countries, where taxes are geared to growth, taxes rise during a boom. The reverse has happened in China. Often newly-rich merchants hide their incomes and so avoid taxes. Farmers, whose tax indebtedness usually is more evident than that of merchants, complain that government agents sometimes beat them if they do not pay taxes. In 1992, the government collected taxes on only 0.79 percent of farm income. The shortfall in revenues probably will make it impossible for China to offer nine years of compulsory education by the end of the century, as promised.

Lacking funds, the government can no longer subsidize industries which in recent years took 75 percent of its tax revenues. Nor does it have the funds to maintain the "iron rice bowl"—the guarantee of food, jobs, and welfare to all citizens. Peasants in Anhui Province recently protested strongly when the government ran out of funds to pay for its schools. This community forced officials to sell their limousines and give up all special privileges. Only in that way, the villagers said, could it conserve vital tax revenues for cultural matters. A rebellion of this kind seems minor when compared to the armed insurrections in other countries. It is significant, though, in a nation whose government was stern enough to massacre students for favoring democracy.

The struggle of women. In the abstract sense, women form the largest of China's growing number of social rebels. They are not always aware of their contribution to change because they have not yet united. Yet as individuals millions of them strive daily for social, political, and economic equality with men. Often they succeed, and because one of every eight humans is a Chinese woman they are causing historic change.

Jiang Caiyun ("Ginger Colorful Cloud") is an example. Married at the age of 22, she needed to supplement her husband's income and went to work in a government transport company. There she saw her job leading nowhere and so asked to be trained as a driver. Her bosses refused this request on grounds that they never teach women or promote them to jobs requiring skill. But Jiang Caiyun persisted, and when she offered to pay for driving lessons herself and take the lessons on her own time, the bosses agreed.

Jiang Caiyun worked day and night, both on the job and as a young woman learning to drive a large truck in competition with men. During her third year as an apprentice she gave birth to a son and was forced to quit her job to care for him. Then once again she found that her husband, who works at a minor government job, did not bring home enough money to keep up with rising costs. She enrolled her son in a government day-care center and, taking a large risk, rented a new Volkswagen sedan from a travel company. Every month she pays the company about $1,000 (U.S.) for the car, plus another $250 for expenses. Nevertheless, by offering constant, expert service to tourists she earns $500-1,000 (U.S.) a month, in contrast to her husband's $200. Now she plans to buy the car and start a small company.

Just a few generations ago, women like Jiang had an identity only as someone's mother, wife, or daughter. Her own grandmother has bound feet. Jiang has become part of a silent revolution in China, and she is contributing to rapid change.

Environmental degradation. The people of Gansu Province, in northwest China, are not noted for rebelling against their government. Still, in 1993 a seemingly obscure issue, the quality of their air, spurred them to rebel. Late in that year they seized a government-owned chemical factory that was polluting their water and air. The plant was releasing clouds of sulfuric acid and carbon disulfide that sent nearby workers into spasms of coughing, fatigue, and dizziness. When officials refused to respond to a petition signed by 200 workers, the rebellion began. At length, after some injuries, it succeeded in shutting down the factory.

This incident pointed to thousands of potential similar rebellions throughout China. If they take place, the cause will be the degradation of China's air, water, soil, raw materials, and ultimately its food supplies. These problems are brought about chiefly by the enormous population and current economic boom. Both have rapidly exhausted the environment in a country that has 22 percent of the world's population but only 8 percent of its resources and 7 percent of its arable land.

At least three hundred Chinese cities lack water. They are diverting it from farms, where 82 million peasants complain they no longer have enough water to irrigate efficiently. Since the 1980's severe declines in rainfall, ranging from 10-20 percent, have compounded the problem. At the same time, government food quotas persuade farmers to increase yields through the use of chemical fertilizers. These forces combined rapidly deplete soils, which erode or flow away.

China recognizes its population problem but tries to solve it in ways that many people, especially outsiders, resent. It restricts families to one child, forcing abortions on women who have conceived more. It also seeks to avoid "abnormal births" by pressing abortions on women with infectious diseases. China has about 50 million physically or mentally retarded people and, fearing more, has tried to prevent them from having children, too.

People in many countries lodged protests against this program when it was announced in 1994.

China's birth control policies have a predictable effect on the country's society. For centuries Chinese families have preferred male children to female on grounds that young men can better support them in their old age. Many couples today, knowing that the law permits them only one child, use modern medical techniques to learn the sex of a fetus. Many abort females and have been known to murder female infants soon after delivery.

China today has 114 boys for every 100 girls, a ratio with far-reaching implications. Pampered, chubby young boys strut beside their parents in every park. These "Little Princes" will want wives one day and find themselves bidding on the limited number of women available. Moreover, the average age of individuals will tend to rise rapidly in a society that barely reproduces itself. Yet the country's population dilemma will become more acute as massive populations accumulate in cities. Even now privacy is barely possible. Some population experts have raised doubts that the economic boom, whether or not sustainable in an environment with limited resources, can keep up with the need for more food, water, and energy. China will not be able to feed its population in the year 2020 as it does today, even if it doubles food production.

FOREIGN RELATIONS

Embittered by its experiences with other nations, Communist China has followed two distinct paths in its foreign policy. At times its government has been arrogant, insisting, as its United Nations delegate did in 1972, that "...we are soberly aware that war is inevitable so long as society is divided into classes and the exploitation of man by man exists." This path reflects China's historic regard for itself as *Zhongguo*—the "Middle Kingdom," as if it were the center of the world. It has long believed that it has much to teach other countries and points to its world leadership before foreigners seized control of its lands.

At other times China, having evaluated its own present situation, recognizes the realistic need to cooperate with other countries. With the failure of Mao Zedong's drive to make China independent of the rest of the world, his successors see this second path as the country's salvation.

The difference in these paths has been made clearer through careful studies of China's foreign policy during the past twenty-five years. During the Cultural Revolution, China recalled more than half of its ambassadors. It shut down many of its embassies or left them in the hands of junior officials. When the turmoil of the Cultural Resolution subsided, it could see it had not gained greater independence. Instead, it faced the possibilities of war with the Soviet Union and economic disaster at home. At that point, China moved to the other path and looked for help from countries it had been calling enemies. This was its basic policy.

Most of the rest of the world, meanwhile, opposed the Communists. Immediately after the Chinese Revolution the West largely followed U.S. policy on China. Western governments recognized the Nationalists on Taiwan and ignored the Communists on the mainland. There were exceptions, though. The Soviet Union and its satellites supplied China with much-needed technical help to set up its industries.

To advance their claim on Taiwan, the Communists refused to cooperate with countries that recognized the Nationalists. Under this second policy they tried to displace the Nationalists in the United Nations and in world trade. Its third major policy was to spread communism. It did this by supporting revolutionary movements throughout Latin America, Africa, and Asia.

A nation's foreign policy must be based not only on its ideology, but also on its physical position and resources. A revolution may change a country's government, but not its climate, topography, and minerals. Thus even after a revolution a country may find it necessary to continue some policies of the government it has overthrown. In one such continuation, Communist China seeks to limit Western influence in Asia, just as it did when American troops approached its border during the Korean War. In 1950 the Chinese, sensing a threat to their industrial heartland, responded to the threat by sending "volunteers" to fight the Americans. They showed a similar determination to keep the Soviet Union from their borders by invading Tibet in 1956. Later, they sent substantial aid, but not soldiers, to help the Vietnamese fight Americans.

The People's Republic has also supported many Asian governments with which it has disagreed. Indonesia was one of these. There a dictator, President Sukarno, became involved in a territorial dispute with a neighbor, the new nation of Malaysia. Because Malaysia had the support of Western powers, particularly Great Britain, the People's Republic backed Sukarno's government. In 1964 the Communist Party of Indonesia tried to seize the government. When it failed, the Indonesians slaughtered many of the Chinese in their country.

The Chinese also supported Prince Sihanouk of Kampuchea (then called Cambodia), a ruler who held aristocratic rather than Communist views. They valued him chiefly because he helped them restrict Western influence in Southeast Asia. When he lost power in 1970, they gave him refuge. Later, they became enemies of Vietnam's Communist government because it moved into Cambodia and formed an alliance with the Soviet Union. Since the collapse of the Soviet Union China has begun improving relations with Vietnam, where an economic boom is expected soon.

The People's Republic of China has taken these specific views with respect to the major powers of the world:

The United States. Chinese Communists long considered the United States, as the world's leading capitalist nation, to be their foremost enemy. In their opinion, the U.S. moved into Asian positions formerly held by such colonial powers as Great Britain, France, and Japan. They believed the American victory in World War II had left a ring of U.S. bases around China. They said the ring included Okinawa, South Korea, the Ryuku Islands, Japan, South Vietnam, and Pakistan.

In response to this, China tried to confront the Americans without committing its own forces. The main test of this policy was over the island of Taiwan, home of the Republic of China. The U.S. guarantees the island's security from attack under a treaty signed in 1955. For years it kept a fleet, in real or in token degrees, in the straits between the mainland and Taiwan.

By 1971 the Chinese concluded, however, that the U.S., while still an enemy, was less dangerous than the Soviet Union. Quiet negotiations between the two countries began, and in a symbolic move, the Chinese invited an American table-tennis team to tour their country (pages 131-32). Apparently believing that the U.S. would disengage in Southeast Asia after its losses in Vietnam, they invited President Nixon to tour the mainland. His visit ended with a joint declaration agreeing, in a wary, diplomatic compromise, "Countries should treat each other with mutual respect....No country should claim infallibility...."

Though the meeting led to mutual recognition, neither of the two countries surrendered alliances with nations hostile to the other one. After replacing the Republic of China in the UN (1971), the People's Republic began to take a broader view of its role in the world. China and the U.S. began exchanges of diplomats, scientists, athletes, and journalists.

Today, China and the U.S. have a closer but still watchful relationship. Taiwan is not the only issue that makes the Chinese wary of the U.S. They also resent what they consider American meddling in their internal affairs. Under President's Reagan and Bush, for example, the U.S. strongly opposed abortion as a means of birth control. Reagan cut off aid funds to countries that did so, provoking strong protests from China. One Chinese leader commented: "We two countries have a different idea of humanitarianism. In China we believe it is wrong to allow a child to grow up starving. Our country will manage its own affairs."

Despite this friction, the People's Republic made the U.S. a leading trading partner. In addition, it invited American technicians to explore for oil and set up new industries in its country. Americans, along with Europeans, received substantial tax credits for developing an import-export trade in China's main coastal cities. Moreover, Chinese executives toured the U.S. to study marketing techniques there. Soon the Chinese were building a large favorable trade balance with the U.S. They shipped the Americans textiles, vegetable oils, canned fruits, and soybeans in exchange for machinery and consumer goods.The Chinese make 6 percent of clothing sold to Americans. In 1993 they sold $26 billion worth of their goods to the U.S. and bought only $7.5 billion in return.

The Americans badly needed foreign trade, too. It pleased them to begin what promised to be a long, profitable relationship. On their West Coast, merchants, seeing how quickly Asia's economies were growing, prepared for a huge trans-Pacific boom. In 1993 they helped to develop an "Asia-Pacific Summit" in Seattle. In addition to the U.S. and China, this conference included Canada, New Zealand, Australia, Indonesia, Malaysia, Hong Kong, Japan, South Korea, Taiwan, Thailand, the Philippines, Singapore, and Brunei. At the meeting, the U.S. announced that its trade with Pacific Rim countries had reached $249 billion a year, compared with the $206 billion it did with members of the European Union.

With an historic handshake, President Nixon and Chairman Mao Zedong, who had long been enemies, began a new era for both the U.S. and China.

This did not prevent the new U.S. President, Bill Clinton, from insisting that China stop imprisoning political prisoners and improve its human rights policies. Clinton warned that China might lose its status as a most-favored nation for trade unless it did so. After this, China made grudging but definite progress in the field of human rights. However, it did nothing to help the U.S. control China's own most belligerent neighbor, North Korea, which threatened the peace of the world by developing nuclear power. Half a million Chinese soldiers died defending North Korea from the Americans in 1950. Now China refused to help the U.S. control the North Koreans. Nor did it heed U.S. demands that it stop selling munitions to countries such as Pakistan and stop its potentially dangerous underground nuclear testing.

Clinton, therefore, groped for a new U.S. policy towards the Chinese. Unlike George Bush, he was reluctant to reward an oppressive, uncooperative government with the fruits of trade. Still, he did not want the U.S. to fall behind in the global rush towards the world's largest and fastest-growing market.

Russia. After the Russian Revolution of 1918, many Communists advanced the theory that growing discontent among the world's industrial workers would destroy capitalism. They thought China could not possibly become Communist soon because it was chiefly an agricultural country. They sent advisers to help Mao Zedong start the Chinese revolution, but they remained skeptical of his ability to defeat the Nationalists. Then, surprised by Mao's success in 1949, they changed their plans and strengthened the alliance by helping set up Chinese industries.

The People's Republic worked with the Soviet Union at first, but historic differences between the two countries proved greater than similarities. Throughout the nineteenth century, Russia tried to establish ports suitable for shipping across the Pacific. In a series of skirmishes and agreements with the weak Qing (Manchu) rulers, the Russians gained Chinese lands along the 1,200-mile border created by the Ussuri and Amur rivers. Advancing across Siberia, Russians annexed these lands as part of their Central Asian empire. The Russian Czars and Manchu emperors signed treaties to confirm the transfers.

The Chinese never recognized these Russian annexations. They pointed out that the Qing rulers were Manchus, foreigner invaders who had no right to sign treaties in China's behalf. They began demanding the land back as early as 1920, when a Soviet government replaced the Czars. Nevertheless, the Soviets refused to return the vast, disputed lands—over 600,000 square miles of valuable territory. By 1949, when the Chinese had their own Communist government, the Soviets had become silent about its former Chinese lands, which they concluded were their property.

Chapter 9 showed how the two Communist giants worked closely together until 1960, when the Soviets pulled out their advisers and canceled their economic aid. In 1969, antagonism between them burst into violence. The Soviets rejected China's demands for a return of the land and rushed troops to the border. Soon the two countries were exchanging gunfire. Angry soldiers fired at each other and threatened war. The Chinese regarded the million Soviet troops on their northern border as an army ready for invasion, not as the defensive force that the Soviets announced. They mobilized and began to build air raid shelters.

The two nuclear giants managed to avoid war, but not the continuation of their quarrel. Each clung to its point of view for nearly a decade. Eventually China, fearing encirclement by an alliance of the Soviet Union and the Vietnamese, called the Soviet Union "even more deceitful than the old-line imperialist countries, and therefore more dangerous." At that point, as a countermeasure, China started down the long road to a relationship with the U.S.

By 1985, it appeared that there was a warming trend in the relationship between the Soviet Union and China. Soviet leadership had changed again; the new chief of state, Mikhail S. Gorbachev, seemed determined to renew Soviet friendship with China. He agreed to help China restore some of the factories that had been standing useless since 1960. By treaty, the two countries agreed to double their trade to $3.9 billion a year by 1990. The Chinese were to trade food, industrial raw materials, and some consumer goods for machinery, transport, and some chemicals.

This treaty was destined to be carried out, but not by the Soviet Union, which collapsed soon after signing it. Russia, the largest survivor of the Soviet Union, took over the obligation instead. Not wishing friction on its border at a time of internal unrest, Russia continued to promise China technology and raw materials. It also prepared a new agreement for signature in 1995. Under it, each of side pledged to avoid a "first strike" against the other. Thus each acted out of fear—the Russians because they feared instability in China when leadership changed, the Chinese because they feared political turmoil would promote instability in Russia.

Japan. Japanese expansion has proved costly to China throughout this century. At times Japan occupied parts of China through military action, and at other times it has been an effective economic competitor. Japan, though in a recession that began in 1993,   has a substantial trade balance with the United States. Its electronics, auto, and banking industries are among the most efficient and productive in the world, and it has substantial capital.

While Japan has no standing army or nuclear force, the Chinese see a military threat in the large population and economic power developing in its neighbor. Specifically, China recalls Japanese aggression from 1931-45 and that for more than fifty years Japan had occupied Taiwan, which China regards as its own province. The Japanese have permitted the United States to establish military bases on Japanese land. Chinese leaders appear to think that the Japan and the United States might join to defend Taiwan against their claim to it.

In 1970 Japan's Premier Sato said, "Taiwan is a most important factor in the security of Japan." This produced a sharp reaction from the Chinese Communists. Sato later tempered his remark with the statement that Communist China's desire for Taiwan was "understandable," but that did little to calm Chinese fears.

Until recently China took Japan to be one of a number of powers, including Australia, Malaysia, and South Korea, that had formed a hostile ring around it. China also criticized Japan's tendency to follow the United States in matters of foreign policy. It softened this hostility greatly, however, after Japan gained a new premier, Kakuei Tanaka. Within three days after he took office, Tanaka announced that he would try to "normalize relations" with China. Seeing China's economy expanding rapidly, Japan evidently had begun to hope that huge markets could be developed on the mainland. At the same time, Japan no doubt wanted to pursue friendly relationships with its rising neighbor. China's nuclear capacity, aircraft and munitions industries, and immense army all seem especially menacing to Japan.

Premier Tanaka himself was once a soldier in a Japanese army that had invaded China. When he reached Beijing to establish friendlier relations, he apologized for his country's past offenses against the Chinese. China's premier, Zhou Enlai, accepted the regrets, saying that it was the militarists of Japan, not the people, who had created the "enormous disasters." The two leaders agreed to establish diplomatic and trade relations. By 1994, China had replaced Germany as Japan's second-largest trading partner. Two-way trade between the two countries reached $30 billion a year, more than twice what it was in the 1980's. Japanese cars, watches, and electronics streamed into huge Chinese markets.

Nevertheless, not all has gone smoothly between the two countries. Trade is greatly in Japan's favor: much-needed Chinese capital flows into Japan at the rate of almost $3 billion a year. Moreover, the Chinese expected capital and technology from Japan but received far less than from the U.S.

There were other persistent reasons for friction between China and Japan. Often the Japanese slip into expressions of patriotism that offend Chinese who suffered during the war. For example, in 1985 the Chinese protested when Prime Minister Nakasone of Japan honored his country's dead soldiers and included those who directed massacres in China. In 1982, the Chinese discovered that Japanese school-children were being taught that Japan's massacre of 300,000 people in Nanjing had been justified in 1937 by Chinese resistance there. The Chinese demanded that the textbooks be changed, the Japanese government agreed. In addition to this re-opening of war-wounds, the Chinese have long been angered by Japan's willingness to continue extensive trade relations with Taiwan.

Despite their mutual problems and troubled pasts, China and Japan are likely to pursue a friendly relationship. Neither can afford a struggle with the other, and each needs the other's skills and markets. Finally, both countries feel threatened by instability in the Pacific and so have a powerful reason to cooperate.

Taiwan. The Chinese Communists regard their revolution as incomplete as long as Nationalist forces occupy Taiwan. This island, about 110 miles off China's southeast coast, is inhabited chiefly by immigrants from South China who came over the past 300 years. As a colony of Japan for fifty years after the Sino-Japanese War of 1895, Taiwan was called Formosa, and its people were taught the Japanese culture and language.

The Japanese were forced to withdraw from Taiwan after their defeat in World War II. Four years later (1949) they were replaced by Jiang Jieshi, who led retreating Nationalists there in 1949. The People's Republic maintains that Taiwan is ruled illegally and must be restored to the mainland government. The Nationalists, on the other hand, insist that they are the rightful government of all China and are gathering strength, while on Taiwan, to resume control of the mainland.

To prevent the mainland Chinese from seizing Taiwan, the United States signed a joint defense treaty with the Nationalists in the early 1950's. The U.S. Seventh Fleet, either in full or in token strength, spent years patrolling the waters of the Taiwan straits, demonstrating America's determination to defend the island.

Although re-conquest of the mainland of China remains the cherished official policy of the Nationalist government, the realities of Communist military power in China, and U.S. diplomatic pressure, have kept the Nationalists from taking aggressive action. They have therefore turned to building a prosperous economy on Taiwan. This large mountainous country, whose eastern slopes rise to 13,000 feet, includes fertile plains on the west. There, the Nationalists have organized efficient industries and farming with the help of the United States, which from 1950-65 gave them $1.5 billion in aid. Taiwan is 240 miles long and is about the size of Massachusetts, Connecticut, and Rhode Island combined.

The Republic of China, as Taiwan is officially known, is in theory ruled by a National Assembly. This body was to have been elected every six years under a constitution endorsed by Jiang Jieshi. In practice, however, assembly members have little power and often do not even attend meetings. Usually fewer than half of the 3,045 seats in the Assembly were taken, for the authority of the President was widely acknowledged.

In 1972, Jiang Jieshi was re-elected to his fifth six-year term as President of the Republic of China. After his death in 1978 he was succeeded by his elder son, Jiang Jingguo, who had been Premier. The son, though, was born in 1910. By the 1980's he was almost ready to yield to a successor.

The issue of what will become of Taiwan is one of the most complex in world diplomacy. With the help of the United States. the Nationalist government has built a strong and vital community on the island. Taiwan has powerful defenses which it is determined to use if necessary. Presumably the United States and other countries would help it in the event of an invasion.

China, however, is equally determined to regain the island. When the Chinese Communists welcomed President Nixon to Beijing in 1972, they first refused to enter complete negotiations without settlement of their claim to Taiwan. The Americans declined to abandon their relationship with the Nationalists. Other nations, such as Great Britain, were willing to recognize that Taiwan is part of the mainland in order to trade with the Communists. Nixon skirted the issue by saying, "Taiwan is a part of China and China is a part of Taiwan." The U.S. finally closed its embassy on Taiwan in 1979, but meanwhile reaffirmed that it would defend the island against invaders.

Since its revolution in 1949, Communist China has used these changing strategies to bring Taiwan back into its fold:

1) In 1950 it began shelling the small offshore islands of Quemoy and Matsu, which the Nationalists also occupy, using large cannons stationed on the mainland. But it did not risk an all-out war with the U.S. by sending landing troops and halted the shelling as the U.S. fleet drew near.

2) During the 1960's and 1970's Communist China sought to replace Taiwan in diplomacy and international trade. Over the strong opposition of the United States, at last it won Taiwan's seat in the

United Nations in 1971. Following this achievement Communist China gained recognition from most Western countries, including the United States. But the Communists were unable to take over Taiwan's markets, as they hoped. This strategy failed because the Nationalists, with U.S. help and their own vitality, developed one of the healthiest economies in Asia. The rate of growth in Taiwan often matched or even exceeded the one in Japan, and the Nationalists remained strong and confident.

3) In 1985 the Chinese Communists offered Taiwan a peaceful solution to the problem of unification. After reaching a settlement with the British Crown Colony on Hong Kong, they made a similar offer to the Nationalists. Basically they assured the people of Hong Kong the right to keep their thriving capitalist economy for at least fifty years after the British lease on the island expires in 1997. Under the agreement, Hong Kong promised to accept a place within the Communist government, though it was not required to adopt a Communist economy or society. The Nationalists on Taiwan refused to consider the offer, hoping that one day they can return to power in Beijing. Nevertheless, the Communists kept the offer open.

Thus the farther the Chinese Communists moved from their violent days of revolution, the more willing they became to negotiate over the issue of Taiwan. Time is on their side. Now stable and with growing production, the Communists seem more willing to wait for the issue to resolve itself. They are establishing freer markets and hope this will persuade the Nationalists to join them. The Nationalists, meanwhile, continue to prosper and are building rapidly on their island fortress.

The Olympic Games of 1984, held in Los Angeles, offered an example of how the two governments may be brought together. Both wanted to compete in the games, but Communist China refused to participate if another country bearing the name China appeared. Eventually both did compete, the Communists under their official name, the People's Republic of China, and the Nationalists as Chinese Taipei. In that way the simple change of a word brought athletes from the two regions into the same playing fields, though they did not compete against one another.

In 1993, the mainland Chinese acknowledged Taiwan's growing importance in its economy and the rest of the world. Their cultural and financial contacts with the wealthy Taiwanese had become a reality too large to hide. They invited the island's leaders to the mainland to discuss cooperation, but not reunification. Then, just a year later, they expressed profound anger with Taiwan for setting its first direct presidential elections in 1996. By doing so, the

Taiwanese raised the possibility of permanent independence from their ancestral homeland. Many of them have given up on the possibility that they will ever regain the mainland, but most want to invest there. Taiwan now has a per capita income of nearly $8,000 a year and has the twenty-fifth largest economy in the world. In 1993 the mainland, with more than 1.1 billion people, still could not match the $115 billion traded by Taiwan's 20 million people.

Tibet and India. In its foreign policy declarations the People's Republic of China stresses "the right of self-determination for all nations." This naturally also emphasizes the independence of China itself. Because of its actions with respect to Tibet and India, as well as Korea, there has been considerable confusion over whether it truly believes in these policies for other nations as well as for itself.

In the past, many observers have described China's foreign policy as belligerent. Certainly its role in the Korean War was interpreted that way, though some historians said that it sent volunteers to fight in Korea as a defensive measure. Two other incidents have also been cited as examples of China's desire for territorial expansion—Tibet and India.

The Tibetan question is a complex one. China claimed to have controlled Tibet since the 1600's, but it had made no attempt to govern it directly at that time. Lying across the world's highest mountains between India and China, Tibet became a buffer state between China, parts of small border kingdoms that have long been under Indian protection, and India itself. These kingdoms include Assam, Bhutan, Nepal, Sikkim, and Ladakh.

In 1959, Tibet's rulers apparently saw that China was preparing to change their feudal monarchy. They revolted, but the Chinese crushed the rebellion and warded off criticism by saying that the issue was a domestic rather than a foreign one. Once in complete control of the country, they introduced land distribution measures that ended the power of the former ruling class. At the same time they imposed the use of their own language and culture, giving rise to cries of imperialism by the Tibetans. In 1985 the Dalai Lama, Tibet's spiritual and political leader, protested that China had killed at least 1.2 million Tibetans, destroyed the country's religion and culture, and threatened to absorb Tibet completely.

The issue of Tibet originated chiefly in population pressures inside of China and in the Soviet troops who seemed so menacing on the Chinese border. In desperate need of territory and buffers against the Soviet Union, the Chinese began to expand. Soon they overwhelmed the six million Tibetans. According to the Dalai Lama, they closed all of Tibet's 5,700 Buddhist monasteries and

500 temples, removing priceless works of art. Like the Manchurians, whose three million people are now ruled by China, Tibetans feared the Chinese and threatened rebellions. East Turkestan experienced a similar loss of land and population when its people became a minority in the China's Xinjiang Province.

The Chinese have declared that they are greatly softening their policies with respect to Tibet. In 1985 they began to return almost thirty tons of precious works of Buddhist art that they had seized during the invasion and the Cultural Revolution. The Tibetans were pleased but still hoped for greater autonomy. "In human society," the Dalai Lama said, "freedom is a basic need, an inalienable right that can never be replaced by temporary improvements in food."

After struggling against the Chinese invaders many Tibetans, including the Dalai Lama, took refuge in India. By permitting this sanctuary and later by befriending the Soviet Union, the Indians infuriated Chinese leaders. China began to create a far-reaching bloc of power extending to the Mediterranean. It formed alliances with Muslim nations which opposed India, among them Pakistan. In 1962, columns of trained Chinese mountain troops stormed over the Himalayas and overran key Indian outposts. One cut deep into Ladakh; another struck to the north of the fertile plains of Assam.

The poorly equipped Indian soldiers could not halt the Chinese advance. It appeared that the Chinese could have gone much further, but they suddenly chose to withdraw to Ladakh. This area became the center of a border dispute. China's continuing quarrel with India caused it to send material support, though not armed forces, to Pakistan during the Pakistani-Indian War of 1971. The United States also aided Pakistan in that war, while the Soviet Union supplied India.

From that time forward, India began favoring the Soviet Union in its foreign policies. Further American aid to Pakistan, given after the Soviet Union invaded the neighboring state of Afghanistan, caused India to strengthen its relationship with the Soviets. This aroused even greater suspicion of India among the Chinese. However India became less dependent on the Soviet Union, and so friendlier with China, after the death of Indira Gandhi in 1984.

Southeast Asia. After the Cambodian government was overthrown by Communist rebels in 1970, the People's Republic invited spokesmen for governments in North Korea, North Vietnam, and Cambodia to a conference. "The Chinese government and people," the meeting was told by Foreign Minister Zhou Enlai, "firmly oppose the United States imperialists' frenzied aggression against the three countries of Vietnam, Laos, and Cambodia, who are fighting against U.S. aggression and for national salvation....The U.S. aggressor troops and their vassal troops must withdraw completely from Indochina so that the Indochinese peoples may respectively settle their problems by themselves."

The United States did eventually withdraw from Indochina, but by that time the results did not please China. After taking control of their own country. Vietnam gave China several reasons to become hostile. The Vietnamese first seized most businesses and gave their owners the choice of becoming farm laborers or leaving the country. Most of these merchants were ethnic Chinese who preferred to escape Vietnam in small boats. Later countless poverty-stricken Vietnamese followed them out to sea. The "boat people," as they became known throughout the world, suffered storms, starvation, and pirate attacks. Tens of thousands of them died before reaching nearby coasts. Even more who managed to land were turned back to deep waters by governments unable to feed them. Communist China tried to rescue many of these people, but the Vietnamese navy beat off its ships.

Vietnam next angered China by seizing control of neighboring Cambodia in 1978. It moved 160,000 troops there, saying it needed to pacify warring factions. Vietnam had previously made Laos a subject state. It now justified its invasion of Cambodia on grounds that millions of people were dying under a Cambodian tyranny. But the invasion had the firm support of the Soviet Union, which the Chinese believed was closing a ring around its southern borders.

Determined to resist encirclement, China rebuked both of its aggressive neighbors. To the Soviets it repeated demands that hostile actions in Afghanistan and on the Sino-Soviet border be ended. To the Vietnamese it raised more dangerous possibilities. In 1979 an army of 170,000 Chinese troops stormed into Vietnam. They burned farms and slaughtered animals, then quickly withdrew. For the next decade China sent arms and money to Vietnam's enemies in Cambodia. Meanwhile it reiterated its historic claims to border lands and offshore islands, chiefly the Paracels, which Vietnam also claimed.

The collapse of the Soviet Union left Vietnam without an major ally and suddenly ended China's fear of the most powerful enemy on its northern borders. Vietnam further reassured China by withdrawing troops from neighboring Kampuchea (Cambodia) and by its efforts to create the kind of flourishing economy which would make it a major trading partner. Immediately upon perceiving this, China invited Vietnam's leaders to Beijing for informal talks. These discussions were certain to lead to mutual recognition and would help restore Chinese influence in one of Southeast Asia's most strategic regions.

Beijing University students created a plastic "Goddess of Liberty" in June 1989 and rallied around it. Afterward, tanks rolled in to crush them.

THE FUTURE OF COMMUNIST CHINA

Toward the end of every dynasty, the Chinese people turned to mysticism, the occult, and hero-worship as a reaction to the disorder in their lives. Today fortune-tellers, seers, and faith-healers roam China's parks and streets. They claim to be in touch with heavenly forces or the spirits of ancestors. They sell advice to anyone confused by the chaos around them. Many people, in a spasm of hero-worship, are buying images of Deng Xiaoping or Mao Zedong to hang on their bicycles, car mirrors, or walls. This phenomenon began in the south, where people claimed Mao's photo protected them from accidents. One man explained why he honored Mao's image: "Now everybody is corrupt and money-grubbing. Under Chairman Mao, people at least were honest and cared for the country."

These hints at change do not necessarily foretell turbulence in China. They do, however, suggest that the Chinese people long for stability and will take unpredictable courses to get it. Above all they do not want to be pawns of their government. They believe that their present boom must lead to more freedom. History shows that every regime, however authoritarian, eventually needs the consent of its people to rule. The one in China will not be an exception.

The chance of turbulence cannot be discounted. In recent months some workers have called violent strikes and sabotage against factories whose managers were preparing to change to capitalist methods. The workers were concerned about layoffs, the end of the "iron rice bowl," and inflation. Fearing an attack, Deng Xiaoping himself began to travel in an armored Cadillac.

Normally such events take place in China when people sense a change in the "Mandate of Heaven." (*See* page 19). If so, China could break up as countries in Eastern Europe have. The vast Chinese population now seems freer than it has been to criticize its government, and many people openly condemn their leaders for massacring students in Tiananmen Square or for allowing the environment to deteriorate. Some are demanding the right to control their own lives. They will do so increasingly if disorder persists. "The Government has already lost control over information," a Chinese writer said. He meant that the Chinese people can now learn about freer societies from satellite television, short-wave radio, fax machines, long-distance telephones, tourists, and imported publications. They glimpse not only prosperity, but at least limited political rights in places as close as Hong Kong, Taiwan, Singapore, and South Korea. Booms have been proceeding in all of those places for years and have increased freedom.

The Chinese government still refuses to acknowledge its increasing loss of control. It does not allow China's rock stars to broadcast songs of protest over state-owned television, for example, but the singers reach people by means of cassettes. "Look all around," the most popular of rock star laments. "We've come to the end of the Golden Road." He points out that drug addiction has become a sign of despair among the young.

Impending changes in Chinese leadership will be a moment of tension in the history of modern China. Deng Xiaoping, approaching his ninetieth year, sought to choose his successor but did not clearly reveal his wishes A struggle for power is certain to follow his death, and it will be a crossroads for the world's most populous country.

During his final years in office Deng Xiaoping took personal responsibility for the Tiananmen Square Massacre. He rejected the possibility of democracy, saying, "Stability takes precedence over all China's problems." But Deng's own solution to China's problems could well lead to the same end. Rapid economic expansion has been costly to morals and the environment.

China is spending its future today, and it may be spending the world's future, too. Massive changes have been taking place in the planet's climate, chiefly caused by such human activities as the addition of excessive carbon dioxide to the atmosphere. China, highly dependent on coal and other carbon products for its energy, has greatly accelerated this process and will continue to do so.

Because the United States has the world's largest economy, it has been sending more petroleum emissions into the atmosphere than any other country. But China now ranks third (just behind the former Soviet Union) and soon will replace the U.S. as earth's major offender. Its smoke and acid rain creep as far as Japan. Its government argues that China has the right to try to catch up with the powers that once dominated its people. To its credit, it is working to replace coal as its primary source of energy. Part of this effort involves a huge hydroelectric project called the Three Gorges on the Yangtzi River. Yet not even this massive effort, combined with nuclear energy, will halt its consumption of coal, which is almost certain to rise from the present 1.1 billion tons a year to more than 1.4 billion tons by the year 2000.

The acceleration of global warming could jeopardize or even destroy life on earth. Moreover, China is a nuclear power with the largest standing army in its region, continuing poverty might trigger violence of another kind. Clearly China and the world's other major powers have at least a brief time in which to learn to cooperate. They have never needed to do so more than now.

Never before in history has a country tried to expand its economy so rapidly with so few resources. Yet China, with the help of foreign investors who seek only profits, has squandered resources. It has poured concrete and asphalt over wheat fields and fouled water supplies by pouring chemical fertilizers over fields. As it spends its future to subsidize its present, it will soon find no more to spend. By 2020-30 its population will have reached 1.5-1.6 billion, despite rigorous birth controls. "Then," said one Chinese member of the Academy of Sciences, "...I am afraid...that all the grain output of the United States could not meet China's needs."

Official statements suggest that China's rulers will continue to demand sacrifices of their people. They will also punish whoever refuses to obey. Promising higher living standards and the need for patriotism, they are likely to insist that political reform is impossible before economic goals are reached. But paradoxically, economic progress stirs greater desire for freedoms as well as greater environmental hazards. As the conflict proceeds, the whole world watches anxiously for signs of irrationality in this atomic power. China has learned that it can no longer isolate itself. Nevertheless, whether it can and will accept its global responsibilities remains one of the most troubling questions of the modern age.

APPENDIX A

ESTIMATED POPULATION GROWTH OF CHINA IN RECENT TIMES

1750—150 million   1950—560 million   1970—803 million
1850—300 million   1960—675 million   1980—970 million
              1990—1,180 million   2000—1,500 million

APPENDIX B

AN ENGLISH-SPEAKER'S
INTRODUCTION TO HANYU PINYIN

Hanyu	English equivalent		Wade-Giles System*
a	(as in)	"far"	(or)	a
b		"boy"		p
c		"ts"		ts
d		"dog"		t
e		"uh"		e
ei		"way"		ei
f		"foot"		f
g		"go"		k
h		"house"		h
i		"eat"		i

In syllables beginning with c, ch, r, s, sh, z, and zh

ie	"yes"	ie
j	"jeep"	j
k	"kind"	k
l	"land"	l
m	"me"	m
n	"no"	n
o	"aw"	o
o(ng)	"look"	o
p	"park"	p
q	"cheek"	ch
r	"run"	j
s	"sister"	s, ss, sz
t	"top"	t
u	"too"	u
unlaut-u	as in German: ue	

187

APPENDIX C

TRANSLITERATION OF COMMON WORDS FROM THE CHINESE

Wade-Giles & Common English	Hanyu Pinyin	Wade-Giles & Common English	Hanyu Pinyin
Amoy	Xiamen	Kwantung	Guangdong
Amur	Heilong	Kweichow	Gueizhou
Annam	Annan	Lao-tzu	Laozi
Anyang	Anyang	Li Po	Li Bo
Canton	Guangzhou	Li Shih-min	Li Shimin
Ch'an	Chan	Li Ssu	Li Si
Chang	Zhang	Li Ta-chao	Li Dazhao
Ch'ang-an	Changan	Liaotung	Liaodong Lin
Ch'i	Qi	Piao	Lin Biao
Chiang Ch'ing	Jiang Qing	Loyang	Luoyang
Chiang Kai-shek	Jiang Jieshi	Lung-men	Longmen
Chin	Jin	Mo Tzu	Mozi
Ch'in	Qin	Nanking	Nanjing
Shih Huang-ti	Shihuangdi	Ningpo	Ningbo
Ch'ing	Qing	Pearl River	Zhu Jiang
Ching-ti	Jingdi	Peking	Beijing
Chou	Zhou	p'i-p'a	pipa
Chou En-lai	Zhou Enlai	Red River	Yuan Jiang
Chu Teh	Zhu De	Shansi	Shanxi
Chung-kuo	Zhongguo	Shantung	Shandong
Chungking	Chongqing	Shensi	Shaanxi
Foochow	Fuzhou	Shen-tsung	Shenzong
Fukien	Fujian	Sian	Xian
Hangchow	Hangzhou	Si	Xi
Honan	Henan	Siang	Xiang
Hopei	Hebei	Singkiang	Xinjiang
Hsiung-nu	Xiongnu	Ssu-ma Ch'ien	Sima Qian
Hwang Ho	Huanghe	Ssu-ma Kuang	Sima Guang
I	Yi	Sun Yat-sen	Sun Yixian
Hsi-hsia	Xixia	Sung	Song
Hsia	Xia	Szechwan	Sichuan
hsien	Xian	Ta-tung	Datong
hsin	Xin	T'ai-p'ing	Taiping
Hwang	Huang	T'ai Tsung	Taizong
I ching	Yijing	T'ang	Tang
jen	ren	Tao	Dao
Juchen	Ruzhen	Tao-te-ching	Daodejing
Jung	Rong	Ti	Di
K'ai-feng	Kaifeng	Tien-an-men	Tiananmen
kan	gan	T'ien Shan	Tianshan
K'ang	Kang	Tientsin	Tianjin
K'ang-hsi	Kangxi	T'opa	Toba
Kansu	Gansu	Tsangpo	Zangbo
Kao-tsung	Gaozong	Tsinling	Qinling
Kaoliang	Gaoliang	Wang An-shih	Wang Anshi
Kiangsi	Jiangxi	Wenchow	Wenzhou
Kuang	Guang	Yangtze	Yangzi
Kuang Hsu	Guangxu	Yung-lo	Yongle
Kwangsi	Guangxi		

APPENDIX D

GLOSSARY

bai (by)—"White" in Chinese.
bei (bay)—"North" in Chinese.
Beijing (bay-zhing)—"Northern capital" in Chinese; China's present capital.

Co-hong (coe-hong)—a group of merchants appointed by the government to deal with foreigners during the Qing (Manchu) period (1644-1912).
commune (cuh-MYUNE)—The now largely abandoned system by which the first Communist government in China organized farmers into groups.
Confucius (con-few-shas)—The Latin form of the name Gungfuzi (joong-foo-dzah), the great philosopher of China's Zhou Dynasty period.

dao (dah-oh)—"The Way": older than, but the basis of, Daoism.
di (dee)—"Earth" in Chinese; used as a suffix with the ruler's name to identify the emperor with "Heaven."
dong (dong)—"East" in Chinese.

he (huh)—"Shallow river" in Chinese.
Huang (hwahng)—"Yellow" in Chinese.

jiang (g-ee-yang)—"Deep river" in Chinese.
jing (g-ing)—"Capital" in Chinese.

Laozi (lah-o-dze)—China's first great Daoist.
Liaoning (lee-aho-nehng)—A northeast province containing a massive peninsula.
ling (ling)—"Range of mountains" in Chinese.
loess (lehs)—The loose, yellowish soil blown southward across North China.

Mandarin (man-dah-rin)—Beijing, or Guanhua speech, called "China's national dialect."
Mao Zedong—(maoh-dzeh-dohng)—The Chinese Communist who led his party to power after World War II.
Mencius (men-see-us)—the Latin form of the name for the first great Confucian, Mengzi (muhn-dzuh), the "Chinese Saint Paul."
Muslim (MUS-lim)—a believer in Islam; a follower of Muhammed (also Moslem.)

nan (nahn)—"South" in Chinese.

Qinling (ching-ling)—Mountain range of Central China, separating North from South China.
Qin Shihuangdi (chin-she-hwang-de)—The ruler who created the first Chinese empire (221-206 B.C.).
ren (run)—An ancient Chinese concept of virtue; "humanitarianism."
Ruzhen (roo-zhun)—A people who lived north of China Proper until their conquest by Jenghis Khan. Their own plural for their name is Ruzhed.

shan (shan)—"Mountain" in Chinese.
shen (shuhn)—"Mountain pass" in Chinese.
Sichuan (suh-choo-ahn)—"Four Rivers," the name of an historically important, mountainous province of China, near Tibet.
si (see)—"West" in Chinese.
Sima Guang (see-mah-goo-ahng)—Historian of China's Han period.

Taiping (tie-ping)—"Great Peace": the name given the rebellion against the Manchus and Westerners in nineteenth-century China.

tian (tee-ahn)—"Heaven" in Chinese.

Uigurs (WEE-gurs)—An originally nomadic people who maintained a kingdom north of China Proper during the Song Dynasty and who later were absorbed China; eastern branch of the Huns. (Also spelled Uighur and Uygur.)

Xia Dynasty (h-see-ya)—a prehistoric period of Chinese history (ca. 1818-1755 B.C.).
xian (h-sayn)—A district or geographical unit of Chiense government.
xiao (h-see-ao)—"Little" or "lesser" in Chinese.

Yangzi (yahng-tse)—The major river of South China.
yin and yang (yin and yang)—The female and male (or positive and negative) principles that exist together in all things, according to many Chinese thinkers.

Zhou (zhoe)—The dynastic period in China (1122-256 B.C.) which produced the major philosophies, including Confucianism and Daoism. zi (zuh)—"Master": the suffix for the names of highly respected figures such as Laozi.

APPENDIX E

STATISTICAL PROFILE OF ASIAN NATIONS

All figures were assembled in 1986, reflecting data obtained earlier. They are given for relative purposes only and should not be considered currently precise.

1. Population in millions.
2. Area of country in 000's sq.mi.
3. Population density per sq. mi.
4. Percentage population increases.*

5. Years for population to double.
6. Average life expectancy at birth.
7. Per capita income in dollars.⫟
8. GNP in billions of dollars.

	1.	2.	3.	4.	5.	6.	7.	8.
Bangladesh	98.7	55	1,775	2.7	27	48	130	105
Burma	37.6	261	144	2.5	28	55	180	5.6
China	1,043	3,696	282	1.2	60	67	296	301
India	768	1,183	605	2.2	32	52	260	190
Indonesia	167	741	226	1.7	42	52	560	87
Japan	121	147	827	0.6	120	76	10,100	1,204
Kampuchea	7.2	69	104	2.5	27	45	159	1.1
Laos	4.1	91	45	1.7	42	50	152	.6
Malaysia	15	127	122	2.4	30	70	1,870	27
Pakistan	100	307	326	2.7	27	50	370	35
Philippines	54	116	472	2.5	28	64	760	39
Singapore	2.5	239	10,704	1.1	65	73	7,100	16
Taiwan	19.1	14	1,376	1.4	51	72	3,040	46
Thailand	51	198	258	1.8	40	63	812	40
Vietnam	60	128	462	2.5	27	52	170	1

*World average, 1.8; U.S, .7
⫟U.S., $16,270

China	India	Japan	Southeast Asia	The West
1964 1st nuclear warhead exploded	1965 Clash with Pakistan	1971 Defense budget doubled	1966 Sukarno overthrown	1964 U.S. launches Gemini spacecraft
1965 Army ranks abolished	1967 Indira Gandhi Prime Minister	1972 Tanaka visits China	1966 U.S. bombs Hanoi	1964 Racial violence in U.S.
1965 Lin Piao foresees world revolution	1967 Clash with China	1973 Tanaka visits United States	1966 U.S. defoliates Vietnam jungles	1964 Johnson elected
1966 Cultural Revolution	1968 Alliance with Russia	1974 Critical inflation	1970 Sihanouk overthrown	1965 1st "walks" in space
1966 Red Guards riot	1969 Banks nationalized		1970 U.S. troops in Cambodia	1965 Peace demonstrations
1967 Cultural Revolution abates	1969 Communist victory in Bengal elections		1971 U.S. troops in Laos	1965 Watts riots
1969 Lin Piao named Mao's successor	1971 Army supports Bangladesh		1972 Martial law, Philippines	1966 U.S. student riots
1969 Border clash with Russians	1972 Bhutto leads Pakistan		1972 U.S. mines Haiphong harbor	1967 Israel wins "6-Day War"
1971 Lin Piao dies	1974 1st nuclear bomb		1973 U.S. bombs Hanoi	1967 "Black Power" movement
1971 Admitted to UN			1973 Armistice in Vietnam	1967 Anti-pollution movement
1972 Nixon's visit			1973 Armistice violations, Vietnam	1968 Martin Luther King dies
1972 Britain recognizes China			1974 War Spreads in Cambodia	1968 Russia invades Czechoslovakia
1973 Increasing world trade				1968 Nixon elected
				1969 My Lai charges
				1970 West German-Russian treaty
				1971 U.S. devalues dollar
				1972 Nixon visits China, Russia
				1972 Army limitation talks (SALT)
				1972 Britain joins Common Market
				1972 Peace negotiations
				1972 Nixon re-elected
				1973 Watergate investigation
				1973 Jupiter probe
				1973 4th Arab—Israeli war
				1973 Arab oil embargo
				1974 New energy sources explored

China	India	Japan	Southeast Asia	The West
1974 Jiang Jieshi dies	1974 Atomic power gained	1972 U.S. returns Okinawa	1975 Communism in Laos	1974 Ford succeeds Nixon
1976 Zhou Enlai dies	1974 Sikkim annexed	1972 Disputes with USSR	1975 Khmer Rouge triumphs	1976 Viking II on Mars
1976 Mao Zedong dies	1975 "National Emergency"	1980 Exports soar	1975 Lon Nol flees	1976 South African riots
1976 Rise of Hua Guofeng	1977 M.R. Desai elected	1981 U.S. warns of tariffs	1975 Vast Thai inflation	1977 Carter defeats Ford
1976 Massive earthquakes	1977 Army seizes Pakistan	1982 Nakasone elected	1976 Kampuchean migrations	1977 First space shuttle
1977 Deng Xiaoping returns	1978 Mrs. Gandhi imprisoned	1983 Tanaka convicted	1976 Vietnam controls Laos	1978 Inflation rages
1978 China raids Vietnam	1980 Mrs. Gandhi reelected	1985 Soaring prosperity	1976 Vietnam united	1979 Thatcher elected
1979 U.S. recognizes China	1980 Muslim-Hindi riots	1986 Increasing trade	1977 Cambodian border war	1979 U.S. hostages in Iran
1981 "Gang of 4" convicted	1982 Bangladeshi martial law		1978 Suharto reelected	1979 3-Mile Island
1981 Incentive programs	1984 Golden Temple stormed		1978 Kampuchean holocaust	1979 Afghanistan invaded
1982 New laws end Maoism	1984 Massacres of Punjabis		1978 "Boat People"	1980 Riots sweep Poland
1985 Huge economic gains	1984 Mrs. Gandhi dies		1978 Soviet-Viet alliance	1980 Rising technology
1986 Growing world trade	1984 Rajiv Gandhi elected		1978 Viets in Kampuchea	1980 Reagan elected
	1984 Bhopal incident		1979 Pol Pot overthrown	1980 Interferon created
	1985 Sikh terrorists		1980 Singapore prospers	1980 Iran-Iraq War
	1985 Zia ends martial law		1983 Suharto's 4th term	1981 Mitterand elected
			1983 B. Aquino murdered	1981 Polish martial law
			1984 Sino-Viet conflict	1982 OPEC weakens
			1985 Khmer Rouge crippled	1982 British-Argentine War
			1986 Marcos deposed	1983 Reagan reelected
			1986 Malaysia prospers	1985 Terrorists in Europe
			1986 Viets raid Thailand	1985 Inflation abates
				1985 Advances in genetics
				1985 Gorbachev heads USSR
				1985 "3rd World" debt soars
				1986 Oil prices plunge
				1986 Economies improve
				1986 South African unrest
				1986 Central American wars
				1986 Space shuttle explodes

APPENDIX G

DR. SUN YIXIAN'S THREE PRINCIPLES OF THE PEOPLE *

(San Min Chu I)

The Principle of Nationalism. What are the *San Min* Principles? They are, by the simplest definition, the principles of our nation's salvation. What is a principle? It is an idea, a faith, and a power. When men begin to study into the heart of a problem, an idea generally develops first; as the idea becomes clearer, a faith arises; and out of the faith a power is born. . . .

What is the Principle of Nationalism? Looking back over the history of China's social life and customs, I would say briefly that the Principle of Nationalism is equivalent to the "doctrine of the state." The Chinese people have shown the greatest loyalty to family and clan with the result that in China there have been family-ism and clan-ism but not real nationalism. Foreign observers say that the Chinese are like a sheet of loose sand. Why? Simply because our people have shown loyalty to family and clan but not to the nation—there has been no nationalism. The family and the clan have been powerful unifying forces; again and again Chinese have sacrificed themselves, their families, their lives in defense of their clan. . . . But for the nation there has never been an instance of the supreme spirit of sacrifice. The unity of the Chinese people has stopped short at the clan and has not extended to the nation. . . .

Considering the law of survival of ancient and modern races, if we want to save China and to preserve the Chinese race, we must certainly promote Nationalism to make this principle luminous for China's salvation, we must first understand it clearly. The Chinese race totals four hundred million people. . . . For the most part, the Chinese people are of the Han or Chinese race with common blood, common language, common religion, and common customs—a single, pure race. . . . But the Chinese people have only family and clan groups; there is no national spirit. Consequently, in spite of four hundred million people gathered together in one China, we are in fact but a sheet of loose sand. We are the poorest and weakest state in the world, occupying the lowest position in international affairs; the rest of mankind is the carving knife and the serving dish, while we are the fish and the meat. Our position now is extremely perilous; if we

---

* Translated by Frank W. Price; edited by L. T. Chen, Ministry of Information of the Republic of China, Chungking, China. 1943.

do not earnestly promote nationalism and weld together our four hundred millions into a strong nation, we face a tragedy—the loss of our country and the destruction of our race. To ward off this danger, we must espouse Nationalism and employ the national spirit to save the country. . . .

China has been under the political domination of the West for a century. . . . During the past century China has lost a huge amount of territory. . . . The Powers' attitude was formerly something like this: since China would never awaken and could not govern herself, they would occupy the points along the coast. . .as bases for "slicing up" China. Then when the Revolution broke out in China, the Powers realized that China still had life, and have given up, but only lately, the idea of partitioning her. When the Powers had their greedy eyes on China, some counter-revolutionists said that revolution would only invite dismemberment; but the result was just the opposite. The Revolution frustrated foreign designs upon China. Further back in history, our territorial losses were Korea, Taiwan (Formosa), the Pescadores, and such places, which, as a result of the Sino-Japanese War, were ceded to Japan. . . . Still further back in the century, we lost Burma and Annam. . . . Still earlier in the history of territorial losses were Amur and Ussuri river basins and before that the areas north of the Ili, Khokand, and Amur Rivers—all of which China gave over with folded hands to the foreigner without so much as a question. In addition there are those small countries which at one time paid tribute to China—the Loochoo Islands, Siam, Borneo, the Sulu Archipelago, Java, Ceylon, Nepal, Bhutan. . . .

After the Chinese Revolution, the Powers realized that it would be exceedingly difficult to dismember China by political force. A China which has learned how to revolt against the control of the Manchus would be sure some day to oppose the political control of the Powers. As this would put them in a difficult position, they are now reducing their political activities against China and are using economic pressure instead to keep us down. . . . They are still using imperialism to forward their economic designs, and economic oppression is more severe than imperialism or political oppression. . . . The common people are easily provoked by political oppression but are hardly conscious of economic oppression. China has already endured several tens of years of economic domination from the Powers, and nobody has felt irritated at all.

The result is that China is everywhere becoming a colony of the Powers. The people of the nation still think we are only a "semi-colony" and comfort themselves with this term, but in reality we are being crushed by the economic strength of the Powers to a greater degree than if we were a full colony. . . . China is not the colony of one nation but of all, and we are not the slaves of one country but of all. . . . So "semi-colony" is not the right designation for China; I think we ought to be called a "hypo-colony."

. . .Now we want to revive China's lost nationalism and use the strength of our four hundred millions to fight for mankind against injustice; this is our divine mission. The Powers are afraid that we will have such thoughts and are setting forth a specious doctrine. They are now advocating cosmopolitanism to inflame us, declaring that, as the civilization of the world advances and as mankind's vision enlarges, nationalism becomes too narrow, unsuited to the present age, and hence that we should espouse cosmopolitanism. In recent years some of China's youths, devotees of the new culture, have been opposing nationalism, led astray by this doctrine. But it is not a doctrine which wronged races should talk about. We, the wronged races, must first recover our position of national freedom and equality before we are fit to discuss cosmopolitanism. . . . We must understand that cosmopolitanism grows out of nationalism; if we want to extend cosmopolitanism we must first establish strongly our own nationalism. If nationalism cannot become strong, cosmopolitanism certainly cannot prosper. . . . If we discard nationalism and go and talk cosmopolitanism. . .we put the cart before the horse. . . .

. . .What means shall we use to revive our nationalism?. . . . Today I shall discuss two ways by which our nationalism can be revived: the first is by awakening our four hundred millions to see where we stand. . . . We must see clearly and then, of course, act. . . . What are the disasters which threaten us and from what direction do they come? They come from the Great Powers, and they are: first, political oppression; second, economic oppression; and third, the more rapid growth of population among the powers. These three disasters from without are already upon our heads, and our people are in a most dangerous situation. . . . If we still do not awake but go on in the way we have been going, even though the foreign diplomatists should sleep on their job, our nation would be ruined in ten years. . . . If we are to recover our lost nationalism, we must have some kind of group unity, large group unity. An easy and successful way to bring about the unity of a large group is to build upon the foundation of small united groups, and the small units we can build upon in China are the clan groups and also the family groups. . . . If we take the clans as our social units and, after improving their internal organization, join them together to form a state, our task will naturally be easier than that of foreign countries which make the individual the unit. Where the individual is the unit, there will be at least millions of units in a country, four hundred million in China; the knitting together of such a huge number of separate units would naturally be very difficult. . . . If three or four hundred clan groups will take thought for the state, there will be a way out for us and, no matter what nation we face, we will be able to resist. . . . If we want to restore our national standing, we must first revive our national spirit. If we want to revive our national spirit, we must fulfill two conditions. First, we must understand that we occupy today a most perilous position; and second, knowing our danger, we must utilize China's ancient social groups, the family and the clan, and consolidate them to form a great national body. When this is accomplished and we have the strength of four hundred millions united to fight, no matter how low our present position, we should be able to lift it up. So, to know and to unite are the two essentials for reviving our nationalism. . . . When our nationalism is revived, we can go a step farther and study how to restore our national standing. . . . If we want to restore our race's standing, besides uniting all into a great national body, we must. . .recover our ancient morality—then, and only then, can we plan how to attain again to the national position we once held.

As for China's old moral standards, they are not yet lost sight of by the people. . . . First come Loyalty and Filial Devotion, then Kindness and Love, then Faithfulness and Justice, then Harmony and Peace. The Chinese still speak of these ancient qualities of character. But since our domination by alien races and since the invasion of foreign culture which has spread its influence all over China, a group intoxicated with the new culture have begun to reject the old morality, saying that the former makes the latter unnecessary. They do not understand that we ought to preserve what is good in our past and throw away only the bad. . . . We must revive not only our old morality but also our old learning. . . . If we want to regain our national spirit we must reawaken the learning as well as the moral ideals which we once possessed. . . . But even if we succeed in reviving our ancient morality, learning, and powers, we will still not be able, in this modern world, to advance China to a first place among the nations. . . . We will still need to learn the strong points of Europe and America before we can progress at an equal rate with them. Unless we do study the best from foreign countries, we will go backward. . . .

If we want to learn from the West, we will have to catch up with the advance line and not chase from behind. In the study of science, for instance, this will mean the saving of two hundred years. We are in such a position today that if we should still slumber on, not commence to struggle, and not know how to restore the standing of our state, our country would be lost and our race wiped out forever. But now that we know how, we ought to follow the world currents and study the best features of Western nations; we certainly should go beyond other countries in what we study and cause the "last to be first." Although we went backward for many centuries, yet now it should take us but a few years to catch up with the rest of the world. Japan is a good example. Her culture was formerly copied from China and was much inferior to ours, but recently Japan has studied only European and American civilization, and within a few decades has become one of the world's great powers. I do not think that our intellectual powers are below those of the Japanese, and it should be easier for us now than for Japan to learn from the West. So the next ten years is a critical period for us; if we can come to life as the Japanese did and all put forth a very sincere effort to elevate the standing of our nation, within a decade we should be able to get rid of foreign political and economic control, the pressure of foreign population increase, and all the various calamities that are now upon us. . . .

After China reaches that place, what then? A common phrase in ancient China was, "Rescue the weak, lift up the fallen." Because of this noble policy, China prospered for thousands of years, and Annam, Burma, Korea, Siam, and other small states were able to maintain their independence. As European influence spread over the East, Annam was overthrown by France, Burma by Great Britain, Korea by Japan. If we want China to rise to power, we must not only restore our national standing, but we must also assume a great responsibility towards the world. If China cannot assume that responsibility, she will be a great disadvantage, not an advantage to the world, no matter how strong she may be. The road which the Great Powers are traveling today means the destruction of other states; if China, when she become strong, wants to crush other countries, copy the Powers' imperialism, and go their road, we will just be following in their tracks. Only if we "rescue the weak and lift up the fallen" will we be carrying out the divine obligation of our nation. . . .

The Principle of Democracy. What is the People's Sovereignty? In order to define this term we must first understand what a "people" is. Any unified and organized body of men is called a "people." What is "sovereignty?" It is power and authority extended to the area of the state. . . . The power to execute orders and to regulate public conduct is called "sovereignty," and when "people" and "sovereignty" are linked together, we have the political power of the people. To understand "political power" we must know what government is. . . . Briefly, government is a thing of the people and by the people; it is control of the affairs of all the people. The power of control is political sovereignty, and where the people control the government we speak of the "people's sovereignty."

. . .The essential question is this: Is China today ripe for democracy? There are some who say that the standards of the Chinese people are too low and that they are not ready for popular government. . . . But if we base our judgment upon the intelligence and the ability of the Chinese people, we come to the conclusion that the sovereignty of the people would be far more suitable for us. Confucius and Mencius two thousand years ago spoke for people's rights. Confucius said, "When the Great Doctrine prevails, all under heaven will work for the common good." He was pleading for a free and fraternal world in which the people would rule. . . . Mencius said, "Most precious are the people; next come the spirits of land and grain; and last, the princes." Again: "Heaven sees as the people see, Heaven hears as the people hear," and "I have heard of the punishment of the tyrant Chou, but never of the assassination of a sovereign." He, in his age, already saw that kings were not absolutely necessary and would not last forever, so he called those who brought happiness to the people holy monarchs, but those who were cruel and unprincipled he called individualists whom all should oppose. Thus China, more than two millenniums ago had already considered the idea of democracy, but at that time she could not put it into operation. Democracy was then what foreigners called a Utopia, an ideal which could not be immediately realized. . . .

Thirty years ago. . .we fellow revolutionists firmly resolved that, if we wanted China to be strong and our revolution to be effective, we must espouse the cause of democracy. But in those days merely to make such a suggestion stirred up opposition not only from Chinese but also from foreigners. . . . Chinese who opposed democracy used to ask what strength there was in our Revolutionary Party to be able to overthrow the Manchu emperor. But in 1911 he fell with one push, another victim of the world tide. This world tendency is like the Yangtze River, which makes crooks and turns, sometimes to the north and sometimes to the south, but in the end flows eastward and nothing can stop it. Just so the life of mankind has flowed from theocracy on to autocracy and from autocracy now on to democracy, and there is no way to stem the current. . . .

Today I am speaking about the people's sovereignty and I want you all to understand clearly what it really means. Unless we do understand clearly, we can never get rid of imperial ambitions among us. . . . When we have a real republic, who will be king? The people, our four hundred millions, will be king. This will prevent everybody from struggling for power and will reduce the war evil in China. . . .

What are the newest discoveries in the way of applying democracy? First, there is the suffrage, and it is the only method in operation throughout the so-called modern democracies. Is this one form of popular sovereignty enough in government? This one power by itself may be compared to the early machines which could move forward only but not back. The second of the newly discovered methods is the power of recall. With this power, the people can pull the machine back. These two rights, the right to elect and the right to recall, give the people control over their officials and enable them to put all government officials in their positions or to move them out of their positions. The coming and going of officials follows the free will of the people just as modern machines move to and fro by the free action of the engine. Another important thing in a state, in addition to officials, is law. . . . What power must the people possess in order to control the laws? If all the people think that a certain law would be of great advantage to them, they should have the power to decide upon this law and turn it over to the government for execution. This third kind of popular power is called the initiative. If everybody thinks that an old law is not beneficial to the people, they should have the power to amend it and to ask the government to administer the revised law and do away with the old law. This is called the referendum and is a fourth form of popular sovereignty. Only when the people have these four powers can we say that there is a full measure of democracy, and only where these four powers are effectively applied can we say that there is thorough going, direct, popular sovereignty. . . . Only then can we speak of government by all the people. . . .

The government's own power to transact business may be called the power to work, to work on behalf of the people. If the people are very powerful, whether the government can work or not and what kind of work it does will depend entirely upon the will of the people. If the government is very powerful, as soon as it starts work it can display great strength, and whenever the people want it to stop, it will have to stop. In a nutshell, if the people are really to have direct control over the power of government, they must be able to command at any time the actions of the government. . . . The political power. . . . is in the hands of the people, the administrative power. . . . is in the hands of the government. The people control the government through the suffrage, the recall, the initiative, and the referendum; the government works for the people through its legislative, judicial, executive, civil examination, and censorship departments. With these nine powers in operation and preserving a balance, the problem of democracy will truly be solved and the government will have a definite course to follow. . . .

If we now want to combine the best from China and the best from other countries and guard against all kinds of abuse in the future, we must take the three Western governmental powers—the executive, legislative, and judicial—add to them the old Chinese powers of examination and censorship and make a finished wall, a quintuple-power government. Such a government will be the most complete and the finest in the world, and a state with such a government will indeed be of the people, by the people, and for the people. . . .

The Principle of Livelihood. . . . The Principle of Livelihood is socialism, it is communism, it is Utopianism. But this principle cannot be explained by a few definitions. . . . The problem of livelihood is now rising like a tide in every country. Yet the problem is comparatively new, with a history of not much over a century. What has caused the sudden emergence of this question in the last hundred years? Briefly, the rapid progress of material civilization all over the world, the great development of industry and the sudden increase in the productive power of the human race. Candidly speaking, the problem arose with the invention of machinery and with the gradual substitution of natural power for human labor in the most civilized nations. . . . Since the invention of machinery, therefore, the world has undergone a revolution in production. Machinery has usurped the place of human labor, and men who possessed machinery have taken wealth away from those who did not have machinery. . . .

If the industries are carried on by the state, the rights and privileges which they bring will be enjoyed by all the people. The people of the whole nation will then have a share in the profits of capital and will not be injured by capital, as in foreign countries, where large capital is in private hands. This concentration of capital among a few private individuals means that a large number of people suffer; class war then breaks out as an attempt to eliminate the suffering. In the solution of the social problem, we have the same object in view as that in foreign countries: to make everybody contented and happy, free from the suffering caused by the unequal distribution of wealth and property. . . .

Our Three Principles of the People mean government "of the people, by the people, and for the people"—that is, a state belonging to all the people, a government controlled by all the people, and rights and benefits for the enjoyment of all the people. If this is true, the people will not only have a communistic share in the state production, but they will have a share in everything. When the people share everything in the state, then will we truly reach the goal of the *Min-sheng* Principle, which is Confucius' hope of a "great commonwealth."

APPENDIX G

DR. SUN YIXIAN'S THREE PRINCIPLES OF THE PEOPLE *

(San Min Chu I)

The Principle of Nationalism. What are the *San Min* Principles? They are, by the simplest definition, the principles of our nation's salvation. What is a principle? It is an idea, a faith, and a power. When men begin to study into the heart of a problem, an idea generally develops first; as the idea becomes clearer, a faith arises; and out of the faith a power is born. . . .

What is the Principle of Nationalism? Looking back over the history of China's social life and customs, I would say briefly that the Principle of Nationalism is equivalent to the "doctrine of the state." The Chinese people have shown the greatest loyalty to family and clan with the result that in China there have been family-ism and clan-ism but not real nationalism. Foreign observers say that the Chinese are like a sheet of loose sand. Why? Simply because our people have shown loyalty to family and clan but not to the nation—there has been no nationalism. The family and the clan have been powerful unifying forces; again and again Chinese have sacrificed themselves, their families, their lives in defense of their clan. . . . But for the nation there has never been an instance of the supreme spirit of sacrifice. The unity of the Chinese people has stopped short at the clan and has not extended to the nation. . . .

Considering the law of survival of ancient and modern races, if we want to save China and to preserve the Chinese race, we must certainly promote Nationalism to make this principle luminous for China's salvation, we must first understand it clearly. The Chinese race totals four hundred million people. . . . For the most part, the Chinese people are of the Han or Chinese race with common blood, common language, common religion, and common customs—a single, pure race. . . . But the Chinese people have only family and clan groups; there is no national spirit. Consequently, in spite of four hundred million people gathered together in one China, we are in fact but a sheet of loose sand. We are the poorest and weakest state in the world, occupying the lowest position in international affairs; the rest of mankind is the carving knife and the serving dish, while we are the fish and the meat. Our position now is extremely perilous; if we

* Translated by Frank W. Price; edited by L. T. Chen, Ministry of Information of the Republic of China, Chungking, China. 1943.

do not earnestly promote nationalism and weld together our four hundred millions into a strong nation, we face a tragedy—the loss of our country and the destruction of our race. To ward off this danger, we must espouse Nationalism and employ the national spirit to save the country. . . .

China has been under the political domination of the West for a century. . . . During the past century China has lost a huge amount of territory. . . . The Powers' attitude was formerly something like this: since China would never awaken and could not govern herself, they would occupy the points along the coast. . .as bases for "slicing up" China. Then when the Revolution broke out in China, the Powers realized that China still had life, and have given up, but only lately, the idea of partitioning her. When the Powers had their greedy eyes on China, some counter-revolutionists said that revolution would only invite dismemberment; but the result was just the opposite. The Revolution frustrated foreign designs upon China. Further back in history, our territorial losses were Korea, Taiwan (Formosa), the Pescadores, and such places, which, as a result of the Sino-Japanese War, were ceded to Japan. . . . Still further back in the century, we lost Burma and Annam. . . . Still earlier in the history of territorial losses were Amur and Ussuri river basins and before that the areas north of the Ili, Khokand, and Amur Rivers—all of which China gave over with folded hands to the foreigner without so much as a question. In addition there are those small countries which at one time paid tribute to China—the Loochoo Islands, Siam, Borneo, the Sulu Archipelago, Java, Ceylon, Nepal, Bhutan. . . .

After the Chinese Revolution, the Powers realized that it would be exceedingly difficult to dismember China by political force. A China which has learned how to revolt against the control of the Manchus would be sure some day to oppose the political control of the Powers. As this would put them in a difficult position, they are now reducing their political activities against China and are using economic pressure instead to keep us down. . . . They are still using imperialism to forward their economic designs, and economic oppression is more severe than imperialism or political oppression. . . . The common people are easily provoked by political oppression but are hardly conscious of economic oppression. China has already endured several tens of years of economic domination from the Powers, and nobody has felt irritated at all.

The result is that China is everywhere becoming a colony of the Powers. The people of the nation still think we are only a "semi-colony" and comfort themselves with this term, but in reality we are being crushed by the economic strength of the Powers to a greater degree than if we were a full colony. . . . China is not the

colony of one nation but of all, and we are not the slaves of one
country but of all. . . . So "semi-colony" is not the right designation
for China; I think we ought to be called a "hypo-colony."

. . .Now we want to revive China's lost nationalism and use the
strength of our four hundred millions to fight for mankind against injustice; this is our divine mission. The Powers are afraid that we will
have such thoughts and are setting forth a specious doctrine. They are
now advocating cosmopolitanism to inflame us, declaring that, as the
civilization of the world advances and as mankind's vision enlarges,
nationalism becomes too narrow, unsuited to the present age, and
hence that we should espouse cosmopolitanism. In recent years some
of China's youths, devotees of the new culture, have been opposing
nationalism, led astray by this doctrine. But it is not a doctrine which
wronged races should talk about. We, the wronged races, must first
recover our position of national freedom and equality before we are
fit to discuss cosmopolitanism. . . . We must understand that
cosmopolitanism grows out of nationalism; if we want to extend
cosmopolitanism we must first establish strongly our own
nationalism. If nationalism cannot become strong, cosmopolitanism
certainly cannot prosper. . . . If we discard nationalism and go and
talk cosmopolitanism. . .we put the cart before the horse. . . .

. . .What means shall we use to revive our nationalism?. . . . Today
I shall discuss two ways by which our nationalism can be revived: the
first is by awakening our four hundred millions to see where we
stand. . . . We must see clearly and then, of course, act. . . . What are
the disasters which threaten us and from what direction do they
come? They come from the Great Powers, and they are: first,
political oppression; second, economic oppression; and third, the
more rapid growth of population among the powers. These three
disasters from without are already upon our heads, and our people
are in a most dangerous situation. . . . If we still do not awake but go
on in the way we have been going, even though the foreign
diplomatists should sleep on their job, our nation would be ruined in
ten years. . . . If we are to recover our lost nationalism, we must have
some kind of group unity, large group unity. An easy and successful
way to bring about the unity of a large group is to build upon the
foundation of small united groups, and the small units we can build
upon in China are the clan groups and also the family groups. . . . If
we take the clans as our social units and, after improving their
internal organization, join them together to form a state, our task will
naturally be easier than that of foreign countries which make the
individual the unit. Where the individual is the unit, there will be at
least millions of units in a country, four hundred million in China;
the knitting together of such a huge number of separate units would

naturally be very difficult. . . . If three or four hundred clan groups will take thought for the state, there will be a way out for us and, no matter what nation we face, we will be able to resist. . . . If we want to restore our national standing, we must first revive our national spirit. If we want to revive our national spirit, we must fulfill two conditions. First, we must understand that we occupy today a most perilous position; and second, knowing our danger, we must utilize China's ancient social groups, the family and the clan, and consolidate them to form a great national body. When this is accomplished and we have the strength of four hundred millions united to fight, no matter how low our present position, we should be able to lift it up. So, to know and to unite are the two essentials for reviving our nationalism. . . . When our nationalism is revived, we can go a step farther and study how to restore our national standing. . . . If we want to restore our race's standing, besides uniting all into a great national body, we must. . .recover our ancient morality—then, and only then, can we plan how to attain again to the national position we once held.

As for China's old moral standards, they are not yet lost sight of by the people. . . . First come Loyalty and Filial Devotion, then Kindness and Love, then Faithfulness and Justice, then Harmony and Peace. The Chinese still speak of these ancient qualities of character. But since our domination by alien races and since the invasion of foreign culture which has spread its influence all over China, a group intoxicated with the new culture have begun to reject the old morality, saying that the former makes the latter unnecessary. They do not understand that we ought to preserve what is good in our past and throw away only the bad. . . . We must revive not only our old morality but also our old learning. . . . If we want to regain our national spirit we must reawaken the learning as well as the moral ideals which we once possessed. . . . But even if we succeed in reviving our ancient morality, learning, and powers, we will still not be able, in this modern world, to advance China to a first place among the nations. . . . We will still need to learn the strong points of Europe and America before we can progress at an equal rate with them. Unless we do study the best from foreign countries, we will go backward. . . .

If we want to learn from the West, we will have to catch up with the advance line and not chase from behind. In the study of science, for instance, this will mean the saving of two hundred years. We are in such a position today that if we should still slumber on, not commence to struggle, and not know how to restore the standing of our state, our country would be lost and our race wiped out forever. But now that we know how, we ought to follow the world currents and study the best features of Western nations; we certainly should go beyond other countries in what we study and cause the "last to be first." Although we went backward for many centuries, yet now it should take us but a few years to catch up with the rest of the world. Japan is a good example. Her culture was formerly copied from China and was much inferior to ours, but recently Japan has studied only European and American civilization, and within a few decades has become one of the world's great powers. I do not think that our intellectual powers are below those of the Japanese, and it should be easier for us now than for Japan to learn from the West. So the next ten years is a critical period for us; if we can come to life as the Japanese did and all put forth a very sincere effort to elevate the standing of our nation, within a decade we should be able to get rid of foreign political and economic control, the pressure of foreign population increase, and all the various calamities that are now upon us. . . .

After China reaches that place, what then? A common phrase in ancient China was, "Rescue the weak, lift up the fallen." Because of this noble policy, China prospered for thousands of years, and Annam, Burma, Korea, Siam, and other small states were able to maintain their independence. As European influence spread over the East, Annam was overthrown by France, Burma by Great Britain, Korea by Japan. If we want China to rise to power, we must not only restore our national standing, but we must also assume a great responsibility towards the world. If China cannot assume that responsibility, she will be a great disadvantage, not an advantage to the world, no matter how strong she may be. The road which the Great Powers are traveling today means the destruction of other states; if China, when she become strong, wants to crush other countries, copy the Powers' imperialism, and go their road, we will just be following in their tracks. Only if we "rescue the weak and lift up the fallen" will we be carrying out the divine obligation of our nation. . . .

The Principle of Democracy. What is the People's Sovereignty? In order to define this term we must first understand what a "people" is. Any unified and organized body of men is called a "people." What is "sovereignty?" It is power and authority extended to the area of the state. . . . The power to execute orders and to regulate public conduct is called "sovereignty," and when "people" and "sovereignty" are linked together, we have the political power of the people. To understand "political power" we must know what government is. . . . Briefly, government is a thing of the people and by the people; it is control of the affairs of all the people. The power of control is political sovereignty, and where the people control the government we speak of the "people's sovereignty."

. . .The essential question is this: Is China today ripe for democracy? There are some who say that the standards of the Chinese people are too low and that they are not ready for popular government. . . . But if we base our judgment upon the intelligence and the ability of the Chinese people, we come to the conclusion that the sovereignty of the people would be far more suitable for us. Confucius and Mencius two thousand years ago spoke for people's rights. Confucius said, "When the Great Doctrine prevails, all under heaven will work for the common good." He was pleading for a free and fraternal world in which the people would rule. . . . Mencius said, "Most precious are the people; next come the spirits of land and grain; and last, the princes." Again: "Heaven sees as the people see, Heaven hears as the people hear," and "I have heard of the punishment of the tyrant Chou, but never of the assassination of a sovereign." He, in his age, already saw that kings were not absolutely necessary and would not last forever, so he called those who brought happiness to the people holy monarchs, but those who were cruel and unprincipled he called individualists whom all should oppose. Thus China, more than two millenniums ago had already considered the idea of democracy, but at that time she could not put it into operation. Democracy was then what foreigners called a Utopia, an ideal which could not be immediately realized. . . .

Thirty years ago. . .we fellow revolutionists firmly resolved that, if we wanted China to be strong and our revolution to be effective, we must espouse the cause of democracy. But in those days merely to make such a suggestion stirred up opposition not only from Chinese but also from foreigners. . . . Chinese who opposed democracy used to ask what strength there was in our Revolutionary Party to be able to overthrow the Manchu emperor. But in 1911 he fell with one push, another victim of the world tide. This world tendency is like the Yangtze River, which makes crooks and turns, sometimes to the north and sometimes to the south, but in the end flows eastward and nothing can stop it. Just so the life of mankind has flowed from theocracy on to autocracy and from autocracy now on to democracy, and there is no way to stem the current. . . .

Today I am speaking about the people's sovereignty and I want you all to understand clearly what it really means. Unless we do understand clearly, we can never get rid of imperial ambitions among us. . . . When we have a real republic, who will be king? The people, our four hundred millions, will be king. This will prevent everybody from struggling for power and will reduce the war evil in China. . . .

What are the newest discoveries in the way of applying democracy? First, there is the suffrage, and it is the only method in operation throughout the so-called modern democracies. Is this one form of popular sovereignty enough in government? This one power by itself may be compared to the early machines which could move forward only but not back. The second of the newly discovered methods is the power of recall. With this power, the people can pull the machine back. These two rights, the right to elect and the right to recall, give the people control over their officials and enable them to put all government officials in their positions or to move them out of their positions. The coming and going of officials follows the free will of the people just as modern machines move to and fro by the free action of the engine. Another important thing in a state, in addition to officials, is law. . . . What power must the people possess in order to control the laws? If all the people think that a certain law would be of great advantage to them, they should have the power to decide upon this law and turn it over to the government for execution. This third kind of popular power is called the initiative. If everybody thinks that an old law is not beneficial to the people, they should have the power to amend it and to ask the government to administer the revised law and do away with the old law. This is called the referendum and is a fourth form of popular sovereignty. Only when the people have these four powers can we say that there is a full measure of democracy, and only where these four powers are effectively applied can we say that there is thorough going, direct, popular sovereignty. . . . Only then can we speak of government by all the people. . . .

The government's own power to transact business may be called the power to work, to work on behalf of the people. If the people are very powerful, whether the government can work or not and what kind of work it does will depend entirely upon the will of the people. If the government is very powerful, as soon as it starts work it can display great strength, and whenever the people want it to stop, it will have to stop. In a nutshell, if the people are really to have direct control over the power of government, they must be able to command at any time the actions of the government. . . . The political power. . . . is in the hands of the people, the administrative power. . . . is in the hands of the government. The people control the government through the suffrage, the recall, the initiative, and the referendum; the government works for the people through its legislative, judicial, executive, civil examination, and censorship departments. With these nine powers in operation and preserving a balance, the problem of democracy will truly be solved and the government will have a definite course to follow. . . .

If we now want to combine the best from China and the best from other countries and guard against all kinds of abuse in the future, we must take the three Western governmental powers—the executive, legislative, and judicial—add to them the old Chinese powers of examination and censorship and make a finished wall, a quintuple-power government. Such a government will be the most complete and the finest in the world, and a state with such a government will indeed be of the people, by the people, and for the people. . . .

The Principle of Livelihood. . . . The Principle of Livelihood is socialism, it is communism, it is Utopianism. But this principle cannot be explained by a few definitions. . . . The problem of livelihood is now rising like a tide in every country. Yet the problem is comparatively new, with a history of not much over a century. What has caused the sudden emergence of this question in the last hundred years? Briefly, the rapid progress of material civilization all over the world, the great development of industry and the sudden increase in the productive power of the human race. Candidly speaking, the problem arose with the invention of machinery and with the gradual substitution of natural power for human labor in the most civilized nations. . . . Since the invention of machinery, therefore, the world has undergone a revolution in production. Machinery has usurped the place of human labor, and men who possessed machinery have taken wealth away from those who did not have machinery. . . .

If the industries are carried on by the state, the rights and privileges which they bring will be enjoyed by all the people. The people of the whole nation will then have a share in the profits of capital and will not be injured by capital, as in foreign countries, where large capital is in private hands. This concentration of capital among a few private individuals means that a large number of people suffer; class war then breaks out as an attempt to eliminate the suffering. In the solution of the social problem, we have the same object in view as that in foreign countries: to make everybody contented and happy, free from the suffering caused by the unequal distribution of wealth and property. . . .

Our Three Principles of the People mean government "of the people, by the people, and for the people"—that is, a state belonging to all the people, a government controlled by all the people, and rights and benefits for the enjoyment of all the people. If this is true, the people will not only have a communistic share in the state production, but they will have a share in everything. When the people share everything in the state, then will we truly reach the goal of the *Min-sheng* Principle, which is Confucius' hope of a "great commonwealth."

APPENDIX H

ON THE PEOPLE'S DEMOCRATIC DICTATORSHIP*

By Mao Zedong

The first of July marks the fact that the Communist Party of China has already lived through twenty-eight years. Like a man, a political party has its childhood, youth, manhood and old age. The Communist Party of China is no longer a child or a lad in his teens but has become an adult. When a man reaches old age, he will die; the same is true of a party. When classes disappear, all instruments of class struggle—parties and the state machinery—will lose their function, cease to be necessary, therefore, gradually wither away and end their historical mission; and human society will move to a higher stage. We are the opposite of the political parties of the bourgeoisie. They are afraid to speak of the extinction of classes, state power and parties. We, on the contrary, declare openly that we are striving hard to create the very conditions which will bring about their extinction. The leadership of the Communist Party and the state power of the people's dictatorship are such conditions. Anyone who does not recognize this truth is no communist. Young comrades who have not studied Marxism-Leninism and have only recently joined the Party may not yet understand the truth. They must understand it—only then can they have a correct world outlook. They must understand that the road to the abolition of classes, to the abolition of state power and to the abolition of parties is the road that all mankind must take; it is only a question of time and conditions. Communists the world over are wiser than the bourgeoisie. They understand the laws governing the existence and development of things, they understand dialectics, and they can see farther. The bourgeoisie does not welcome this truth because it does not want to be overthrown. To be overthrown is painful. . . But for the working class, the laboring people and the Communist Party the question is not one of being overthrown, but of working hard to create the conditions in which classes, state power and political parties will die out very naturally and mankind will enter the realm of Great Harmony. . . .

* In commemoration of the twenty-eighth anniversary of the Communist Party of China, June 30, 1949; from the *Selected Works of Mao Tse-tung*, Volume IV, Foreign Language Press, 1961, Peking, China.

As everyone knows, our Party passed through these twenty-eight years not in peace but amid hardships, for we had to fight enemies, both foreign and domestic, both inside and outside the Party. We thank Marx, Engels, Lenin and Stalin for giving us a weapon. This weapon is not a machine-gun, but Marxism-Leninism.

...It was through the Russians that the Chinese found Marxism. Before the October Revolution, the Chinese were not only ignorant of Lenin and Stalin, they did not even know of Marx and Engels. The salvos of the October Revolution brought us Marxism-Leninism. The October Revolution helped progressives in China, as throughout the world, to adopt the proletarian world outlook as the instrument for studying a nation's destiny and considering anew their own problems. Follow the path of the Russians—that was their conclusion. In 1919, the May 4th Movement took place in China. In 1921, the Communist Party of China was founded. Sun Yat-sen, in the depth of despair, came across the October Revolution and the Communist Party of China. He welcomed the October Revolution, welcomed Russian help to the Chinese and welcomed cooperation with the Communist Party of China. Then Sun Yat-sen died and Chiang Kai-shek rose to power. Over a long period of twenty-two years. Chiang Kai-shek dragged China into ever more hopeless straits. In this period, during the anti-fascist Second World War in which the Soviet Union was the main force, three big imperialist powers were knocked out, while two others were weakened. In the whole world, only one big imperialist power, the United States of America, remained uninjured. But the United States faced a grave domestic crisis. It wanted to enslave the whole world; it supplied arms to help Chiang Kai-shek slaughter several million of Chinese. Under the leadership of the Communist Party of China, the Chinese people, after driving out Japanese imperialism, waged the People's War of Liberation for three years and have basically won victory....

Twenty-four years have passed since Sun Yat-sen's death, and the Chinese revolution, led by the Communist Party of China, has made tremendous advances both in theory and practice and has radically changed the face of China. Up to now the principal and fundamental experience the Chinese people have gained is twofold:

(1) Internally, arouse the masses of the people. That is, unite the working class, the peasantry, the urban petty bourgeoisie and the national bourgeoisie, form a domestic united front under the leadership of the working class, and advance from this to the establishment of a state which is a people's democratic dictatorship under the leadership of the working class and based on the alliance of workers and peasants.

(2) Externally, united in a common struggle with those nations of

the world which treat us as equals and unite with the peoples of all countries. That is, ally ourselves with the Soviet Union, with the People's Democracies and with the proletariat and the broad masses of the people in all other countries, and form an international united front.

"You are leaning to one side." Exactly. The forty-years' experience of Sun Yat-sen and the twenty-eight years' experience of the Communist Party have taught us to lean to one side, and we are firmly convinced that in order to win victory and consolidate it we must lean to one side. . . . Sitting on the fence will not do, nor is there a third road. . . .

"You are too irritating." We are talking about how to deal with domestic and foreign reactionaries, the imperialists and their running dogs, not about how to deal with anyone else. With regard to such reactionaries, the question of irritating them or not does not arise. Irritated or not irritated, they will remain the same because they are reactionaries. Only if we draw a clear line between reactionaries and revolutionaries, expose the intrigues and plots of the reactionaries, arouse the vigilance and attention of the revolutionary ranks, heighten our will to fight and crush the enemy's arrogance can we isolate the reactionaries, vanquish them or supersede them. We must not show the slightest timidity before a wild beast. We must learn from Wu Sung on the Chingyang Ridge. As Wu Sung saw it, the tiger on Chingyang Ridge was a man-eater, whether irritated or not. Either kill the tiger or be eaten by him—one or the other.

"We want to do business." Quite right, business will be done. We are against no one except the domestic and foreign reactionaries who hinder us from doing business. . . . When we have beaten the internal and external reactionaries by uniting all domestic and international forces, we shall be able to do business and establish diplomatic relations with all foreign countries on the basis of equality, mutual benefit and mutual respect for territorial integrity and sovereignty.

"Victory is possible even without international help." This is a mistaken idea. In the epoch in which imperialism exists, it is impossible for a genuine people's revolution to win victory in any country without various forms of help from the international revolutionary forces, and even if victory were won, it could not be consolidated. . . . Internationally, we belong to the side of the anti-imperialist front headed by the Soviet Union, and so we can turn only to this side for genuine and friendly help, not to the side of the imperialist front.

"You are dictatorial." My dear sirs, you are right, that is just what we are. All of the experience the Chinese people have accumulated through several decades teaches us to enforce the people's democratic dictatorship, that is, to deprive the reactionaries of the right to speak and let the people alone have that right.

Who are the people? At the present stage in China, they are the
working class, the peasantry, the urban petty bourgeoisie and the
national bourgeoisie. These classes, led by the working class and the
Communist Party, united to form their own state and elect their own
government; they enforce their dictatorship over the running dogs of
imperialism—the landlord class and bureaucratic-bourgeoisie, as
well as the representatives of those classes, the Kuomintang
reactionaries and their accomplices—suppress them, ask them only to
behave themselves and not to be unruly in word or deed. If they speak
or act in an unruly way, they will be promptly stopped and punished.
Democracy is practiced within the ranks of the people, who enjoy the
rights of freedom of speech, assembly, association and so on. The
right to vote belongs only to the people, not to the reactionaries. The
combination of these two aspects, democracy for the people and
dictatorship over the reactionaries, is the people's democratic
dictatorship. . . .

"Don't you want to abolish state power?" Yes, we do, but not right
now; we cannot do it yet. Why? Because imperialism still exists,
because domestic reaction still exists, because classes still exist in our
country. Our present task is to strengthen the people's state
apparatus—mainly the people's army, the people's police and the
people's courts—in order to consolidate national defense and protect
the people's interests. Given this condition, China can develop
steadily, under the leadership of the working class and the
Communist Party, from an agricultural into an industrial country
and from a new-democratic into a socialist and communist society,
can abolish classes and realize the Great Harmony. The state
apparatus, including the army, the police and the courts, is the
instrument by which one class oppresses another. It is an instrument
for the oppression of antagonistic classes; it is violence and not
"benevolence." "You are not benevolent!" Quite so. We definitely do
not apply a policy of benevolence to the reactionaries and towards the
reactionary activities of the reactionary classes. Our policy of
benevolence is applied only within the ranks of the people, not
beyond them to the reactionaries or to the reactionary activities of
reactionary classes.

The people's state protects the people. Only when the people have
such a state can they educate and remould themselves on a
countrywide scale by democratic methods and, with everyone taking
part, shake off the influence of domestic and foreign reactionaries....
rid themselves of the bad habits and ideas acquired in the old society,
not allow themselves to be led astray by the reactionaries, and
continue to advance—to advance towards a socialist and communist
society.

Here, the method we employ is democratic, the method of persuasion, not of compulsion. When anyone among the people breaks the law, he too should be punished, imprisoned or even sentenced to death; but this is a matter of a few individual cases, and it differs in principle from the dictatorship exercised over the reactionaries as a class.

As for the members of the reactionary classes and individual reactionaries, so long as they do not rebel, sabotage or create trouble after their political power has been overthrown, land and work will be given to them as well in order to allow them to live and remould themselves through labor into new people. If they are not willing to work, the people's state will compel them to work. Propaganda and educational work will be done among them, too, and will be done moreover, with as much care and thoroughness as among the captured army officers in the past. This, too, may be called a "policy of benevolence" if you like, but it is imposed by us on the members of the enemy classes and cannot be mentioned in the same breath with the work of self-education which we carry on within the ranks of the revolutionary people.

Such remoulding of members of the reactionary classes can be accomplished only by a state of the people's democratic dictatorship under the leadership of the Communist Party. When it is well done, China's major exploiting classes, the landlord class and the bureaucratic bourgeoisie (the monopoly capitalist class), will be eliminated for good. There remain the national bourgeoisie; at the present stage, we can already do a good deal of suitable educational work with many of them. When the time comes to realize socialism, that is, to nationalize private enterprise, we shall carry the work of educating and remoulding them a step further. The people have a powerful state apparatus in their hands—there is no need to fear rebellion by the national bourgeoisie.

The serious problem is the education of the peasantry. The peasant economy is scattered, and the socialization of agriculture, judging by the Soviet Union's experience, will require a long time and painstaking work. Without socialization of agriculture, there can be no complete, consolidated socialism. The steps to socialize agriculture must be co-ordinated with the development of a powerful industry having state enterprise as its backbone. The state of the people's democratic dictatorship must systematically solve the problem of industrialization. . . .

To sum up our experience and concentrate it into one point, it is: the people's democratic dictatorship under the leadership of the working class (through the Communist Party) and based upon the alliance of workers and peasants. This dictatorship must unite as one with the international revolutionary forces. This is our formula, our principal experience, our main program. . . .

APPENDIX I

THE TIANANMEN SQUARE MASSACRE

The Student View

Wu'er Kaixi was a 21-year-old student at Beijing University who helped to organize the Democracy Movement there in 1989. Threatened with execution after the Tiananmen Square Massacre, he fled to Hong Kong. These are excerpts from a press conference that he gave immediately after his escape:

All fellow countrymen who passionately love freedom and democracy, all the Chinese people: I am Wu'er Kaixi of Beijing Normal University, the head of the Beijing Independent Students Union. I am also one of the twenty-one "anti-revolutionary hoodlums" on the so-called wanted list issued by the illegal government. ...

I want simply to state that June 4 was the republic's darkest day. Our motherland was ill. In Tiananmen Square the reactionary warlords, the reactionary government, and the fascist army had Li Peng and Yang Shangkun as their chiefs and directors, with Deng Xiaoping as the executive producer behind the scene. Their ugly fascist faces were completely exposed in the early hours of June 4 in Tiananmen Square when they fired at thousands of peaceful pleading students and innocent peaceful residents of Beijing.

... that night one could have counted at least 1,000 people who died. During the whole bloody crackdown in Beijing there were more than 10,0000 casualties. ... We all know that in the few days after the massacre gunshots were heard at all hours in Beijing alone. Many people were killed in the streets. ... I myself saw many of my classmates and fellow countrymen being beaten by those merciless and inhuman beasts—the fascist army with their guns and clubs. In the ambulance that took me away I clearly saw a student who had been shot in the head and abdomen. The head was blasted apart, the abdomen still bubbled out blood.

We had been peacefully petitioning! We had all been peaceful! ... I have many classmates who were crushed by the tanks, totally flattened to death by the tanks in Tiananmen Square. Many of their corpses were scooped up one-by-one with metal shovels. (The soldiers used) plastic bags to bundle up those corpses of our students and then then pack them into (more) plastic bags; then they piled them together and cremated them.

A student at Quinghua University told me that one of his classmates held hands with another two and stood up against a tank. These three were all shot, and the tank still ran over them.

I think they announced that our Beijing Independent Students Union is illegal. We are not illegal. We are completely legal. . . . They are illegal. This government no longer can represent the people. A government that can no longer represent the people and fires at the people is naturally an illegal government. . . .

The people's hearts may feel discouraged and temporarily find things difficult. However, they will never have a reason for ultimate failure. The history of these few days tells us that this is entirely a people's movement and an anti-government movement. This government, I predict, (will fall) at the earliest in half a year—seven or eight months—and at the most three years. . . . The people will certainly control their own political power once again. . . .

Our burden becomes heavier when we think of the fellow students who will forever remain on Changan Avenue and the fellow students on Tiananmen Square. I do not know how many of those heroic souls are still enraged and wish them a peaceful eternal rest on that street called "Avenue of Eternal Peace" (Changan Avenue).

We the living, our lives no longer belong to our individual selves. Our lives now envelope those of our fellow students and those of our fellow countrymen who paid with their lives for democracy, freedom, our beautiful motherland and for the prosperity of the motherland. Their lives have already been absorbed into ours.

We must resolutely throw out our chests, stand tall and keep on living, as well as carry on their will. We must carry through this great patriotic democracy movement to the end. . . .

What is democracy? Many; people have asked me this. I want to reply that democracy; is people controlling political power, not political power controlling the people; it is people choosing their own political and economic lifestyles according to their own wills. This is democracy. What we have to do is awaken this concept, this democratic concept, this rich historical responsibility, this glorious concept, in the minds of every citizen of the People's Republic of China. . . .

We must admit, due to educational crises over the past many; years, what we have accomplished in our education has been poor. So, all we youth in the republic, our quality is very low. Every citizen's average quality is very low. One of our missions is to raise this quality.

Moreover, we who are in the student movement truly want to advance democracy, to advance China and to make her prosperous and strong. All the people do not want actual upheaval; none of us wants to see upheaval. We only want to quickly destroy this reactionary regime. . . . What we want is not merely the overthrow of Li Peng, but the establishment of a kind of democratic political balance of power in China—a political balance of power among the people, to make a kind of true democratic function exist in China and to establish it.

The Official View

Three days after the Tiananmen Square Massacre Deng Xiaoping, China's paramount leader, addressed commanders of the People's Liberation Army in Beijing. These are excerpts from his speech:

This storm was bound to happen sooner or later. As determined by the international and domestic climate, it was bound to happen and was independent of human will. It was just a matter of time and scale. It has turned out in our favor, for we still have a large group of veterans who have experienced many storms and have a thorough understanding of things. They were on the side of taking resolute action to counter the turmoil. Although some comrades may not understand this now they will understand eventually and will support the decision of the Central Committee....

. . . Actually what we faced was not just some ordinary people who were misguided, but also a rebellious clique and a large quantity of the dregs of society. The key point is that they wanted to overthrow our state and the party. Failing to understand this means failing to understand the nature of the matter....

Their goal was to establish a bourgeois republic entirely dependent on the West. Of course we accept people's demands for combatting corruption. We are even ready to listen to some persons with ulterior motives when they raise the slogan about fighting corruption. However, such slogans were just a front. Their real aim was to overthrow the Communist Party and topple the socialist system.

During the course of quelling the rebellion, many comrades of ours were wounded or even sacrificed their lives. Some of their weapons were also taken from them by the rioters. Why? Because bad people mingled with the good, which made it difficult for us to take the firm measures that were necessary.

Handling this matter amounted to a severe political test for our army, and what happened shows that our People's Liberation Army passed muster. If tanks were used to roll over people, this would have created a confusion between right and wrong among the people nationwide. That is why I have to thank the P.L.A. officers and men for using this approach to handle the rebellion.

The P.L.A. losses were great, but this enabled us to win the support of the people and made those who can't tell right from wrong change their viewpoint. They can see what kind of people the P.L.A. are, whether there was bloodshed at Tiananmen, and who were those that shed blood....

. . . we should never forget how cruel our enemies are. For them we should not have an iota of forgiveness....

We have already accomplished our first goal of doubling the gross national product. We plan to use twelve years to attain our second goal of doubling the GNP. In the fifty years after that we hope to reach the level of a moderately developed country. A two percent annual growth rate is sufficient. That is our strategic goal. . . . It will be an unbeatable achievement for a country with (over one billion) people like ours to reach the level of a moderately developed nation after sixty-one years. . . .

Promoting plain living must be a major objective of education, and this should be the keynote for the next sixty to seventy years. The more prosperous our country becomes, the more important it is to keep hold of the enterprising spirit. The promotion of this spirit and plain living will also be helpful for overcoming decay.

After the People's Republic was founded we promoted plain living. Later on, when life became a little better, we promoted spending more, leading to wastage everywhere. This, in addition to lapses in theoretical work and an incomplete legal system, resulted in backsliding.

I once told foreigners that our worst omission of the past ten years was in education. What I meant was political education, and this doesn't apply to schools and students alone, but to the masses as a whole. . . .

Is there anything wrong with the basic concept of reforms and openness? No. Without reforms and openness how could we have what we have today? There has been a fairly satisfactory rise in the standard of living, and it may be said that we have moved one step further. The positive results of ten years of reforms must be properly assessed even though there have emerged such problems as inflation. Naturally in reform and adopting the open policy we run the risk of importing evil influences from the West, and we have never under-estimated such influences. In the early 1980's, when we established special economic zones, I told our Guangdong comrades that on the one hand they should persevere with reforms and openness, and on the other hand they should deal severely with economic crimes. . . .

. . . we must persist in the coordination between a planned economy and a market economy. There cannot be any change. . . . (We) must place more emphasis on planning in the adjustment period. At other times there can be a little more market adjustment so as to allow more flexibility. The future policy should still be a marriage between the planned and market economies.

What is important is that we should never change China back into a closed country. Such a policy would be most detrimental. We don't even have a good flow of information. Nowadays, are we not talking about the importance of information?

. . . If there is any inadequacy, then I should say our reforms and openness have not proceeded adequately enough. The problems we face in implementing reforms are far greater than those we encounter in opening our country. In political reforms we can affirm one point: We have to insist on implementing the system of the National People's Congress and not the American system of the separation of three powers. The U.S. berates us for suppressing students. But when they handled domestic student unrest and turmoil, didn't they send out police and troops, arrest people and shed blood? They were suppressing students and the people, but we are putting down counter-revolutionary rebellion. What qualifications do they have to criticize us? From now on, however, we should pay attention to such problems. We should never allow them to spread.

APPENDIX J

CONSTITUTION OF THE PEOPLE'S REPUBLIC OF CHINA

PREAMBLE

China is one of the countries with the longest histories in the world. The people of all nationalities in China have jointly created a splendid culture and have a glorious revolutionary tradition.

Feudal China was gradually reduced after 1840 to a semi-colonial and semi-feudal country. The Chinese people waged wave upon wave of heroic struggles for national independence and liberation and for democracy and freedom.

Great and earth-shaking historical changes have taken place in China in the 20th century.

The Revolution of 1911, led by Dr. Sun Yixian, abolished the feudal monarchy and gave birth to the Republic of China. But the Chinese people had yet to fulfil their historical task of overthrowing imperialism and feudalism.

After waging hard, protracted and tortuous struggles, armed and otherwise, the Chinese people of all nationalities led by the Communist Party of China with with Chairman Mao Zedong as its leader ultimately, in 1949, overthrew the rule of imperialism, feudalism and bureaucrat-capitalism, won the great victory of the new-democratic revolution, and founded the People's Republic of China. Thereupon the Chinese people took state power into their own hands and became masters of the country.

After the founding of the People's Republic, the transition of Chinese society from a new-democratic to a socialist society was effected step by step. The socialist transformation of the private ownership of the means of production was completed, the system of exploitation of man by man eliminated and the socialist system established. The people's democratic dictatorship led by the working class and based on the alliance of workers and peasants, which is in essence the dictatorship of the proletariat, has been consolidated and developed. The Chinese people and the Chinese People's Liberation Army have thwarted aggression, sabotage and armed provocations by imperialists and hegemonists, safeguarded China's national independence and security and strengthened its national defence. Major successes have been achieved in economic development. An independent and fairly comprehensive socialist system of industry has in the main been established. There has been a marked increase in agricultural production. Significant progress has been made in educational, scientific, cultural and other undertakings, and socialist ideological education has yielded noteworthy results. The living standards of the people have improved considerably.

Both the victory of China's new-democratic revolution and the successes of its socialist cause have been achieved by the Chinese people of all nationalities under the leadership of the Communist Party of China and the guidance of Marxism-Lenism and Mao Zedong Thought, and by upholding truth, correcting errors and overcoming numerous difficulties and hardships. The basic task of the nation in the years to come is to concentrate its effort on socialist modernization. Under the leadership of the Communist Party of China and the guidance of Marxism-Lenism and Mao Zedong Thought, the Chinese people of all nationalities will continue to adhere to the people's democratic dictatorship and follow the socialist road, steadily improve socialist institutions, develop socialist democracy, improve the socialist legal system and work hard and self-reliantly to modernize industry, agriculture, national defence and science and technology step by step to turn China into a socialist country with a high level of culture and democracy.

The exploiting classes as such have been eliminated in our country. However, class struggle will continue to exist within certain limits for a long time to come. The Chinese people must fight against those forces and elements, both at home and abroad, that are hostile to China's socialist system and try to undermine it.

Taiwan is part of the sacred territory of the People's Republic of China. It is the lofty duty of the entire Chinese people, including our compatriots in Taiwan, to accomplish the great task of reunifying the motherland.

In building socialism it is imperative to rely on the workers, peasants and intellectuals and unite with all the forces that can be united. In the long years of revolution and construction, there has been formed under the leadership of the Communist Party of China a broad patriotic united front that is composed of democratic parties and people's organizations and embraces all socialist working people, all patriots who support socialism and all patriots who stand for reunification of the motherland. This united front will continue to be consolidated and developed. The Chinese People's Political Consultative Conference is a broadly representative organization of the united front, which has played a significant historical role and will continue to do so in the political and social life of the country, in promoting friendship with the people of other countries and in the struggle for socialist modernization and for the reunification and unity of the country.

The People's Republic of China is a unitary multinational state built up jointly by the people of all its nationalities. Socialist relations of equality, unity and mutual assistance have been established among them and will continue to be strengthened. In the struggle to safeguard the unity of the nationalities, it is necessary to combat big-nation chauvinism, mainly Han chauvinism, and also necessary to combat local-national chauvinism. The state does its utmost to promote the common prosperity of all nationalities in the country.

China's achievements in revolution and construction are inseparable from support by the people of the world. The future of China is closely linked with that of the whole world. China adheres to an independent foreign policy as well as to the five principles of mutual respect for sovereignty and territorial integrity, mutual non-aggression, non-interference in each other's internal affairs, equality and mutual benefit, and peaceful coexistence in developing diplomatic relations and economic and cultural exchanges with other countries; China consistently opposes imperialism, hegemonism, and colonialism, works to strengthen unity with the people of other countries, supports the oppressed nations and the developing countries in their just struggle to win   and   preserve   national   independence   and   develop   their national economies, and strives to safeguard world peace and promote the cause of human progress.

This Constitution affirms the achievements of the struggles of the Chinese people of all nationalities and defines the basic system and basic tasks of the state in legal form; it is the fundamental law of the state and has supreme legal authority. The poeple of all nationalities, all state organs, the armed forces, all political parties and public organizations and all enterprises and undertakings in the country must take the Constitution as the basic norm of conduct, and they have the duty to uphold the dignity of the Constitution and ensure its implementation.

CHAPTER ONE

GENERAL PRINCIPLES

ARTICLE 1

The People's Republic of China is a socialist state under the people's democratic dictatorship led by the working class and based on the alliance of workers and peasants.

The socialist system is the basic system of the People's Republic of China. Sabotage of the socialist system by any organization or individual is prohibited.

ARTICLE 2

All power in the People's Republic of China belongs to the people.

The organs through which the people exercise state power are the National People's Congress and the local people's congresses at different levels.

The people administer state affairs and manage economic, cultural and social affairs through various channels and in various ways in accordance with the law.

ARTICLE 3

The state organs of the People's Republic of China apply the principle of democratic centralism.

The national People's Congress and the local people's congresses at different levels are instituted through democratic election. They are responsible to the people and subject to their supervision.

All administrative, judicial and procuratorial organs of the state are created by the people's congresses to which they are responsible and under whose supervision they operate.

The division of functions and powers between the central and local state organs is guided by the principle of giving full play to the initiative and enthusiasm of the local authorities under the unified leadership of the central authorities.

ARTICLE 4

All nationalities in the People's Republic of China are equal. The state protects the lawful rights and interests of the minority nationalities and upholds and develops the relationship of equality, unity and mutual assistance among all of China's nationalities. Discrimination against and oppression of any nationality are prohibited; any acts that undermine the unity of the nationalities or instigate their secession are prohibited.

The state helps the areas inhabited by minority nationalities speed up their economic and cultural development in accordance with the peculiarities and needs of the different minority nationalities.

Regional autonomy is practiced in areas where people of minority nationalities live in compact communities; in these areas organs of self-government are established for the exercise of the right of autonomy. All the national autonomous areas are inalienable parts of the People's Republic of China.

The people of all nationalities have the freedom to use and develop their own spoken and written languages and to preserve or reform their own ways and customs.

ARTICLE 5

The state upholds the uniformity and dignity of the socialist legal system.

No law or administrative or local rules and regulations shall contravene the Constitution.

ARTICLE 6

The basis of the socialist economic system of the People's Republic of China is socialist public ownership of the means of production, namely, ownership by the working people.

The system of socialist public ownership supersedes the system of exploitation of man by man; it applies the principle of "from each according to his ability, to each according to his work."

ARTICLE 7

The state economy is the sector of socialist economy under ownership by the whole people; it is the leading force in the national economy. The state ensures the consolidation and growth of the state economy.

ARTICLE 8

Rural people's communes, agricultural producers' cooperatives, and other forms of cooperative economy such as producers' supply and marketing, credit and consumers cooperatives, belong to the sector of the socialist economy under collective ownership by the working people. Working people who are members of rural economic collectives have the right, within the limits prescribed by law, to farm plots of cropland and hilly land allotted for private use, engage in household sideline production and raise privately-owned livestock.

The various forms of cooperative economy in the cities and towns, such as those in the handicraft, industrial, building, transport, commercial and service trades, all belong to the sector of socialist economy under collective ownership by the working people.

The state protects the lawful rights and interests of the urban and rural economic collectives and encourages, guides and helps the growth of the collective economy.

ARTICLE 9

Mineral resources, waters, forests, mountains, grassland, unreclaimed land, beaches and other natural resources are owned by the state, that is, by the whole people, with the exception of the forests, mountains, grassland, unreclaimed land and beaches that are owned by collectives in accordance with the law.

The state ensures the rational use of natural resources and protects rare animals and plants. The appropriation of or damage of natural resources by any organization or individual by whatever means is prohibited.

ARTICLE 10

Land is the cities is owned by the state.

Land in the rural and suburban areas is owned by collectives except for those portions which belong to the state in accordance with the law; house sites and privately farmed plots of cropland and hilly land are also owned by collectives.

The state may in the public interest take over land for its use in accordance with the law.

No organization or individual may appropriate, buy, sell or lease land, or unlawfully transfer land in other ways.

All organizations and individuals who use land must make rational use of the land.

ARTICLE 11

The individual economy of urban and rural working people, operated within the limits prescribed by law, is a complement to the socialist public economy. The state protects the lawful rights and interests of the individual economy.

The state guides, helps, and supervises the individual economy by exercising administrative control.

ARTICLE 12

Socialist public property is sacred and inviolable.

The state protects socialist public property. Appropriation or damage of state or collective property by any organization or individual by whatever means is prohibited.

ARTICLE 13

The state protects the right of citizens to own lawfully-earned income, savings, houses and other lawful property.

The state protects by law the right of citizens to inherit private property.

ARTICLE 14

The state continuously raises labor productivity, improves economic results and develops the productive forces by enhancing the enthusiasm of the working people, raising the level of their technical skill, disseminating advanced science and technology, improving the system of economic administration and enterprise operation and management, instituting the socialist system of responsibility in various forms and improving organization of work.

The state practices strict economy and combats waste.

The state properly apportions accumulation and consumption, pays attention to the interests of the collective and the individual as well as of the state and, on the basis of expanded production, gradually improves the material and cultural life of the people.

ARTICLE 15

The state practices economic planning on the basis of socialist public ownership. It ensures the proportionate and coordinated growth of the national economy through overall balancing by economic planning and the supplementary role of regulation by the market.

Disturbance of the orderly functioning of the social economy or disruption of the state economic plan by any organization or individual is prohibited.

ARTICLE 16

State enterprises have decision-making power in operation and management within the limits prescribed by law, on condition that they submit to unified leadership by the state and fulfil all their obligations under the state plan.

State enterprises practice democratic management through congresses of workers and staff and in other ways in accordance with the law.

ARTICLE 17

Collective economic organizations have decision-making power in conducting independent economic activities, on condition that they accept the guidance of the state plan and abide by the relevant laws.

Collective economic organizations practice democratic management in accordance with the law, with the entire body of their workers electing or removing their managerial personnel and deciding on major issues concerning operation and management.

ARTICLE 18

The People's Republic of China permits foreign enterprises, other foreign enterprises, other foreign economic organizations and individual foreigners to invest in China and to enter into various forms of economic cooperation with Chinese enterprises and other economic organizations in accordance with the law of the People's Republic of China.

All foreign enterprises and other foreign economic organizations in China, shall abide by the law of the People's Republic of China. Their lawful rights and interests are protected by the law of the People's Republic of China.

ARTICLE 19

The state develops socialist educational undertakings and works to raise the scientific and cultural level of the whole nation.

The state runs schools of various types, makes primary education compulsory and universal, develops secondary, vocational and higher education and promotes preschool education.

The state develops educational facilities of various types in order to wipe out illiteracy and provide political, cultural, scientific, technical and professional education for workers, peasants, state functionaries and other working people. It encourages people to become educated through independent study.

The state encourages the collective economic organizations, state enterprises and undertakings and other social forces to set up educational institutions of various types in accordance with the law.

The state promotes the nationwide use of "Putonghua" (Common Speech based on Beijing pronounciation).

ARTICLE 20

The state promotes the development of the natural and social sciences, disseminates scientific and technical knowledge, and commends and rewards achievements in scientific research as well as technological discoveries and inventions.

ARTICLE 21

The state develops medical and health services, promotes modern medicine and traditional Chinese medicine, encourages and supports the setting-up of various medical and health facilities by the rural economic collectives, state enterprises and undertakings and neighborhood organizations, and promotes public health activities of a mass character, all to protect the people's health.

The state develops physical culture and promotes mass sports activities to build up the people's physique.

ARTICLE 22

The state promotes the development of literature and art, the press, broadcasting and television undertakings, publishing and distribution services, libraries, museums, cultural centers and other cultural undertakings, that serve the people and socialism, and sponsors mass cultural activities.

The state protects places of scenic and historical interest, valuable cultural monuments and treasures and other important items of China's historical and cultural heritage.

ARTICLE 23

The state trains specialized personnel in all fields who serve socialism, increases the number of intellectuals and creates conditions to give full scope to their role in socialist modernization.

ARTICLE 24

The state strengthens the building of socialist spiritual civilization through spreading education in high ideals and morality, general education and education in discipline and the legal system, and through promoting the formulation and observance of rules of conduct and common pledges by different sections of the people in urban and rural areas.

The state advocates the civil virtues of love of the motherland, of the people, of labor, of science and of socialism; it educates the people in patriotism, collectivism, internationalism and communism and in dialectical and historical materialism; it combats capitalist, feudal and other decadent ideas.

ARTICLE 25

The state promotes family planning so that population growth may fit the plan for economic and social development.

ARTICLE 26

The state protects and improves the living environment and the ecological environment, and prevents and remedies pollution and other public hazards.

The state organizes and encourages afforestation and the protection of forests.

ARTICLE 27

All state organs carry out the principle of simple and efficient administration, the system of responsibility for work and the system of training functionaries and appraising their work in order constantly to improve quality of work and efficiency and combat bureaucratism.

All state organs and functionaries must rely on the support of the people, keep in close touch with them, heed their opinions and suggestions, accept their supervision and work hard to serve them.

ARTICLE 28

The state maintains public order and suppresses treasonable and other counter-revolutionary activities; it penalizes actions that endanger public security and disrupt the socialist economy and other criminal activities, and punishes and reforms criminals.

ARTICLE 29

The armed forces of the People's Republic of China belong to the people. Their tasks are to strengthen national defense, resist aggression, defend the motherland, safeguard the people's peaceful labor, participate in national reconstruction, and work hard to serve the people.

The state strengthens the revolutionization, modernization, and regularization of the armed forces in order to increase the national defense capability.

ARTICLE 30

The administrative division of the People's Republic of China is as follows:
1) The country is divided into provinces, autonomous regions and municipalities directly under the Central Government;
2) Provinces and autonomous regions are divided into autonomous prefectures, counties, autonomous counties and cities;

3) Counties and autonomous counties are divided into townships, nationality townships and towns.

Municipalities directly under the Central Government and other large cities are divided into districts and counties. Autonomous prefectures are divided into counties, autonomous counties, and cities.

All autonomous regions, autonomous prefectures and autonomous counties are national autonomous areas.

ARTICLE 31

The state may establish special administrative regions when necessary. The systems to be instituted in special administrative regions shall be prescribed by law enacted by the National People's Congress in the light of the specific conditions.

ARTICLE 32

The People's Republic of China protects the lawful rights and interests of foreigners within Chinese territory, and while on Chinese territory foreigners must abide by the law of the People's Republic of China.

The People's Republic of China may grant asylum to foreigners who request it for political reasons.

CHAPTER TWO

THE FUNDAMENTAL RIGHTS AND DUTIES OF CITIZENS

ARTICLE 33

All persons holding the nationality of the People's Republic of China are citizens of the People's Republic of China.

All citizens of the People's Republic of China are equal before the law.

ARTICLE 34

All citizens of the People's Republic of China who have reached the age of 18; have the right to vote and stand for election, regardless of nationality, race, sex, occupation, family background, religious belief, education, property status, or length of residence, except persons deprived of political rights according to law.

ARTICLE 35

Citizens of the People's Republic of China enjoy freedom of speech, of the press, of assembly, of association, of procession and of demonstration.

ARTICLE 36

Citizens of the People's Republic of China enjoy freedom of religious belief.

No state organ, public organization or individual may compel citizens to believe in, or not to believe in, any religion; nor may they discriminate against citizens who believe in, or do not believe in, any religion.

The state protects normal religious activities. No one may make use of religion to engage in activities that disrupt public order, impair the health of citizens or interfere with the educational system of the state.

Religious bodies and religious affairs are not subject to any foreign domination.

ARTICLE 37

The freedom of person of citizens of the People's Republic of China is inviolable.

No citizen may be arrested except with the approval or by decision of a people's procuratorate or by decision of a people's court, and arrests must be made by a public security organ.

Unlawful deprivation or restriction of citizens' freedom of person by detention or other means is prohibited; and unlawful search of the person of citizens is prohibited.

ARTICLE 38

The personal dignity of citizens of the People's Republic of China is inviolable. Insult, libel, false charge or frame-up directed against citizens by any means is prohibited.

ARTICLE 39

The home of citizens of the People's Republic of China is inviolable. Unlawful search of, or intrusion into, a citizen's home is prohibited.

ARTICLE 40

The freedom and privacy of correspondence of citizens of the People's Republic of China are protected by law. No organization or individual may, on any ground, infringe upon the freedom and privacy of citizens' correspondence except in cases where, to meet the needs of state security or of investigation into criminal offenses, public security or procuratorial organs are permitted to censor correspondence in accordance with procedures prescribed by law.

ARTICLE 41

Citizens of the People's Republic of China have the right to criticize and make suggestions to any state organ or functionary. Citizens have the right to make to relevant state organs complaints and charges against, or exposures of, any state organ or functionary for violation of the law or dereliction of duty; but fabrication or distortion of facts for the purpose of libel or frame-up is prohibited.

The state organ concerned must deal with complaints, charges or exposures made by citizens in a responsible manner after ascertaining the facts. No one may suppress such complaints, charges and exposures, or retaliate against the citizens making them.

Citizens who have suffered losses through infringement of their civic rights by any state organ or functionary have the right to compensation in accordance with the law.

ARTICLE 42

Citizens of the People's Republic of China have the right as well as the duty to work.

Using various channels, the state creates conditions for employment, strengthens labor protection, improves working conditions and, on the basis of expanded production, increases remuneration for work and social benefits.

Work is the glorious duty of every able-bodied citizen. All working people in state enterprises and in urban and rural economic collectives should perform their tasks with an attitude consonant with their status as masters of the country. The state promotes socialist labor emulation and commends and rewards model and advanced workers. The state encourages citizens to take part in voluntary labor.

The state provides necessary vocational training to citizens before they are employed.

ARTICLE 43

Working people in the People's Republic of China have the right to rest.

The state expands facilities for rest and recuperation of working people and prescribes working hours and vacations for workers and staff.

ARTICLE 44

The state prescribes by law the system of retirement for workers and staff in enterprises and undertakings and for functionaries of organs of state. The livelihood of retired personnel is ensured by the state and society.

ARTICLE 45

Citizens of the People's Republic of China have the right to material assistance from the state and society when they are old, ill or disabled. The state develops the social insurance, social relief, and medical and health services that are required to enable citizens to enjoy this right.

The state and society ensure the livelihood of disabled members of the armed forces, provide pensions to the families of martyrs and give preferential treatment to the families of military personnel.

The state and society help make arrangements for the work, livelihood and education of the blind, deaf-mutes and other handicapped citizens.

ARTICLE 46

Citizens of the People's Republic of China have the duty as well as the right to receive education.

The state promotes the all-round moral, intellectual and physical development of children and young people.

ARTICLE 47

Citizens of the People's Republic of China have the freedom to engage in scientific research, literary and artistic creation and other cultural pursuits. The tate encourages and assists creative endeavors conducive to the interests of the people that are made by citizens engaged in education, science, technology, literature, art, and other cultural work.

ARTICLE 48

Women in the People's Republic of China enjoy equal rights with men in all spheres of life, political, economic, cultural and social, including family life.

The state protects the rights and interests of women, applies the principle of equal pay for equal work for men and women alike and trains and selects cadres from among women.

ARTICLE 49

Marriage, the family and mother and child are protected by the state.

Both husband and wife have the duty to practice family planning.

Parents have the duty to rear and educate their minor children, and children who have come of age have the duty to support and assist their parents.

Violation of the freedom of marriage is prohibited. Maltreatment of old people, women and children is prohibited.

ARTICLE 50

The People's Republic of China protects the legitimate rights and interests of Chinese nationals residing abroad and protects the lawful rights and interests of returned overseas Chinese and of the the family members of Chinese nationals residing abroad.

ARTICLE 51

The exercise by citizens of the People's Republic of China of their freedoms and rights may not infringe upon the interests of the state, of society and of the collective, or upon the lawful freedoms and rights of other citizens.

ARTICLE 52

It is the duty of citizens of the People's Republic of China to safeguard the unity of the country and the unity of all its nationalities.

ARTICLE 53

Citizens of the People's Republic of Cina must abide by the Constitution and the law, keep state secrets, protect public property and observe labor discipline and public order and respect social ethics.

ARTICLE 54

It is the duty of citizens of the People's Republic of China to safeguard the security, honor and interests of the motherland; they must not commit acts detrimental to the security, honor and interests of the motherland.

ARTICLE 55

It is the sacred obligation of every citizen of the People's Republic of China to defend the motherland and to resist aggression.

It is the honorable duty of citizens of the People's Republic of China to perform military service and join the militia in accordance with the law.

ARTICLE 56

It is the duty of citizens of the People's Republic of China to pay taxes in accordance with the law.

CHAPTER THREE

THE STRUCTURE OF THE STATE

SECTION I

The National People's Congress

ARTICLE 57

The National People's Congress of the People's Republic of China is the highest organ of state power. Its permanent body is the Standing Committee of the National People's Congress.

ARTICLE 58

The National People's Congress and its Standing Committee exercise the legislative power of the state.

ARTICLE 59

The National People's Congress is composed of deputies elected by the provinces, autonomous regions and municipalities directly under the Central Government, and by the armed forces. All the minority nationalities are entitled to appropriate representation.

Election of deputies to the National People's Congress is conducted by the Standing Committee of the National People's Congress.

The number of deputies to the National People's Congress and the manner of their election are prescribed by law.

ARTICLE 60

The National People's Congress is elected for a term of five years.

Two months before the expiration of the term of office of a National People's Congress, its Standing Committee must ensure that the election of deputies to the succeeding National People's Congress is completed. Should exceptional circumstances prevent such an election, it may be postponed by decision of a majority vote of more than two-thirds of all those on the Standing Committee of the current National People's Congress, and the term of office of the current National People's Congress may be extended. The election of deputies to the succeeding National People's Congress must be completed within one year after the termination of such exceptional circumstances.

ARTICLE 61

The National People's Congress meets in session once a year and is convened by its Standing Committee. A session of the National People's Congress may be convened at any time the Standing Committee deems it necessary or when more than one-fifth of the deputies to the

National People's Congress so proposes.

When the National People's Congress meets, it elects a presidium to conduct its session.

ARTICLE 62

The national People's Congress exercises the following functions and powers:

1) to amend the Constitution;
2) to supervise the enforcement of the Constitution;
3) to enact and amend basic statutes concerning criminal offenses, civil affairs, the state organs and other matters;
4) to elect the President and the Vice-President of the People's Republic of China;
5) to decide on the choice of the Premier of the State Council upon nomination by the President of the People's Republic of China, and to decide on the choice of the Vice-Premiers, State Councillors, Ministers in charge of ministries or commissions and the Auditor-General and the Secretary-General of the State Council upon nomination by the Premier;
6) to elect the Chairman of the Central Military Commission and, upon nomination by the Chairman, to decide on the choice of all the others on the Central Military Commission;
7) to elect the President of the Supreme People's Court;
8) to elect the Procurator-General of the Supreme People's Procuratorate;
9) to examine and approve the plan for national economic and social development and the report on its implementation;
10) to examine and approve the state budget and the report on its implementation;
11) to alter or annul inappropriate decisions of the Standing Committee of the National People's Congress;
12) to approve the establishment of province, autonomous regions, and munipalities directly under the Central Government;
13) to decide on the establishment of special administrative regions and the systems to be instituted there;
14) to decide on questions of war and peace; and
15) to exercise such other function and powers as the highest organ of state power should exercise.

ARTICLE 63

The National People's Congress has the power to recall or remove from office the following persons:

1) The President and the Vice-President of the People's Republic of China;
2) the Premier, Vice-Premiers, State Councillors, Ministers in charge of ministries or commissions and the Auditor-General and the Secretary-General of the State Council;
3) the Chairman of the Central Military Commission and others on the Commission;
4) the President of the Supreme People's Court; and
5) the Procurator-General of the Supreme People's Procuratorate.

ARTICLE 64

Amendments to the Constitution are to be proposed by the Standing Committee of the National People's Congress or by more than one-fifth of the deputies to the National People's Congress and adopted by a majority vote of more than two-thirds of all the deputies to the Congress.

Statutes and resolutions are adopted by a majority vote of more than one half of all the deputies to the National People's Congress.

ARTICLE 65

The Standing Committee of the National People's Congress is composed of the following: the Chairman; the Vice-Chairmen; the Secretary-General; and members.

Minority nationalities are entitled to appropriate representation on the Standing Committee of the National People's Congress.

The National People's Congress elects, and has the power to recall, all those onits Standing Committee.

No one on the Standing Committee of the National People's Congress shall hold any post in any of the administrative, judicial or procuratorial organs of the state.

ARTICLE 66

The Standing Committee of the National People's Congress is elected for the same term as the National People's Congress; it exercises its functions and powers until a new Standing Committee is elected by the succeeding National People's Congress.

The Chairman and Vice-Chairmen of the Standing Committee shall serve no more than two consecutive terms.

ARTICLE 67

The Standing Committee of the National People's Congress exercises the following functions and powers:

1) to interpret the Constitution and supervise its enforcement;
2) to enact and amend statutes with the exception of those which should be enacted by the National People's Congress;
3) to enact, when the National People's Congress is not in session, partial supplements and amendments to statutes enacted by the National People's Congress provided that they do not contravene the basic principles of these statutes;
4) to interpret statutes;
5) to examine and approve, when the National People's Congress is not is session, partial adjustments to the plan for national economic and social development and to the state budget that prove necessary in the course of their implementation;
6) to supervise the work of the State Council, the Central Military Commission, the Supreme People's Court and the Supreme People's Procuratorate;
7) to annul those administrative rules and regulations, decisions or orders of the State Council that contravene the Constitution or the statutes;
8) to annul those local regulations or decisions of the organs of state power of provinces, autonomous regions and municipalities directly under the Central Government that contravene the Constitution, the statutes, or the administrative rules and regulations;
9) to decide, when the National People's Congress is not in session, on the choice of Ministers in charge of ministries or commissions or the Auditor-General and the Secretary-General of the State Council upon nomination by the Premier of the State Council;
10) to decide, upon nomination by the Chairman of the Central Military Commission, on the choice of others on the Commission, when the National People's Congress is not in session.
11) to appoint and remove Vice-Presidents and judges of the Supreme People's Court, members of its Judicial Committee and the President of the Military Court at the suggestion of the President of the Supreme People's Court;
12) to appoint and remove Deputy Procurators-General and procurators of the Supreme People's Procuratorate, members of its Procuratorial Committee and the Chief Procurator of the Military Procuratorate at the suggestion of the Procurator-General of the Supreme People's Procuratorate, and to approve the appointment and removal of the chief procurators of the people's procuratorates of provinces, autonomous regions and municipalities directly under the Central Government;
13) to decide on the appointment and recall of plenipotentiary representatives abroad;
14) to decide on the ratification and abrogation of treaties and important agreements concluded with foreign states;
15) to institute systems of titles and ranks for military and diplomatic personnel and of other specific titles and ranks;
16) to institute state medals and titles of honor and decide on their conferment;
17) to decide on the granting of special pardons;
18) to decide, when the National People's Congress is not in session, on the proclamation of a state of war in the event of an armed attack on the country or in fulfilment of

international treaty obligations concerning common defense against aggression;

19) to decide on general mobilization or partial mobilization;

20) to decide on the enforcement of martial law throughout the country or in particular provinces, autonomous regions or municipalities directly under the Central Government; and

21) to exercise such other functions and powers as the National People's Congress may assign to it.

ARTICLE 68

The Chairman of the Standing Committee of the National People's Congress presides over the work of the Standing Committee and convenes its meetings. The Vice-Chairmen and the Secretary-General assist in the work of the Chairman.

Executive meetings with the participation of the Chairman, Vice-Chairmen and Secretary-General handle the important day-to-day work of the Standing Committee of the National People's Congress.

ARTICLE 69

The Standing Committee of the National People's Congress is responsible to the National People's Congress and reports on its work to the Congress.

ARTICLE 70

The National People's Congress establishes a Nationalities Committee, a Law Committee, a Financial and Economic Committee, a Financial and Economic Committee, an Education, Science, Culture and Public Health Committee, a Foreign Affairs Committee, an Overseas Chinese Committee and such other special committees as are necessary. These special committees work under the direction of the Standing Committee of the National People's Congress when the Congress is not in session.

The special committees examine, discuss and draw up relevant bills and draft resolutions under the direction of the National People's Congress and its Standing Committee.

ARTICLE 71

The National People's Congress and its Standing Committee may, when they deem it necessary, appoint committees of inquiry into specific questions and adopt relevant resolutions in the light of their reports.

All organs of state, public organizations and citizens concerned are obliged to supply the necessary information to those committees of inquiry when they conduct investigations.

ARTICLE 72

Deputies to the National People's Congress and all those on its Standing Committee have the right, in accordance with procedures prescribed by law, to submit bills and proposals within the scope of the respective functions and powers of the National People's Congress and its Standing Committee.

ARTICLE 73

Deputies to the National People's Congress during its sessions, and all those on its Standing Committee during its meetings, have the right to address questions, in accordance with procedures prescribed by law, to the State Council or the ministries and commissions under the State Council, which must answer the questions in a responsible manner.

ARTICLE 74

No deputy to the National People's Congress may be arrested or placed on criminal trial without the consent of the Presidium of the current session of the National People's Congress or, when the National People's Congress is not in session, without the consent of its Standing Committee.

ARTICLE 75

Deputies to the National People's Congress may not be called to legal account for their speeches or votes at its meetings.

ARTICLE 76

Deputies to the National People's Congress must play an exemplary role in abiding by the Constitution and the law and keeping state secrets and, in production and other work and their public activities, assist in the enforcement of the Constitution and the law.
Deputies to the National People's Congress should maintain close contact with the units which elected them and with the people, listen to and convey the opinions and demands of the people and work hard to serve them.

ARTICLE 77

Deputies to the National People's Congress are subject to the supervision of the units which elected them. The electoral units have the power, through procedures prescribed by law, to recall deputies whom they elected.

ARTICLE 78

The organization and working procedures of the National People's Congress and its Standing Committee are prescribed by law.

SECTION II

The President of the People's Republic of China

The President and Vice-President of the People's Republic of China are elected by the National People's Congress.
Citizens of the People's Republic of China who have the right to vote and to stand for election and who have reached the age of 45 are eligible for election as President or Vice-President of the People's Republic of China.
The term of office of the President and Vice-President of the People's Republic of China is the same as that of the National People's Congress, and they shall serve no more than two consecutive terms.

ARTICLE 80

The President of the People's Republic of China, in pursuance of decisions of the National People's Congress and its Standing Committee, promulgates statutes; appoints and removes the Premier, Vice-Premiers, State Councillors, Ministers in charge of ministries or commissions, and the Auditor-General and the Secretary-General of the State Council; confers state medals and titles of honor; issues orders of special pardons; proclaims a state of war; and issues mobilization orders.

ARTICLE 81

The President of the People's Republic of China receives foreign diplomatic representatives on behalf of the People's Republic of China and, in pursuance of decisions of the Standing Committee of the National People's Congress, appoints and recalls plenipotentiary representatives abroad, and ratifies and abrogates treaties and important agreements concluded with foreign states.

ARTICLE 82

The Vice-President of the People's Republic of China assists in the work of the President.
The Vice-President of the People's Republic of China may exercise such parts of the functions and powers of the President as may be deputed by the President.

ARTICLE 83

The President and Vice-President of the People's Republic of China exercise their functions and powers until the new President and Vice-President elected by the succeeding National Congress assume office.

ARTICLE 84

In case the office of the President of the People's Republic of China falls vacant, the Vice-President succeeds to the office of President.

In case the office of the Vice-President of the People's Republic of China falls vacant, the National People's Congress shall elect a new Vice-President to fill the vacancy.

In the event that the offices of both the President and the Vice-President of the People's Republic of China fall vacant, the National People's Congress shall elect a new President and a new Vice-President. Prior to such election, the Chairman of the Standing Committee of the National People's Congress shall temporarily act as the President of the People's Republic of China.

SECTION III

The State Council

ARTICLE 85

The State Council, that is, the Central People's Government, of the People's Republic of China is the executive body of the highest organ of state power; it is the highest organ of state administration.

ARTICLE 86

The State Council is composed of the following: the Premier; the Vice-Premiers; the State Councillors; the Ministers in charge of ministries; the Ministers in charge of commissions; the Auditor-General; and the Secretary-General.

The Premier has overall responsibility for the State Council. The ministers have overall responsibility for the ministries or commissions under their charge.

The organization of the State Council is prescribed by law.

ARTICLE 87

The term of office of the State Council is the same as that of the National People's Congress.

The Premier, Vice-Premiers, and State Councillors shall serve no more than two consecutive terms.

ARTICLE 88

The Premier directs the work of the State Council. The Vice-Premiers and State Councillors assist in the work of the Premier.

Executive meetings of the State Council are composed of the Premier, the Vice-Premiers, the State Councillors and the Secretary-General of the State Council.

ARTICLE 89

The State Council exercises the following functions and powers:

1) to adopt administrative measures, enact administrative rules and regulations and issue decisions and orders in accordance with the Constitution and the statutes;
2) to submit proposals to the National People's Congress or its Standing Committee;
3) to lay down the tasks and responsibilities of the ministries and commissions of the State Council, to exercise unified leadership over the work of the ministries and commissions and to direct all other administrative work of a national character that does not fall within the jurisdiction of the ministries and commissions;
4) to exercise unified leadership over the work of local organs of state administration at different levels throughout the country, and to lay down the detailed division of functions and powers between the Central Government and the organs of state administra-

tion of provinces, autonomous regions and municipalities directly under the Central Government;

5) to draw up and implement the plan for national economic and social development and the state budget;

7) to direct and administer affairs of education, science, culture, public health, physical culture and family planning;

8) to direct and administer civil affairs, public security, judicial administration, supervision and other related matters;

9) to conduct foreign affairs and conclude treaties and agreements with foreign states;

10) to direct and administer the building of national defense;

11) to direct and administer affairs concerning the nationalities, and to safeguard the equal rights of minority nationalities and the right of autonomy of the national autonomous areas;

12) to protect the legitimate rights and interests of Chinese nationals residing abroad and protect the lawful rights and interests of returned overseas Chinese and of the family members of Chinese nationals residing abroad;

13) to alter or annul inappropriate orders, directives and regulations issued by the ministries or commissions;

14) to alter or annul inappropriate decisions and orders issued by local organs of state administration at different levels;

15) to approve the geographic division of provinces, autonomous regions and municipalities directly under the Central Government, and to approve the stablishment and geographic division of autonomous prefectures, counties, autonomous counties and cities;

16) to decide on the enforcement of martial law in parts of provinces, autonomous regions and municipalities directly under the the Central Government;

17) to examine and decide on the size of administrative organs and, in accordance with the law, to appoint, remove and train administrative officers, appraise their work and reward or punish them; and 18) to exercise such other functions and powers as the National People's Congress or its Standing Committee may assign it.

ARTICLE 90

The Ministers in charge of ministries or commissions of the State Council are responsible for the work of their respective departments and convene and preside over ministerial meetings or commission meetings that discuss and decide on major issues in the work of their respective departments.

The ministries and commissions issue orders, directives and regulations within the jurisdiction of their respective departments and in accordance with the statutes and the administrative rules and regulations, decisions, and orders issued by the State Council.

ARTICLE 91

The State Council establishes an auditing body to supervise through auditing the revenue and expenditure of all departments under the State Council and of the local governments at different levels, and those of the state financial and monetary organization and of enterprises and undertakings.

Under the direction of the Premier of the State Council, the auditing body independently exercises its power to supervise through auditing in accordance with the law, subject to no interference by any other administrative organ or any public organization or individual.

ARTICLE 92

The State Council is responsible, and reports on its work, to the National People's Congress or, when the National People's Congress is not in session, to its Standing Committee.

SECTION IV

The Central Military Commission

ARTICLE 93

The central Military Commission of the People's Republic of China directs the armed forces of the country.

The Central Military Commission is composed of the following: the Chairman; the Vice-Chairman; and members. The Chairman of the Central Military Commission has overall responsibility for the Commission.

The term of office of the Central Military Commission is the same as that of the National People's Congress.

ARTICLE 94

The Chairman of the Central Military Commission is responsible to the National People's Congress and its Standing Committee.

SECTION V

LOCAL GOVERNMENTS

ARTICLE 95

People's congresses and people's governments are established in provinces, municipalities directly under the Central Government, counties, cities, municipal districts, townships, nationality townships and towns.

The organization of local people's congresses and local people's governments at different levels is prescribed by law.

Organs of self-government are established in autonomous regions, autonomous prefectures and autonomous counties. The organization and working procedures of organs of self-government are prescribed by law in accordance with the basic principles laid down in Sections V and VI of Chapter Three of the Constitution.

ARTICLE 96

Local people's congresses at different levels are local organs of state power.

Local people's congresses at and above the county level establish standing committees.

ARTICLE 97

Deputies to the people's congresses of provinces, municipalities directly under the Central Government, and cities divided into districts are elected by the people's congresses at the next lower level; deputies to the people's congresses at the next lower level; deputies to the people's congresses of counties, cities not divided into districts, municipal districts, townships, nationality townships and towns are elected directly by their constituencies.

The number of deputies to local people's congresses at different levels and the manner of their election are prescribed by law.

ARTICLE 98

The term of office of the people's congresses of provinces, municipalities directly under the Central Government and cities divided into district is five years. The term of office of the people's congresses of counties, cities not divided into districts, municipal districts, townships, nationality townships and towns is three years.

ARTICLE 99

Local people's congresses at different levels ensure the observance and implementation of the Constitution, the statutes and the administrative rules and regulations in their respective administrative areas. Within the limits of their authority as prescribed by law, they adopt and issue resolutions and examine and decide on plans for local economic and cultural development and for the development of public service.

Local people's congresses and above the county level examine and approve the plans for economic and social development and the budgets of their respective administrative areas, and examine and approve reports on their implementation. They have the power to alter or annul inappropriate decisions of their own standing committees.

The people's congresses of nationality townships may, within the limits of their authority as prescribed by law, take specific measures suited to the peculiarities of the nationalities concerned.

ARTICLE 100

The people's congresses of provinces and municipaliteis directly under the Central Government, and their standing committees, may adopt local regulations, which must not contravene the Constitution, the statutes and the administrative rules and regulations, and they shall report such local regulations to the Standing Committee of the National People's Congress for the record.

ARTICLE 101

At their respective levels, local people's congresses elect, and have the power to recall, governors and deputy governors, or mayors and deputy mayors, or heads and deputy heads of counties, districts, townships and towns.

Local people's congresses at and above the county level elect, and have the power to recall, presidents of people's courts and chief procurators of people's procuratorates at the corresponding level. The election or recall of chief procurators of people's procuratorates shall be reported to the chief procurators of the people's procuratorates at the next higher level for submission to the standing committees of the people's congresses at the corresponding level for approval.

ARTICLE 102

Deputies to the people's congresses of provinces, municipalities directly under the Central Government and cities divided into districts are subject to supervision by the units which elected them; deputies to the people's congresses of counties, cities not divided into districts, municipal districts, townships, nationality townships and towns are subject to supervision by their constituencies.

The electoral units and constituencies which elect deputies to local people's congresses at different levels have the power, according to procedures prescribed by law, to recall deputies whom they elected.

ARTICLE 103

The standing committee of a local people's congress at and above the county level is composed of a chairman, vice-chairmen and members, and is responsible, and reports on its work, to the people's congress at the corresponding level.

The local people's congress at and above the county level elects, and has the power to recall, anyone on the standing committee of the people's congress at the corresponding level.

No one on the standing committee of a local people's congress at and above the county level shall hold any post in state administrative, judicial and procuratorial organs.

ARTICLE 104

The standing committee of a local people's congress at and above the county level discusses and decides on major issues in all fields of work in its administrative area; supervises the work of the people's government, people's court and people's procuratorate at the corresponding level; annuls inappropriate decisions and orders of the people's government at the corresponding level; annuls inappropriate resolutions of the people's congress at the next lower level; decides on the appointment and removal of functionaries of state organs within the limits of its authority as prescribed by law; and, when the people's congress at the corresponding level is not in session, recalls individual deputies to the people's congress at the next higher level and elects individual deputies to fill vacancies in that people's congress.

ARTICLE 105

Local people's governments at different levels are the executive bodies of local organs of state power as well as the local organs of state administration at the corresponding level.

Local people's governments at different levels practice the system of overall responsibility by governors, mayors, county heads, district heads, township heads and town heads.

ARTICLE 106

The term of office of local people's governments at different levels is the same as that of the people's congresses at the corresponding level.

ARTICLE 107

Local people's governments at and above the county level, within the limits of their authority as prescribed by law, conduct the administrative work concerning the economy, education, science, culture, public health, physical culture, urban and rural development, finance, civil affairs, public security, nationalities affairs, judicial administration, supervision and family planning in their respective administrative areas; issue decisions and orders; appoint, remove and train administrative functionaries, appraise their work and reward or punish them.

People's governments of townships, nationality townships and towns carry out the resolutions of the people's congress at the corresponding level as well as the decisions and orders of the state administrative organs at the next higher level and conduct administrative work in their respective administrative areas.

People's governments of provinces and municipalities directly under the Central Government decide on the establishment and geographic division of townships, nationality townships and towns.

ARTICLE 108

Local people's governments at and above the county level direct the work of their subordinate departments and of people's governments at lower levels, and have the power to alter or annul inappropriate decisions of their subordinate departments and people's governments at lower levels.

ARTICLE 109

Auditing bodies are established by local people's governments at and above the county level. Local auditing bodies at different levels independently exercise their power to supervise through auditing in accordance with the law and are responsible to the people's government at the corresponding level and to the auditing body at the next higher level.

ARTICLE 110

Local people's governments at different levels are responsible, and report on their work, to people's congresses at the corresponding level. Local people's governments at and above the county level are responsible, and report on their work, to the standing committee of the people's congress at the corresponding level when the congress is not in session.

Local people's governments at different levels are responsible, and report on their work, to the state administrative organs at the next higher level. Local people's governments at different levels throughout the country are state administrative organs under the unified leadership of the State Council and are subordinate to it.

ARTICLE 111

The residents' committees and villagers' committees established among urban and rural residents on the basis of their place of residence are mass organizations of self-management at the grass-roots level. The chairman, vice-chairmen and members of each residents' or villagers' committee are elected by the residents. The relationship between the residents' and villagers' committees and the grassroots organs of state power is prescribed by law.

The residents' and villagers' committees establish committees for people's mediation, public security, public health and other matters in order to manage public affairs and social services in their areas, mediate civil disputes, help maintain public order and convey residents' opinions and demands and make suggestions to the people's government.

SECTION VI

Organs of Self-Government of National Autonomous Areas

ARTICLE 112

The organs of self-government of national autonomous areas are the people's congresses and people's governments of autonomous regions, autonomous prefectures and autonomous counties.

ARTICLE 113

In the people's congress of an autonomous region, prefecture or county, in addition to the deputies of the nationality or nationalities exercising regional autonomy in administrative area, the other nationalities inhabiting the area are also entitled to appropriate representation.

The chairmanship and vice-chairmanships of the standing committee of the people's congress of an autonomous region, prefecture or county shall include a citizen or citizens of the nationality or nationalities exercising regional autonomy in the area concerned.

ARTICLE 114

The administrative head of an autonomous region, prefecture or county shall be a citizen of the nationality, or one of the nationalities, exercising regional autonomy in the area concerned.

ARTICLE 115

The organs of self-government of autonomous regions, prefectures and counties exercise the functions and powers of local organs of state as specified in Section V of Chapter Three of the Constitution. At the same time, they exercise the power of autonomy within the limits of their authority as prescribed by the Constitution, the law of regional national autonomy and other laws, and implement the laws and policies of the state in the light of the existing local situation.

ARTICLE 116

People's congresses of national autonomous areas have the power to enact autonomy regulations and specific regulations in the light of the political, economic and cultural characteristics of the nationality or nationalities in the areas concerned. The autonomy regulations and specific regulations of autonomous regions shall be submitted to the Standing Committee of the National People's Congress for approval before they go into effect. Those of autonomous prefectures and counties shall be submitted to the standing committees of the people's congresses of provinces or autonomous regions for approval before they go into effect, and they shall be reported to the Standing Committee of the National People's Congress for the record.

ARTICLE 117

The organs of self-government of the national autonomous areas have the power of autonomy in administering the finances of their areas. All revenues accruing to the national autonomous areas under the financial system of the state shall be managed and used by the organs of self-government of those areas on their own.

ARTICLE 118

The organs of self-government of the national autonomous areas independently arrange for and administer local economic development under the guidance of state plans.

In exploiting natural resources and building enterprises in the national autonomous areas, the state shall give due consideration to the interests of those areas.

ARTICLE 119

The organs of self-government of the national autonomous areas independently administer educational, scientific, cultural, public health and physical culture affairs in their respective areas, protect and cull through the cultural heritage of the nationalities and work for the development and flourishing of their cultures.

ARTICLE 120

The organs of self-government of the national autonomous areas may, in accordance with the military system of the state and concrete local needs and with the approval of the State Council, organize local public security forces for the maintenance of public order.

ARTICLE 121

In performing their functions, the organs of self-government of the national autonomous areas, in accordance with the autonomy regulations of the respective areas, employ the spoken and written language or languages in common use in the locality.

ARTICLE 122

The state gives financial, material and technical assistance to the minority nationalities to accelerate their economic and cultural development.

The state helps the ntional autonomous areas train large numbers of cadres at different levels and specialized personnel and skilled workers of different professions and trades from among the nationality or nationalities in those areas.

SECTION VII

The People's Courts and the People's Procuratorates

The people's courts in the People's Republic of China are the judicial organs of the state.

ARTICLE 124

The People's Republic of China establishes the Supreme People's Court and the local people's courts at different levels, military courts and other special people's courts.

The term of office of the President of the Supreme People's Court is the same as that of the National People's Congress; the President shall serve no more than two consecutive terms.

The organization of people's courts is prescribed by law.

ARTICLE 125

All cases handled by the people's courts, except for those involving special circumstances as specified by law, shall be heard in public. The accused has the right of defense.

ARTICLE 126

The people's courts shall, in accordance with the law, exercise judicial power independently and are not subject to interference by administrative organs, public organizations or individuals.

ARTICLE 127

The Supreme People's Court is the highest judicial organ.

The Supreme People's Court supervises the administration of justice by the local people's courts at different levels and by the special people's courts; people's courts at higher levels supervise the administration of justice by those at lower levels.

ARTICLE 128

The Supreme People's Court is responsible to the National People's Congress and its Standing Committee. Local people's courts at different levels are responsible to the organs of state power which created them.

ARTICLE 129

The people's procuratorates of the People's Republic of China are state organs for legal supervision.

ARTICLE 130

The People's Republic of China establishes the Supreme People's Procuratorate and the local people's procuratorates at different levels, military procuratorates and other special people's procuratorates.

The term of office of the Procurator-General of the Supreme People's Procuratorate is the same as that of the National People's Congress; the Procurator-General shall serve no more than two consecutive terms.

The organization of people's procuratorates is prescribed by law.

ARTICLE 131

People's procuratorates shall, in accordance with the law, exercise procuratorial power independently and are not subject to interference by administrative organs, public organizations or individuals.

ARTICLE 132

The Supreme People's Procuratorate is the highest procuratorial organ.

The Supreme People's Procuratorate directs the work of the local people's procuratorates at different levels and of the special people's procuratorates; people's procuratorates at higher levels direct the work of those at lower levels.

ARTICLE 133

The Supreme People's Procuratorate is responsible to the National People's Congress and its Standing Committee. Local people's procuratorates at different levels are responsible to the organs of state power at the corresponding levels which created them and to the people's procuratorates at the higher level.

ARTICLE 134

Citizens of all nationalities have the right to use the spoken and written languages of their own nationalities in court proceedings. The people's courts and people's procuratorates should provide translation for any party to the court proceedings who is not familiar with the spoken or written languages in common use in the locality.

In an area where people of a minority nationality live in a compact community or where a number of nationalities live together, hearings should be conducted in the language or languages in common use in the locality; indictments, judgments, notices and other documents should be written, according to actual needs, in the language or languages in common use in the locality.

ARTICLE 135

The people's courts, people's procuratorates and public security organs shall, in handling criminal cases, divide their functions, each taking responsibility for its own work, and they shall coordinate their efforts and check each other to ensure correct and effective enforcement of law.

APPENDIX K

BIBLIOGRAPHY

The mark (*) indicates a book especially useful for young readers, as well as for adults.

Journals & Periodicals (to 1986)

Encyclopedia Brittanica Yearbook, Asian Survey (Berkeley: University of California Press); American-Asian Review (New York: St. John's University); Asian Pacific Community (Tokyo: Asian Club).

Books: General

BUNGE, FREDERICA M.; SHINN, RINN-SUP; & WHITAKER, DONALD P. *China: A Country Study.* Washington, D.C.: U.S. Department of the Army, 1981.
   One of the distinguished series published by the federal government with the aid of American University.

COHEN, JOAN L. & COHEN, JEROME A. *China Today and Her Ancient Treasures.* New York: Abrams, 1985.
   Contains hundreds of beautifully printed photographs of artifacts, as well as a precise and useful text.

*CREEL, H.G. *The Birth of China.* New York: F.A. Ungar, 1954.
   An outstanding study of the Shang and Chou dynasties.

*DEBARY, W.T. (ed.). *Sources of Chinese Tradition.* New York: Columbia University Press, 1960.
   The best single compilation of original materials in this field.

EBERHARD, WOLFRAM. *A History of China.* Berkeley: University of California Press, 1960.
   An excellent interpretation, by a sociologist.

FAIRBANK, JOHN K. *et al. A History of East Asia.* Boston: Houghton-Mifflin, 1973.
   A standard in its field.

FAIRBANK, JOHN K. (ed.). *The Cambridge History of China (vol. 12): Republican China.* Cambridge: Cambridge University Press, 1983.
   One of the most scrupulous, detailed reference work of its kind.

FITZGERALD, C.P. *China: A Short Cultural History.* Boulder: Westview, 1985.
   A widely admired paperback which focuses on all cultural aspects.

*GROUSSET, RENE. *The Rise and Splendour of the Chinese Empire.* Berkeley: University of California Press, 1958.
   A survey of Chinese civilization, with emphasis on art and culture.

HSU, IMMANUEL, C. *Readings in Modern Chinese History.* London: Oxford University Press, 1971.
   A valuable collection.

HSU, IMMANUEL C. *The Rise of Modern China.* Oxford: Oxford University Press, 1983.
   Surveys the causes and consequences of revolution.

KEIGHTLEY, DAVID N. *The Origins of Chinese Civilization.* Berkeley: University of California Press, 1983.
   A scholarly but readily accessible study.

*LATOURETTE, K.S. *The Chinese: Their History and Culture.* New York: The Macmillan Company, 1946.
   A standard work, complete, although now dated.

MATHEWS, JAY & LINDA. *One Billion: A China Chronicle.* New York: Ballentine Books, 1983.
   One of the best popular surveys of every aspect of life in modern China.

NEEDHAM, JOSEPH. *Science and Civilization in China.* 5 vols. Cambridge: Cambridge University Press, 1954, 1956, 1959, 1963, 1983.
   A monumental work of scholarship which stands alone in its field.

REISCHAUER, E. & FAIRBANK, J.K. *A History of East Asian Civilizations.* 2 vols. Boston: Houghton-Mifflin Company, 1961-64.
   A brilliant study of China and Japan, by two of the most noted scholars in the field.

241

RONAN, COLIN A. *A Shorter Science & Civilization in China* (Vol. 1) Cambridge: Cambridge University Press, 1980.
An effort to make Joseph Needham's superb work (*op. cit.*) accessible to a larger public.
*SCHELL, ORVILLE. *Watch Out for the Foreign Guests!* New York: Penguin, 1985.
Written for the widest public, by a Berkeley scholar who has often traveled in Ching.
*SENCE JONATHAN. *The Memory Palace of Matteo Ricci.* New York: Penguin, 1985.
A beautifully researched and written essay probing the mental process of the 17th-century Jesuit who lived in two distinct worlds, Italy and China.
TSOU, TANG. *Cultural Revolution & Post-Mao Reforms: A Historical Perspective.* Chicago: University of Chicago Press, 1986.
A detailed study of one of the key events of modern times.
*POLO MARCO. *Travels.* Baltimore: Penguin Books. (Paperback).
R.E. Latham's translation of the classic first published in 1477.
RODZINSKI, W.A. *A History of China.* (2 vols.) New York: Pergamon, 1979 & 1983.
A detailed study, the more concise version of which was published for the same author in 1984.
SALISBURY, HARRISON E. *The Long March.* New York: Harper & Row, 1985.
The knowledgable former New York *Times* writer retraces the heroic journey with journalistic clarity.
SCHAFER, EDWARD H. *Ancient China.* Boston: Little, Brown, 1970.
An illustrated work by a fine writer and noted scholar.
*SCHURMANN, FRANZ & SCHELL, ORVILLE. *The China Reader.* (4 vols.) New York: Random House, 1967.
A fine source of original material from the Imperial, Republican, Communist, and Communist-Nationalist stages.
TWITCHETT, DENIS et al. (eds.). *Cambridge History of China.* Cambridge: Cambridge University Press, 1979-86.
Ongoing research which compiles work of many of the best thinkers in this field.
UNITED NATIONS. *Economic Survey of Asia and the Far East.* New York: United Nations Publishing Service, 1981.
The most complete data available to the date of publication.
*VAN GULICK, ROBERT. *The Chinese Gold Murders.*
*_____. *The Chinese Bell Murders.* New York: Avon (paperback), 1963.
Highly readable mysteries by a Dutch diplomat illuminate medieval China.

Politics & Government

CLUBB, D.E. *Twentieth-Century China.* New York: Columbia University Press, 1972.
A former U.S. diplomat's view of the sources of change.
FAIRBANK, JOHN K. *The United States & China.* Cambridge: Harvard University Press, 1979.
A revised edition of a widely read book dealing with both Chinese and American attitudes.
FAIRBANK, JOHN K. & REISCHAUER, EDWIN O. *China: Tradition & Transformation.* Boston: Houghton-Mifflin, 1978.
Two of the world's most honored Asian scholars relate history to the present in an illustrated text.
LIU, ALAN P. *How China is Ruled.* New York: Prentice-Hall, 1986.
An illustrated survey of contemporary government.
*MALRAUX, ANDRE. *Man's Fate.* New York: Random House, 1969.
A novel written during the Gaullist diplomat's early, radical period, regarded as one of the most important works of revolutionary fiction.
MAO ZEDONG. *Selected Works.* New York: International Publishers. 1954-56.
Original works by one of the most influential humans of modern times.
SNOW, EDGAR. *China: The Long Revolution.* New York Random House, 1972.
A famed, sympathetic American's last book about a country he loved.
TUCHMAN, BARBARA, W. *Stilwell and the American Experience in China: 1911-1945.* New York: Macmillan, 1971.
A disturbing exposition of a crucial struggle in America's China policy.
YU–MING SHAW (ed.). *Mainland China: Politics, Economics & Reform.* Boulder: Westview, 1985.

Religion & Philosophy

*CHAMPION, S.G., and SHORT, D. (eds.). *Readings from World Religions.* New York: Fawcett-World, 1968 (Paperback)
Succinct essays about, and readings from, the texts of the world's eleven most influential religions.

CREEL, H.G. *Chinese Thought from Confucius to Mao Tse-Tung.* Chicago: University of Chicago Press, 1953.
An aging but standard popular survey of Chinese intellectual activity.

*KRAMER, SAMUEL NOAH (ed.). *Mythologies of the Ancient World.* New York: Doubleday & Company, 1961 (Anchor Paperback).
One of the world's leading antiquarians includes excellent sections on the mythologies of China, India, and Japan, among others.

WEBER, MAX *The Religions of China.* Glencoe: Free Press, 1957.
The pioneering sociologist's analysis of China's major faiths.

Sociology & Customs

CHU, GODWIN C. & HSU, FRANCIS I. (eds.). *China's New Social Fabric.* London: Routledge & Kegan, 1983.
A symposium which both reports on recent change and speculates about the future.

*FAIRBANK, J.K. (ed.). *Thought and Institutions.* Chicago: University of Chicago Press, 1959.
Thirteen penetrating essays tracing the history of ideas in China.

JOHNSON, KAY A. *Women, the Family & Peasant Revolution in China.* Chicago: University of Chicago Press, 1983.
An effort to assemble needed data about a much discussed but insufficiently studied subject.

MOSHER, STEVEN W. *Broken Earth: The Rural Chinese.* Glencoe: Free Press, 1984.
Vividly describes the life of the majority of the people of China.

*MYRDAL, JAN. *Report from a Chinese Village.* New York: New American Library, 1965. (Paperback)
A famed Swedish sociologist's thorough observations.

*MYRDAL, JAN. *Return to a Chinese Village.* New York: Pantheon, 1984.
The noted Swedish sociologist revisits the community which he previously made famous in *Report from a Chinese Village.*

*WELLS, IRENE, and BOTHWELL, JEAN. *Fun and Festival.* New York: Friendship Press.
A series of booklets by the Commission on Missionary Education, giving games, dress, recipes, language, music, and stories about China, Japan, India, Pakistan, and Ceylon.

YANG, C.K. *Chinese Family in the Communist Revolution.* Cambridge: Harvard University Press, 1959.
An excellent study of the impact of modernization and revolution.

*YUTANG, LIN (ed.). *The Wisdom of China and India.* New York: Random House, 1942.
A Chinese popularizer's selections from the literature of Asia's seminal cultures.

Literature & Art

*BIRCH, CYRIL (ed.). *Anthology of Chinese Literature.* Vol. 1. *From Early Times to the Fourteenth Century,* 1965; Vol. 2: *From the Fourteenth Century to the Present Day,* 1972. New York: Grove Press (Paperback).
The best two-volume survey of its kind.

*BREWITT–TAYLOR (trans.). *Romance of the Three Kingdoms,* by Lo Kuan Chung. 2 vols. Rutland: Tuttle, 1959.
A good translation of one of China's most influential historical novels.

*BUCK, PEARL. (trans.). *All Men Are Brothers.* New York: Grove Press, 1957.
A novel, set in the thirteenth century, dealing with a Chinese Robin Hood.

*BUCK PEARL. *The Good Earth.* New York: Pocket Books (Paperback), 1958.
A famous American novel of Chinese peasant life.

*CARTER, T.F. *The Invention of Printing in China and Its Spread Westward.* New York: The Ronald Press, 1955.
A widely respected study of early creativity in China.

CHIANG, YEE. *Chinese Calligraphy: An Introduction to its Aesthetics and Technique.* London: Methuen, 1954.

A fine analysis of one of China's most abstract arts.

DEFRANCIS, JOHN. *Beginning Chinese.* New Haven: Yale University Press, 1976.

One of the clearest and most complete methods of language instruction, which should be combined with tapes available from Seton Hall University, South Orange, N.J. 07079.

*FENOLLOSA, E. *Epochs of Chinese and Japanese Art.* 2 vols. Baltimore: Dover Publications, 1963.

A good introduction to the history and aesthetics of Chinese and Japanese art.

HSIA, C.T. *A History of Modern Chinese Fiction.* New Haven: Yale University Press, 1961.

A critical survey of modern writing, showing the impact of the revolution

LIU HSIEH. *The Literary Mind and the Carvings of Dragons.* New York: Columbia University Press, 1962.

An examination of the patterns of thought in Chinese literature.

*STRAITS TIMES COLLECTION. *Fun With Chinese Characters.* Singapore: Federal Publications, 1985.

A series of books which use cartoons, standard brush strokes, and proverbs to show how Chinese characters were developed and are created.

*SULLIVAN, MICHAEL. *Chinese Art: A History.* Berkeley: University of California Press, 1974.

One of the best general surveys of its kind.

*WU, NELSON I. *Chinese and Indian Architecture.* New York: Braziller, 1963.

A splendidly illustrated an annotated short survey.

*WALEY, ARTHUR (trans.). *Translations from the Chinese.* New York: Knopf, 1941.

A masterful translation and analysis of Chinese poetry, especially the Tang.

*_____. *Monkey.* New York: Grove Press, 1958.

A humorous classic novel which mocks Chinese manners.

*WANG, CHI-CHEN (trans.). *Dream of the Red Chamber.* New York: Twayne, 1958.

A superb novel of family life in Ming China.

WILLETS, WILLIAM. *Chinese Calligraphy: Its History & Aesthetic Motivation.* Oxford: Oxford University Press, 1981.

Explains the fascination which the Chinese have for this subtle art form.

*YOHANNAN, JOHN D. (ed.). *A Treasury of Asian Literature.* New York: John Day, 1956. (Also Mentor Paperback).

Well chosen excerpts from the works which helped to shape Asian history.

INDEX

Abahai, 72
abortions, 170, 173-74
Academy of Letters, 50
acupuncture, 148
Afghanistan, 62, 183
Africa, 172
agriculture, 12*ff.*
Amoy, 72. *See also* Xiamen.
Amur River, 5
Analects, 28
animals, domestic, 13
An Lushan, 51
Annan (Annam), 37, 68, 94
Anyang, 18, 20
Arabs, 58, 70
architecture, 42
arts, 42, 57, 151-52
Asia-Pacific Summit of 1993, 174
"Asian Perspective," 57
Assam, 181, 182
astronomy, 41
atomic bomb, 146
"Awakening Society," the, 119

Bactria, 42
Ban Chao, 39
"barefoot doctors," 149-50
Ban Yong, 39
Beijing, 14, 54, 60, 62, 65, 66, 97, 101, 126
Beijing Opera, 151
Beijing University, 98, 114
Bengal, 67
Bhutan, 181
birth control, 171, 186
Book of Changes, 85. See also *Yijing.*
Book of History. See *Shujing*.
Book of Odes. See *Shijing*.
books, 52, 58
Boxer Rebellion, 82, 83, 93
boy-girl ratio, 171
Brahmaputra River. *See* Zangbo.

British, 70, 75-78, 80, 94, 107, 180. *See also* Great Britain.
British East India Company, 76
brush painting, 45
bronze, 20
Buddhism, 43, 45, 49, 51, 68, 164. *See also* Chan Buddhism.
Burma Road, 108
bureaucracy, 53-54, 87
Bush, President George, 173, 175

"capitalist restoration." *See* Cultural Revolution.
"Chinese melon, Cutting the," 94
"Classic of the Way and Values." *See* Daodejing.
Cairo Conference, 109
calendar, 41
calligraphy, 45
Cambodia, 163, 182-83
canals, 14. *See also* Grand Canal.
cannon, development of, 75
Cantlie, Sir James, 83
Canton. *See* Guangzhou.
Cao Cao, 44
Cao Pei, 44
carpeting, 65
Cathay, 67
Catholics, 70, 72, 75
cattle, 12
Censorate, 99
Central Asia, 45
Chan Buddhism, 49, 57, 59
Changan, 51
Chen Boda, 128
Chen Duxiu, 98, 100
Chen Province, 36
Chiang Kai-shek. *See* Jiang Jieshi.
China Proper, 4, 5
Chou Dynasty. *See* Zhou Dynasty.
Christianity, 65, 79, 82,164
Churchill, Sir Winston, 109

245